Jump Start Health!

Practical Ideas to Promote Wellness in
Kids of All Ages

Jump Start Health!

Practical Ideas to Promote Wellness in Kids of All Ages

David Campos

Teachers College, Columbia University
New York and London

Published by Teachers College Press, 1234 Amsterdam Avenue, New York, NY 10027

Library of Congress Cataloging-in-Publication Data

Campos, David.
  Jump start health! : practical ideas to promote wellness in kids of all ages / David Campos.
       p. cm.
    Includes bibliographical references and index.
    ISBN 978-0-8077-5178-7 (pbk. : alk. paper)
    ISBN 978-0-8077-5179-4 (hardcover : alk. paper)
       1. Children—Health and hygiene. 2. Health education. I. Title.
    RJ101.C324 2011
    613′.0432—dc22   2010049623

ISBN 978-0-8077-5178-7 (paper)
ISBN 978-0-8077-5179-4 (hardcover)

Printed on acid-free paper
Manufactured in the United States of America

18 17 16 15 14 13 12 11   8 7 6 5 4 3 2 1

For my father,
Agapito D. Campos,
who dreamed his sons would work far from the crop fields
in which he once labored

Contents

Preface

I began writing *Jump Start Health!* in January 2008. I intended this book to serve as the sequel to another I had written on the topic of childhood obesity that was largely theoretical and conceptual in nature. It had a wealth of information, but it was not practical enough for the everyday classroom teacher. I empathize with busy teachers who have—what seems—a never-ending flow of demands placed on them. And to comb through pages of an academic text to construct lessons to teach not only can prove to be cumbersome, but also can exhaust treasured time and energy. In fact, many teachers become annoyed with that process and abandon that idea to do so altogether. I do not blame them; after all, they have a sea of standards to meet, expectations to fulfill, added curricula to teach alongside the core subjects, and so forth.

Yet still, there is something innately different about the topic of childhood obesity that warrants the scrutiny to accentuate what needs to be efficiently imparted to children. And that is that this is about the course of children's health, which can be altered for the better by teaching children that health is a worthy lifelong pursuit. I wanted this book to be practical enough for teachers and youth-serving professionals to easily convey this knowledge to children, and hence reinforce the likelihood that they will enjoy a better quality of life. To that end, the purposes of *Jump Start Health!* are threefold: to inform about the critical issue affecting childhood today, the obesity crisis; to provide a knowledge base on healthy diet and physical activity practices; and to offer practical approaches to impart that knowledge to children in school settings.

As I wrote this book, I noticed increasing media coverage on health and weight issues, which is unmistakably well deserved. That these matters now garner national attention is valuable because we are an overweight and obese society and health needs to hold a prominent position in the public consciousness. Pick any mainstream magazine, like *U.S. News and World Report* (childhood obesity was its cover feature on September 10, 2007) and *Time* (with featured articles with titles such as "Should Parents of Obese Kids Lose Custody?" "Do Obese Kids Become Obese Adults?" and "Lifelong Effects of Childhood Obesity"), or watch any news show, and an aspect of health is certain to be covered. Of course, some of this is sensationalized, but the publicity nonetheless raises the awareness that behavioral changes are essential to improved health. One news piece from September 21, 2009, that caught my attention featured the photo of an adorable 8-month-old—and boy, was he huge. *Newsweek* titled the piece "Born to Be Big? Are Some Kids Fated to Be Fat?" I was shocked by the reported results of a Harvard study: Obesity levels in infants had risen 73% since 1980.

A wide range of sources confirms that our nation has a serious problem with obesity. Nearly 60% of Americans are overweight or obese (Begley, 2009), and in some states, one out of three adults is obese (Trust for America's Health, 2009). Moreover, the number of children considered overweight or obese is larger than ever before. There is no denying that excess weight is an epidemic in this country. Despite good news about children's health (immunizations have reduced the incidence of chicken pox, measles, and mumps alone), nothing can overshadow the notion that childhood obesity is an important challenge of our age that has to be addressed through a variety of forums; school happens to be one of them.

Children have to learn early on that the choices they make now contribute to their long-term health. To happen upon this information in adolescence or adulthood is too late. As most adults can attest, it is difficult to break old habits and start new ones—not to mention that obesity is difficult to reverse (Katan & Ludwig, 2010). Even though news coverage on health is widespread, there are far too many parents who do not—and cannot—model good health because they too are set in their ways or they simply do not know how. And left to their own devices, children do not always make decisions that are best for their health (McDevitt & Ormrod, 2010). In fact, they often ascribe to crazes that contradict health. Inevitably, many children adopt poor dietary and physical activity habits that they carry well into adulthood. Because children are just starting to make their own decisions and assume increasing responsibilities, it makes sense to introduce the tenets of healthy lifestyles in childhood. This is the opportune time to empower them with the knowledge and skills to make decisions that positively contribute toward their health. Without that knowledge, they will not always make the right decisions. Actually, research has shown that as children start making their own decisions, their nutrition deteriorates (McDevitt & Ormrod, 2010).

Schools are the ideal medium of this knowledge because of the two labs where teachers can reinforce the concepts of good dietary and physical activity practices: the cafeteria and the gym. More than that, schools are the very places where most people learn what life should be like. Health is such an essential part of life that why would we not teach the concepts that lead to it? Besides, schools already offer children knowledge with a preventative function (e.g., dental care, antismoking and antidrug campaigns, fire safety, and stranger-danger precautions), so that they develop a body of skills that will serve to protect them throughout their lifespan. So too should obesity prevention be designated with that degree of significance—not to mention that classroom teachers are professionally trained to deliver instruction in meaningful and challenging ways. They know their students best, and they know how to tailor health resources to fulfill the unique needs of their students.

On that score, why consider *Jump Start Health!* a health resource? Readers will find that this book is a tool kit of background matter associated with excess weight, healthy eating, and physical activity coupled with practical approaches to teaching children how to live healthier. The first section of the book, "Coming to Terms with Childhood Obesity," encompasses two chapters. Chapter 1 is an overview of childhood obesity. Supporting data are cast purposefully throughout the discussion to underscore the impact of excess weight on individual and social health. In Chapter 2, a discussion ensues over the notion of health and wellness. Health is a far more comprehensive concept than that of feeling and looking good, and if readers fail to fully understand its complexity, they will have a difficult time convincing children that it is a worthy pursuit. Health affects many aspects of life, and readers need to know exactly how poor dietary and sedentary behaviors influence the seven dimensions of wellness so that they can effectively communicate it to children. The discussion then transitions to the media's fixed hold on personal health. It is well established that the media can influence a number of health issues, including sex; drugs; aggressive behavior; suicide; and the topic at hand, obesity (Strasburger, 2007; Strasburger, Wilson, & Jordan, 2009). Readers and children alike should recognize how the media can provoke these self-destructive behaviors. Toward the end of the chapter, federal campaigns are discussed so that readers understand how childhood obesity is being addressed at the national level.

The next section, "Nurturing Healthy Dietary Habits," consists of Chapters 3 and 4. Chapter 3 presents the material that teachers should know to augment the Ideas. The discussion focuses on the nutritional aspects of healthy eating and aligns with each of the food groups identified on the federal diagram MyPyramid. Readers are provided a snapshot of the benefits of each group, what the recommended daily amounts encompass, and how Americans fare in their consumption. Chapter 4 presents the first set of Ideas. The discussion begins with the assumptions that frame the Ideas and pivots to the considerations to be made in their delivery to children. All the Ideas were designed with the National Health Education Standards in mind, and include a rationale, objectives, suggestions to motivate the students and frame the discussion, a step-by-step approach to the lesson, guided and independent activities, and ways to conclude.

The third section, "Promoting Regular Physical Activity," parallels the pattern set in the former two chapters. The primary difference, of course, is that Chapters 5 and 6 are centered on physical activity. The discussion in this section begins with the benefits associated with regular physical activity and the problems with inactivity and then shifts to support for why the Ideas should be implemented. Readers are reminded that there is not enough time in the school day to be physically active, and children have to be encouraged to pursue physical activity. After all, it is still voluntary to be physically active, and they have far too many attractive sedentary options.

There are bound to be teachers who think that there are more important things than health and physical activity to be teaching children. In their minds, if the issue of childhood obesity was not stressed before, why now? Make no mistake, though, we have an unprecedented epidemic on our hands and children's quality of life is at stake. As a classroom teacher, you hold considerable power to educate children on matters related to academics, social skills, and values. You also hold it within you to alter a child's ability to chart his or her health for a lifetime.

The time has come to intervene in the childhood obesity crisis. *Jump Start Health!* is one way to do so.

Acknowledgments

I could not have successfully completed this book if not for the support of a number of people. Most notably, I remain grateful to my parents, Agapito and Guadalupe Campos, who have provided me steadfast love and unwavering support throughout my life. They sacrificed considerably so that my brothers and I could earn an education and break free of migrant work. I am equally indebted to the wisdom of my brothers, Ernie and John, who have contributed significantly to my life and remain a source of inspiration for my work.

I extend a special thanks to friends and colleagues who have given me a solid base from which I can build. I am fortunate to have the continuing encouragement and unconditional support of Dr. Valerie Janesick, who generously shares her talents and expertise; Dr. Kenneth A. Perez, who is always insightful and at hand to answer my medical questions; and my friends Koran Kanaifu, Bobby Coronado, Simon Chow, Alex Clemenzi, and Ericka Knudson, who provide me with much needed balance in my life. I am lucky to know you all.

Last, I extend my deepest gratitude to the production team at Teachers College Press, and especially to my editor, Brian Ellerbeck, for his role in the development of this book. He believed in me and the potential value of this book from the beginning and, through his vision and patient support, guided me through the 2½ years it took me to write *Jump Start Health!*.

Part I

COMING TO TERMS WITH CHILDHOOD OBESITY

CHAPTER 1

Overview

The advocacy organization Trust for America's Health released its report *F as in Fat: How Obesity Policies Are Failing in America* in July 2009. The news was not good, nor was it a big surprise: Obesity rates across the nation climbed in 23 states and no state witnessed a decline. Mississippi became the first state to crest at 32.5%, which means that about one in three adults in that state is obese. Three other states—Alabama, Tennessee, and West Virginia—followed closely behind with percentages that ranged above 30.2%. The bulletin about the weight status of youth was just as dismal. There are nearly 25 million children who are obese or overweight—an unprecedented number in our nation's history—which is triple as many from 1980 (Trust for America's Health, 2007). Particularly sobering is that the number of overweight youth is escalating at a high rate. It does not take a rocket scientist to infer that because weight and health are closely linked, the health status of these children is rapidly declining.

With these revealing findings that give a glimpse into the modern-day conditions of children's health, it makes sense to delve into the topic of childhood obesity to understand the measures that teachers can take to help children surmount the common challenges associated with pursuing better health. In this introductory chapter, childhood obesity is explored in four sections:

- The Childhood Obesity Epidemic
- Concern over Childhood Obesity
- Time to Address the Childhood Obesity Epidemic
- About *Jump Start Health!*

THE CHILDHOOD OBESITY EPIDEMIC

By now there is hardly an American around who has not heard of this nation's childhood obesity crisis. What many do not know is that the United States is not alone at the crossroad of youth and overweight. Industrialized countries, as far away as Australia, Japan, Taiwan, Ireland, and Greece, are wrestling with their own overweight youth as well. In this country, the rate of childhood obesity is increasing across the board regardless of where a child lives or his or her race, ethnicity, age, gender, or family's income level. With more and more children becoming overweight and obese, it is apparent why newspaper headlines, daily news programs, health experts, and youth-serving professionals are sounding the alarm, calling this crisis an epidemic.

But what has happened in the past few decades to cause this surge of overweight and obese youth? Health experts believe that most Americans lack energy balance. That is, the energy going into our bodies (by way of calories consumed) is not balanced with the energy going out (by way of calories being expended). Quite simply, the nation as a whole is eating too much of the wrong foods and exercising too little. This pertains to children and adolescents. They simply do not have the knowledge and skills that can guide them to improve their dietary habits and increase their daily physical activity. Moreover, the adults in their lives model poor lifestyle behaviors, and often their caretakers make poor healthy decisions for them by feeding them nutrient-inferior meals and snacks. All the while, youth influence one another to conform to what is standard and acceptable (e.g., eating hamburgers and fries, snacking on candy bars, and watching hours of television).

In the following, I discuss what we know about the root causes of child obesity, namely poor dietary and physical activity habits.

A Diet of the Wrong Foods

An unprecedented number of Americans have unhealthy eating patterns. Adults are far from ideal role models with only 12% consuming a healthy diet, according to the U.S. Department of Agriculture Healthy Eating Index. Between 1978 and 1995 the number of calories that the average adult consumed on a daily basis jumped from 1,876 to 2,043 (Center for Science in the Public Interest, 2003a). Reportedly, only 22.6% of Americans consume the recommended daily serving of five or more fruit and vegetables (Centers for Disease Control, 2003a). As with their adult counterparts, what youth eat, how often they eat, and the size of their portions have shifted in a direction that leaves nutritionists and other health experts aghast.

The foods youth consume today are generally nutrient-inferior products, high in calories and fat. More than 80% of youngsters in our country consume too much fat (over 30% of total calories from fat), and 90% consume too much saturated fat (Action for Healthy Kids, 2005b). One study of 3,000 infants and toddlers found that even the very young consume too many high-calorie foods, too much sodium, and too few fruit and vegetables (Mathematica Policy Research, 2006). The U.S. Department of Agriculture (2001) reported that only 2% of all school-age youth meet the federal recommendations of eating foods from all major groups, and the Centers for Disease Control (CDC) (2006) indicated that only one youth in five eats five servings of fruit and vegetables a day. In fact, children's and adolescents' vegetable consumption decreased by 42% and 32%, respectively, between 1997 and 2002 (Centers for Disease Control, 2003a).

Milk consumption—or lack thereof—is a problem, too. The CDC noted that fewer than one in five schoolchildren drinks three or more glasses of milk a day. Throughout the years, milk drinking has fallen by the wayside as soda drinking has gained in popularity. Researchers have found that among youth, daily soda consumption has grown by roughly 100 grams from the mid-1970s to the mid-1990s (Sturm, 2005). It is particularly frightening that adolescents drink twice as much soda as milk (U.S. Department of Agriculture, 2007). This generation of youth also snacks more frequently than those of the past. In fact, snacking is a way of life for Americans, considering that nearly a third of the calories consumed are from snacks (Institute of Medicine, 2004). One study found that about 90% of 6- to 18-year-olds reported eating three snacks a day, and over 50% ate five or more snacks daily (American Dietetic Association, 2004). Youth today consume about 10 more grams of snacks a day than did their counterparts of the 1970s (Sturm, 2005). In all, snacking can add about 610 calories to a young person's diet, which would not be such a great problem *if* the snacks were healthy (Jahns, Siega-Riz, & Popkin, 2001).

Reportedly, adults and children alike consume more of the bad foods. The pattern becomes more apparent when portion sizes are explored. The portion sizes of food we eat today are larger than ever before. As an example, the average bagel today weighs between 2 and 5 ounces more than those of the 1950s. Then, a family-size bottle of Coke was 26 ounces; today a single-serving bottle alone is 20 ounces. Then, the average McDonalds meal—original burger, fries, and 12-ounce Coke—was about 590 calories. Today, the supersize Extra Value Meal—Quarter Pounder with cheese, supersize fries, and supersize Coke—equates to 1,550 calories (National Alliance for Nutrition and Activity, 2002). To complicate matters, families today eat out more often than ever before. At one time, eating out was reserved for special occasions. Now, it is commonplace for many. In 1970, Americans spent about 26% of their food dollars on meals and foods prepared outside the home; that figure is now closer to half (46%) (Center for Science in the Public Interest, 2003a). Accordingly, a third of the calories consumed by the average American comes from foods prepared by fast-food establishments and other restaurants. Some researchers claim that on average, individuals as young as 8 eat 218 restaurant meals a year (National Restaurant Association, 2002).

This may not sound like a bad trend, because, after all, eating out is a treat that the whole family can enjoy. It is convenient for parents. There is no cooking or cleaning involved, the meals are palatable and consistent, the meals are perceived as more economical than preparing them at home, and there is an array of options for the most finicky eater. Young people enjoy eating out because it is fun and entertaining, especially when there is a toy that accompanies the meal and a commercial playscape to explore. But there is a high price for eating out often: weight gain, which occurs because the portions tend to be large (especially when there is value associated with or- dering larger portions by way of marketing euphemisms such as *Supersize*, *Biggie*, *Colossal*, and *Kingsize*, adding substantially to calorie and fat con- tent (National Alliance for Nutrition and Activity, 2002). In other words, fast-food and other restaurant meals are generally higher in saturated fat, so- dium, and sugar and lower in fiber, iron, calcium, and cholesterol than foods that are prepared at home (Center for Science in the Public Interest, 2003a).

The Sedentary Lifestyles of Youth

A root cause of weight gain is lack of daily physical activity. Children and youth today are more physically inactive than ever before. Less than one in four children gets 20 minutes of vigorous physical activity a day, and only a quarter of all youth get at least 30 minutes of daily exercise (Action for Healthy Kids, 2003). About one in four youngsters (older than 12) reports no vigorous physical daily activity, and 14% report no physi- cal activity at all (U.S. Department of Agriculture, 2005b). Among 9- to 13-year-olds, 61.5% do not participate in organized physical activity during nonschool hours and nearly one out of four does not engage in free-time physical activity (Centers for Disease Control, 2003b).

Modern technology and conveniences are to blame for much of the sed- entary lifestyles youth lead today. In the war between exercise and technol- ogy, technology is far more attractive in the eyes of youth because they can use it in the comfortable confines of their home well within reach of their favorite snacks. The availability of video games, computers, the Internet, cable television, DVD players, and so forth make for popular pastimes, but they require very little exercise. Some researchers have found that youth over 2 years old average about 4 hours a day watching TV or videos, play- ing video games, or using the computer, and 17% watch more than 5 hours of TV each day (Michigan Department of Education, 2001). It should come as no surprise that youth who watch a lot of TV are 8.3 times more likely to be overweight than their counterparts who watch less than 2 hours (Michi- gan Department of Education, 2001).

The conveniences in children's lives also rob them of physical activity opportunities. Yesteryear, youth got a lot more exercise because they walked or biked to their destinations, including school. In 1969, half of all children walked or biked to school (U.S. Department of Transportation, 1969); now, about 85% of children travel to school by car or bus, and only 13% walk or bike (U.S. Environmental Protection Agency, 2003). The Centers for Disease Control (n.d.b) writes:

> Today, only about 1 out of every 10 trips to school are made by walking and bicycling. Of school trips one mile or less, a low 31% are made by walking; within two miles of school, just 2% are made by bicycling. (p. 2)

The way of life in our environment is also one that encourages very little physical activity. In addition to having the comforts of elevators and escalators that make travel within a building easier, youth are seemingly chauffeured everywhere. One cannot blame parents. After all, most do not even think of walking or biking with their children to the nearest store because the roads, which generally do not promote that kind of activity (especially in commercial districts), are enough to send the would-be pedestrian into hysteria. So the premium mode of transportation is the car. Think of how establishments serve their customers in cars. It is feasible that a parent and accompanying children could run errands without ever leaving their car. They could drop off letters at the post office, buy coffee and bakery goods at a coffee shop, drop laundry off at the cleaners, pick up medication at the pharmacy, deposit money at the bank, and pick up dinner by way of a fast-food restaurant drive-thru without ever stepping on the ground. Driving around is easy, convenient, socially acceptable, and perhaps safe, but on a jaunt like this, children exercise away very few calories.

Finally, youth do not get enough exercise at school. Youngsters in the elementary grades often have recess and PE, but as they get into the upper grades, opportunities for exercise decrease. Indeed, in some school districts, recess has fallen by the wayside to make way for increased instructional time. In a given week, one out of five high school students is physically active for 20 minutes or more, and nearly 11% do not engage in any moderate or vigorous physical activity during the week (Marr, 2004). One study found that children in Iowa spent about 30 minutes each day participating in some sort of aerobic activity, while the older youth averaged about 8 minutes. The Centers for Disease Control (2004) noted that about 70% of high school freshmen participated in regular physical activity, but only 55% of their senior counterparts did so. PE is available in schools throughout the country, but most are surprised to learn that only a fraction of youth have regular PE. Burgeson et al. (2001) found that 8% of elementary school, 6.4% of middle or junior high schools, and 5.8% of high schools offered PE on a regular basis for the whole student body, for the whole school year. With no federal mandate for PE, there is very little consistency for how it is delivered among states, districts, schools, and grade levels. Datar and Sturm (2004) write:

Although guidelines recommend that students have daily classes, receive a sub-stantial percentage of their weekly amount of in-school physical activity in PE classes, and be physically active for at least half of the PE class time, only a small minority of children have daily classes, and active class time is far below 50%. (p. 1501)

CONCERN OVER CHILDHOOD OBESITY

Without question, eating a lot of the wrong foods and getting little exercise can lead to weight gain. But what effect does excess weight have on chil-dren's health status? Not a good one. Carrying excess weight for an extended period is bad for health and well-being. In fact, one out of four overweight 5- to 10-year-olds has high blood pressure, high cholesterol levels, or other early warning signs for disease (Center for Science in the Public Interest, 2003b). Given that 70% to 80% of overweight youth become overweight adults (U.S. Department of Health and Human Services, 2001, cited in Cali-fornia Pan-Ethnic Health Network, 2005), there should be concern. An ar-ray of serious health problems are commonly associated with overweight and obesity, namely, type 2 diabetes, high blood pressure, heart disease, stroke, sleep disorders, certain types of cancer, arthritis and other bone and joint problems, gall bladder disease, and abnormal cholesterol levels, all of which can follow overweight youth well into their adulthood. According to the U.S. Department of Health and Human Services, unhealthy eating and physical inactivity are the primary causes of between 310,000 and 580,000 premature deaths a year (Center for Science in the Public Interest, 2003a).

Of these, type 2 diabetes has health experts especially concerned be-cause it can cause kidney disease, blindness, nerve disorders, and amputa-tions if not managed properly (Moore, 2002). Particularly worrisome is that the prevalence of type 2 diabetes among youth has increased by 33% in the past 15 years, and now more than 13,000 youth are diagnosed with diabe-tes each year (Peterson, Silverstein, Kaufman, & Warren-Boulton, 2007). This surge in type 2 diabetes cases is not by happenstance; the increasing trend coincides with the prevalence of overweight and obese youth. In fact, type 2 diabetes was once considered "adult onset" diabetes because it was seldom seen in youth, but the medical profession has had to adapt the name to reflect the growing trend. If the trend continues, the Centers for Disease Control warns, a third of all children born in 2000 will become diabetic (Action for Healthy Kids, 2003). An increasing number of youth must exert the time and energy to keep the devastating effects of type 2 diabetes at bay, and of those who do not, diabetic complications will likely develop when they are in their 30s to 40s (Center for Science in the Public Interest, 2003b).

These kinds of health risks strongly suggest that being overweight or obese (and inactive) can lead to a diminished quality of life. Ritchie and colleagues (2001) have found that adults who have been overweight since childhood are more likely to have a lower quality of life and die prematurely than their normal-weight counterparts. The Weight-Control Information Network (U.S. Department of Health and Human Services, 2006b) confirms:

> Most studies show an increase in mortality rates associated with obesity. Individuals who are obese have a 10 to 50% increased risk of death from all causes, compared with healthy weight individuals (BMI 18.5 to 24.9). Most of the increased risk is due to cardiovascular causes. Obesity is associated with about 112,000 excess deaths per year in the US population relative to healthy weight individuals. (p. 6)

Others have noted that being overweight and obese can result in disability and loss of independence from stroke and heart diseases, or blindness and limb amputation from diabetes.

What many fail to realize is that overweight and obesity can leave an indelible mark on a child's self-esteem and confidence. In fact, the psychosocial effects of excess weight are often experienced far before any of the maladies. Undoubtedly, excess weight in our culture is a stigma. Sure, youth might feel awkward about being too tall or too short, not conforming to gender roles, having to wear glasses or braces, or fumbling at sports. But these are not related to severe stigmas; overweight and obesity are. Youth who happen to be overweight or obese worry about not fitting in, standing out, and not being as coordinated as their leaner peers. In addition, their clothes are generally bigger and their bodies are often larger, both of which are grounds for the meanest form of child's play: teasing and alienation. In learning communities nationwide, children use words like *pig*, *whale*, *hippo*, and *rhino*, as well as *fatso*, *fatty*, and *blimp*, to cut deep into another child's spirit. If that were not bad enough, children and youth are exposed to overweight characters in movies and literature who are bumbling, clumsy, and jolly, perpetuating an unfavorable image. Youth report that being socially marginalized and discriminated against are the worst aspects of being overweight (Puhl & Brownell, 2001). It should come as no surprise that carrying excess weight can negatively affect the social and psychological development of children and adolescents (Birdwell, 2006). Overweight and obese youngsters suffer from poor self-esteem, depression, feelings of isolation, and anxiety disorders (Schwimmer, Burwinkle, & Varni, 2003).

Excess weight can also affect a child's performance in the classroom. Health experts agree that poor nutrition and a lack of consistent physical activity are factors associated with lower academic achievement (Bogden, 2000).

When children do not eat well or exercise regularly they are not healthy, leading to attention, concentration, and motivation problems that adversely affect their learning. Some studies have found that severely overweight youth

- were four times more likely to report "impaired school functioning" (Schwimmer et al., 2003);
- were likely to have abnormal scores on the Child Behavior Checklist (Tershakovic, Weller, & Gallagher, 1994); and
- were two times more likely to be in special education or remedial classes (Tershakovic, Weller, & Gallagher).

A growing body of evidence suggests that when youth are overweight or obese, they have health problems that force them to miss school. One study found that severely overweight children miss four times as much school as their normal-weight peers (Schwimmer et al., 2003). This is problematic for school districts because many rely heavily on attendance for state funding. When one student misses a single day of school, a district can forfeit from $9 to $20 (Action for Healthy Kids, 2005a). If youth miss 1 day a month, districts like Los Angeles Unified could lose about $15 million, New York City's public schools about $28 million, and Chicago Public Schools $9 million in important state aid (Action for Healthy Kids, 2005a).

TIME TO ADDRESS THE CHILDHOOD OBESITY EPIDEMIC

Unmistakably, youth who carry excess weight for extended periods can experience dreadful outcomes in their lifetime. The time has come to help youngsters understand that the health-related decisions they make today have lifelong effects on their health and well-being. They already make decisions about what they eat and when they exercise, they simply lack the tools to fully understand the essentials of eating right and exercising. They *can* learn how to make smart decisions (without the aid of diet pills, fad diets, or other popular shortcuts) and manage a healthy lifestyle. When children are given the knowledge associated with eating right and exercising, and are supported and encouraged to use that knowledge routinely, they are likely to experience a wide range of healthy results, including sound self-esteem, a lean body, strong bones and muscles, boosts in energy, improved school performance, increased physical performance, and a reduced risk of developing obesity-related diseases.

Schools, then, are the apparent mechanism from which to positively redirect the health lives of children. Youth already learn knowledge, skills, and behaviors to succeed in life. Why not provide them with correct and consistent instruction on food and fitness so that they can develop a practice that leads to a lifetime of physical, mental, and emotional health? Parents can certainly endorse whatever the students learn at school, but because many of them are too busy or simply do not understand wellness, they cannot be held solely responsible for advising children about eating right and exercise. Schools are ideal vessels because they have a captive audience, of about 56 million youth, for nearly 7 hours a day. No community organization, medical group, or wellness foundation could come close to attracting that many pupils for a health-promotion program. Imagine the logistical nightmare if these kinds of entities *were* the only means. In fact, schools have two perfect laboratories where youth can reinforce what they have learned in the classroom: the cafeteria and the gym. Many youth already eat most of their meals at school and some take PE regularly, so learning about food and fitness at school is practical.

Because habit development does not happen overnight, it makes good sense for children to be taught healthy living in the elementary grades. With a head start on health, teachers can collaborate with parents to engineer the framework on which children base their decision-making skills. An added benefit of early instruction is that health messages can be reinforced yearly, and as children grow they will begin to influence others, particularly adults. Indeed, the earlier they are started, the more time they have to improve their health. Teachers play a fundamental role in establishing the framework. As the instructional delivery expert, teachers know child and adolescent development well and are familiar with their students' culture and habits. In effect, teachers can tailor food and fitness instruction to meet students' unique needs; they can make the right connections with home life; they have the clout to influence children in positive ways. In short, teachers can empower youth with the right tools.

ABOUT *JUMP START HEALTH!*

Jump Start Health! is a comprehensive text with tools designed to help teachers and health practitioners improve the dietary and physical activity habits of youngsters nationwide. Twenty-eight practical ideas are provided in this book: 15 are found in Chapter 4, and 13 are in Chapter 6. They underscore the importance of eating right and engaging in routine physical activity, which support the overarching theme that a balance must exist in their lives with what they eat with what they do. Imagine these Ideas as starting blocks paving the way toward meeting the federal recommendations outlined in *Dietary Guidelines for Americans*, MyPyramid, and *Healthy People 2010*.

Jump Start Health! is teacher friendly and easy to navigate. Each of the 28 Ideas has a rationale and clear objectives, includes an instructional sequence that aims to fulfill national standards, has guided and independent activities, and has tips to extend the Idea. Moreover, the supplementary reproducibles, which are available at the Teachers College Press website (http://www.teacherscollegepress.com), can be photocopied so that the students—in small or large groups—can complete them in class or at home. By design, the Ideas impel students to examine what they eat and how much exercise they get, to think critically about committing to an appropriate lifestyle change, and to share their health knowledge with their family and friends.

Today there are many federal, state, and local initiatives that implore you to augment the standard curriculum, which may make it feel like the weight of the world is on your shoulders. With so much to accomplish in a given day, you may ask yourself, Why should I use *Jump Start Health!* in my classroom? The answer, quite simply, is to reduce youngsters' risk of becoming overweight or obese, thereby reducing their risk of developing chronic diseases. Indeed, youth need the decision-making skills to choose the right foods to consume and the right amount to exercise. Unlike other commercial health curricula, *Jump Start Health!* offers 28 Ideas—teaching materials that not only address the National Health Education Standards (The Joint Committee on National Health Education Standards, 2007) and National Standards for Physical Education (NASPE, 2004), but also promote and reinforce the message that healthy living is empowering.

A salient feature of the 28 Ideas is that they can be taught in sequence, or they can be used according to the needs of your learning community. It is strongly recommended, however, that the ideas be taught in a consecutive fashion so that the children consistently get the nutrition and physical activity education information, followed with opportunities to apply what they have learned in interactive activities. *Jump Start Health!* is encouraging because it can also be your own starting point for making lifestyle changes. Use it to design your own personal action plan to make the right choices, and then share your experiences with students. In all, if used accordingly, this text has the potential to enhance users' health, which leads to feeling better, moving with ease in physical activities, and learning better.

Jump Start Health! also communicates healthy practices in a fun way. Positive messages are used in a nonthreatening style to encourage youngsters to adopt, develop, and apply smart choices for their health. There is an emphasis that they have the capability to improve the quality of their health by adjusting their behaviors. At no time is dieting or weight loss suggested, nor are overweight or obese children singled out with demoralizing messages that can lead to irrevocable emotional damage. Instead, the messages are ones of acceptance and health at any size.

Finally, the 28 Ideas can extend the lessons at home, which reinforces the intended messages. This is particularly important because youngsters, by their very circumstance in life, depend on parents and (sometimes) older siblings to make the right decisions to meet their unique needs. The 28 Ideas lend themselves to shaping role models who can reaffirm that optimal health is important. After all, some parents may have never had health education or have incorrect assumptions about food and exercise.

CONCLUSION

That an increasing number of youngsters tend to eat the wrong foods and that modern conveniences and technology are steering them toward a sedentary lifestyle is compelling enough to counter the trend, especially since there appears to be little sign of the obesity crisis slowing down. While some school personnel may find that there is no harm when a youngster has a prodigious girth (because the effects are not readily seen), the signs suggest otherwise. Indeed, there are negative health consequences associated with extra weight, not to mention that discrimination in the form of teasing, insults, and bullying can have untoward effects on a youngster's socio-emotional condition. Moreover, if youngsters do not learn about eating right and exercise early in their lives, they are more likely to develop a lifetime of bad habits that spoil their health and wellness.

The time has come to address childhood obesity and *Jump Start Health!* can be a valuable tool to do so. In all, this text is intended to enhance the lives of youngsters. The 28 Ideas use the very recommendations proposed by the federal government to challenge and equip children with the knowledge to make smart choices. Children need *Jump Start Health!* and similar curricula because—make no mistake—health and wellness play a considerable role in their performance in school. The next chapter explores the dimensions of health and wellness giving rise to the confirming need to carry out the 28 Ideas.

CHAPTER 2

The Significance of Health and Wellness

Our country is in the throes of a serious health problem. With child obesity levels so high, it is self-evident that children today are simply not as healthy as children of a decade or 2 ago. Because excess weight on a child's body can wreak havoc on his or her physical and emotional health, youth-serving professionals are obligated to embrace the long-term challenge to give youngsters access to healthy foods and provide them with ample opportunities for daily physical activity, both of which play a pivotal role in maintaining a healthy body. As glib as it may sound, there are no simple answers for crises, but in the case of the childhood obesity epidemic, there may be: getting children to fully understand that the choices they make now can improve the quality of their lives. More specifically, children need help in developing the habits that lead to and maintain good health.

To get children to thrive now and in the future, we need to equip them with the knowledge and skills that lead to health and wellness. The Ideas presented in *Jump Start Heath*, specifically Chapters 4 and 6, aim to do just that. But before approaching the behaviors that enhance (and threaten) health and wellness, let's explore the dimensions associated with these two interdependent concepts:

- What is health and wellness?
- Media and body image
- The federal government and health and wellness

THE STATE OF HEALTH AND WELLNESS

So often we read and hear about the importance of health and wellness. While most adults may have a general understanding of health and know the behaviors that are detrimental to wellness, children, because of their limited experiences, often do not. Discussing the terms *health* and *wellness* is significant because we cannot expect youth to commit time and effort to

FIGURE 2.1. Top 10 Leading Causes of Death in the United States

Heart disease
Cancer
Stroke (cerebrovascular diseases)
Chronic lower respiratory diseases
Accidents
Diabetes
Alzheimer's disease
Influenza and Pneumonia
Nephritis, nephrotic syndrome, and nephrosis
Septicemia

Source: National Center for Health Statistics. (2009). *Number of deaths for leading causes of death*. Retrieved December 26, 2009, from http://www.cdc.gov/nchs/FASTATS/lcod.htm.

developing positive habits, if they cannot recognize the assumptions, concepts, and practices associated with these two terms.

Health is often perceived as an aspect of life that unavoidably affects humans, or better yet, is assumed to be a condition that is predestined, is inevitable, and cannot be controlled or mastered. Typically, the assumption is that people are fortunate to have been graced with good health or ill-fated because of bad health. Added to that fallacious notion is the impression that one day a person awakens to bad health by chance. Sure, there are acute diseases—diseases that appear suddenly, have identifiable causes, are generally treatable, and vanish in a short time—like appendicitis and pneumonia, but most diseases are chronic (Anspaugh, Hamrick, & Rosato, 2006). Chronic illnesses—heart disease, diabetes, hypertension—are gradual, are caused by multiple factors, endure indefinitely, and are often caused by long-standing lifestyle habits (Anspaugh et al., 2006). In fact, most illnesses in life are preventable. A cursory examination of the common causes of death finds that most people—about 65% of all deaths—die from, or from a complication of, heart disease, cancer, and stroke (American Academy of Family Physicians, 2008). (See Figure 2.1 for the top 10 leading causes of death). Most of these diseases are largely attributed to long-term lifestyle habits such as eating unbalanced diets, living sedentarily, and smoking.

Another popular image of health is absence of illness and disease, which is understandable, considering that being sick, encumbered with a disease, or unable to perform common physical activities do not necessarily invoke affirming images of health. However, the framework of health is far more intricate than these two commonly held views. According to the World Health Organization (2001), health is defined as a state of complete physical, mental, and social well-being and not merely the absence of disease or infirmity. . . . Health is a cumulative state, to be promoted throughout life in order to ensure that the full benefits are enjoyed in later years. Good health is vital to maintain an acceptable quality of life in older individuals and to ensure the continued contributions of older persons to society. (p. 10)

The *American Heritage Stedman's Medical Dictionary* (2008) defines health as "the overall condition of an organism at a given time" and "soundness, especially of body or mind; freedom from disease or abnormality." Others have added that health is an individual quality, personal and unique (Bounds, Shea, Agnor, & Darnell, 2006); does not imply perfection (Anspaugh, Hamrick, & Rosato, 2006); and to a great extent is self-controlling, implying that—after weighing the ostensible effects of personal hereditary—the habits of today can influence health for decades (Hoeger & Hoeger, 2007).

It is difficult to define or discuss health without mention of wellness because the two terms are closely interwoven. Essentially, the definition of health encompasses wellness, which is considered the sense of well-being in all aspects of life, that is, to find work, personal relationships, and life meaningful so that pervasive feelings of happiness and satisfaction are fostered. Corbin, Welk, Corbin, and Welk (2008) assert, "Wellness reflects how one feels (a sense of well-being) about life, as well as one's ability to function effectively" (p. 5). Hoeger and Hoeger (2007) affirm, "Wellness implies a constant and deliberate effort to stay healthy and achieve the highest potential for well-being. Wellness requires implementing positive lifestyle habits to change behavior and thereby improve health and quality of life, prolong life, and achieve total well-being" (p. 8). And Anspaugh and colleagues (2006) add:

> Wellness is defined as a lifelong process that at any given time produces a positive state of personal well-being, of feeling good about yourself; of optimal physical, psychological, and social functioning; and the control and minimization of both internal and external risk factors for both diseases and negative health conditions. Wellness is a process rather than a goal. It implies a choice, a way of life. It means integrating the body, mind, and spirit. It symbolizes acceptance of yourself. It suggests that what you believe, feel, and do have an influence on your health. (p. 2)

Health experts have identified seven dimensions of wellness. To achieve and maintain ultimate health, individuals must commit their fullest personal ability to the forces associated with emotional, intellectual, social, spiritual, physical, occupational, and environmental wellness. Distinct as these are, the seven dimensions function congruously as they overlap, interact, and affect one another.

Emotional Wellness

This dimension is about the personal ability to cope with the ups and downs of life. People remain emotionally stable despite daily stresses and occasional life disappointments. They accept their limitations and do not let them hamper their outlook on life. They keep their emotions in check and respond to burdensome situations in positive and constructive ways.

Intellectual Wellness

This dimension is characterized by having an actively engaged mind that seeks information on how to keep aspects of life—health, career, or personal development—in harmony. Those who exhibit intellectual wellness are lifelong learners who engender learning opportunities to enhance their lives. Open-mindedness and acceptance are salient traits in this dimension (Hoeger & Hoeger, 2007).

Social Wellness

Individuals who have social wellness easily develop positive relationships with others, be it intimate connections with family and friends or more professional ones with work associates. Relationships are enhanced because of an authentic concern for the wellbeing of others, and an outwardly show of respect is delivered to others even when differences are apparent. In short, a person's social and familial network is enhanced because of his or her inclusion.

Spiritual Wellness

Most often associated with prayer, meditation, and serving others, this dimension is about the personal relationship with a greater power that stimulates tranquility, inner strength, and ability. The faith in a Supreme Being generates sound morals, values, ethics, and beliefs and is an ending source of guidance. A fulfilled life in this venue is not contingent upon a specific religion or creed. Moreover, because spiritual wellness encompasses keeping purpose in life, working toward balance through life, and having principles throughout life, people who do not believe in a Supreme Being can also develop spiritual wellness.

Physical Wellness

This dimension is about attending to and being able to use the physical body efficiently to endure the demands of daily life, and committing to an exercise regimen that develops the components of health-related physical fitness, known as body composition, flexibility, strength, cardiovascular fitness, and muscular endurance (Corbin et al., 2008).

Individuals with sound physical wellness avoid harmful matters that may hamper their fitness, such as the abuse of drugs or alcohol.

Occupational Wellness

This dimension embodies the balance of personal life and work, career, and all matters that lead to occupation, including schooling, parenting, and volunteering. Persons with occupational wellness find reward in building and developing a career; take satisfaction at work, knowing that their abilities and potential are tapped; and seek opportunities to create new skills and refines those they have. Hoeger and Hoeger (2007) comment, "Occupational wellness encourages collaboration and interaction among co-workers, which fosters a sense of teamwork and support" (p. 13). In short, work is not a nuisance, but a mechanism for personal and professional growth.

Environmental Wellness

While some might find it odd that the environment is considered a dimension of wellness, it is crucial to our very survival. Without clean, safe food, water, air, and shelter, humans may very well be subjected to the range of diseases that were visited upon society just a century ago. A person who manifests environmental wellness is conscientious about the current and future standard of living and serves the environment through local, national, and worldwide projects that make for a better ecosystem.

In sum, health and wellness are about the general emotions and behaviors associated with the mental, physical, and psychosocial spheres of everyday life. People with sound health and wellness have affirming feelings about their quality of life, feel good about themselves, exude a genuine aura of welfare, and avoid behaviors and substances that can devastate their well-being. Conversely, health and wellness are not about being thin or about weight loss, but unfortunately, in the eyes of many youth they are. For some, dieting and weight loss are serious goals because the body image that is often promoted in the media through celebrities and other slender pop culture icons in magazines, on TV, in movies, and in other outlets is largely an unrealistic one. But how exactly does the media shape an unhealthy body image?

THE MEDIA AND BODY IMAGE

The effect that the media has on body image is an important topic. Youth are barraged with messages that potentially mold how they feel about their bodies: Being thin is the norm, and the fashion, for attractive and successful individuals. What should be avoided is the tendency to use the Ideas in this text and other health resources to intensify the impression that being svelte is desirable above all. With such a message, youth are likely to assume that being overweight or obese is an abysmal way of life and they may begin to engage in unsafe weight-loss practices (e.g., diet pills and smoking), which can make for irreparable body damage. Moreover, when they do not reach their ideal weight—an unrealistic one, nonetheless—they are likely to develop a poor sense of self, not to mention that such recurring messages will wreak havoc on the self-esteem of those who are overweight and obese.

Body image is a dynamic psychosocial occurrence associated with the feelings and values people have about their body. Body image is the way that a person feels in and about his or her body (Witmer, 2008). Based on perception rather fact, body image is individually constructed by way of the social influences of people with whom they interact and of the mass media. Moreover, body image is shaped by how parents, family, peers and others react to a person's body shape and size (National Institute on Media and the Family, 2008). As youth mature they become increasingly aware of what is considered the ideal body from continual exposure to the value that is assigned to certain body types. In short, if individuals see images repeated often enough, they begin to believe that they are a version of reality (Schooler & Ward, 2006).

In their position statement on media violence, the American Academy of Pediatrics (2001b) indicated, "Children are influenced by media—they learn by observing, imitating, and making behaviors their own. . . . They are uniquely vulnerable to learning and adopting as reality the circumstances, attitudes, and behaviors portrayed by entertainment media" (p. 1223). While this is a position about violence, it is not inconceivable that media can leave youth with lasting impressions about what is considered ideal physically. In fact, studies have confirmed that media icons have great influence on how people feel about their bodies. The National Institute on Media and the Family (2008) reports on these studies:

- Tiggemann and Pickering (1996) reported a correlation between the amount of time adolescents watched music videos, movies, and soap operas and personal degree of body satisfaction;
- Harrison and Cantor (1997) found that media influenced undergraduate males to strive for trim bodies and undergraduate females to develop body dissatisfaction;

- Hargreaves and Tiggeman (2002) noted that adolescent girls grew less confident and dissatisfied with their bodies and appearance after watching commercials of unrealistically thin beauties;
- a study of fifth graders found that they became dissatisfied with their bodies after watching a video of Britney Spears or a clip from the sitcom *Friends* (Mundell, 2002); and
- one Australian study of 1,500 youth in Grades 8 through 11 found that boys were vulnerable to becoming body obsessed (i.e., being lean and muscular) after watching music videos (cited in Mundell, 2005).

Particularly disturbing is that popular media seem to perpetuate a supposed ideal body—generally a slender one for girls and a trim and muscular one for boys—through pervasive, yet discreet, casual images and messages (National Institute on Media and the Family, 2008). Indeed, the media are powerful by their very nature because they create and define what is good, attractive, successful, strong, positive, and capable and without mention of the antitheses circumscribes what is not. By design, popular media wield glamorous people, appealing features, and alluring products to attract consumers and convince them of what they need. An unfortunate byproduct is benchmarks for appearance, body weight, size, and shape.

At some point in life people may be conscientious about their body, hanker for physical change, and adapt their appearance to reflect a social fad. This phenomenon is nothing new. After all, Chinese women bound their feet to make them smaller, and 19th-century Western women wore corsets to give the impression of an hourglass figure. But a striking difference between industrialized societies past and modern is that our forebears lived in confined communities with little or no media. The only influence contributing to their body image came from their immediate social circles. Now, easily accessible technology allows for widely disseminated images of the ideal body, one that keeps getting thinner.

Iconic beauties of the 1950s—like Marilyn Monroe and Jayne Mansfield—who were heavier and bustier have been replaced by the gaunt ingénue seen repeatedly in pop media. Today, the average model is 5'10" and weighs about 110 pounds; the average woman is 5'4" and weighs 145 pounds (U.S. Department of Health and Human Services, 2008c). Fox (1997) explains:

> In 1917, the physically perfect woman was about 5ft 4 tall and weighed nearly 10 stone. Even 25 years ago, top models and beauty queens weighed only 8% less than the average woman, now they weigh 23% less. The current media ideal for women is achievable by less than 5% of the female population—and

that's just in terms of weight and size. If you want the ideal shape, face, it's probably more like 1%.

Even modern-day TV sitcoms sport female characters who are typically underweight. Only 1 in 20 is above average size and unsurprisingly, that character's weight is often the target of criticism from male characters, paired with audience laughter (Fouts & Burggraf, 2000).

Another influence on youth and their body image are their toys, particularly Barbie and action figures, which are often marketed in commercials during TV shows popular with children. Barbie has been a popular toy since Mattel debuted the doll in 1959. The curvaceous doll has perfect features, coupled with a stick-thin waist (not to mention nearly every material possession imaginable!). Many young girls are unaware that if Barbie (and similar dolls) were human, her body would be wracked by unending ailments. According to the Media Awareness Network (2008):

> Barbie-doll proportions, for example, found that her back would be too weak to support the weight of her upper body, and her body would be too narrow to contain more than half a liver and few centimeters of bowel. A real woman built that way would suffer from chronic diarrhea and eventually die from malnutrition.

Young boys are vulnerable to the influence of action figures. Like Barbie, their toys evince some exceptional features, albeit more muscular ones. The UCLA Student Nutrition and Body Image Action Committee (2008) point out, "If GI Joe Extreme were life-size, he would have a 55 inch chest and 27 inch bicep. In other words, his bicep would be almost as big as his waist and bigger than most competitive body builders."

Today's youth must persevere through what must be distressing predicaments because of the perpetual contradiction. Youth are continually exposed to two groups of people—the everyday commoners who are likely overweight, and the unrealistically thin models in the media—and they are charged with a challenging mental task: to reconcile the two images and develop a healthy one. Imagine their psychological unease when they witness a commercial for their favorite junk food promoted by slender models.

Having the perfect body resonates with many Americans—if not, the multimillion-dollar diet industry would not exist—but weight loss and that unrealistically thin body is not a healthy goal for youth; health and wellness are. There are many resources in addition to *Jump Start Health!* that can help youth attain that goal, some of which are largely promoted by the federal government.

THE FEDERAL GOVERNMENT AND HEALTH AND WELLNESS

The U.S. government has had a keen interest in the country's health for some time. After all, a country is only as strong and healthy as its people. The federal agency charged with the task of promoting and protecting the public's health is the U.S. Department of Health and Human Services (which houses the Centers for Disease Control, National Institute of Health, and a range of other agencies), and to some extent, other federal branches collaborate accordingly to produce guidelines and create programs that foster general well-being. The resources include *Healthy People 2010*, *Dietary Guidelines for Americans*, MyPyramid: Steps to a Healthier You, Let's Move, *HealthierUS*, Centers for Disease Control and Prevention: BAM! and U.S. Department of Agriculture: Eat Smart, Play Hard.

Healthy People 2010

Healthy People covers a wide range of realistic goals that guide Americans toward improving their well-being. The nearly 30-year-old comprehensive framework began in 1979 as a surgeon general report that became the 1980 document *Promoting Health/Preventing Disease: Objectives for the Nation*. It was regarded as a 10-year action plan, which set into motion *Healthy People 2000* and the current 2010 version. (The 2020 edition is in the works). *Promoting Health/Preventing Disease* concentrated on disease prevention alone, while *Healthy People 2000* incorporated health promotion (Corbin et al., 2008). A federal circular announced:

> *Healthy People 2010* offers a simple but powerful idea: Give our country clear health objectives in a way that allows diverse groups to combine their efforts and work together as a team. *Healthy People 2010* is the basis for coordinated public health action on the national, state, and local levels and has been used as a teaching tool for the next generation of public health leaders. (U.S. Department of Health & Human Services, 2005d)

Healthy People 2010 addresses the 10 most important health issues of our time. They are known as *Leading Health Indicators* and include physical activity, overweight and obesity, tobacco use, substance abuse, responsible sexual behavior, mental health, injury and violence, environmental quality, immunization, and access to health care. The indicators operate within two overarching goals, to increase people's quality and years of healthy lives and to eliminate health disparities in disease, and encompass 467 science-based objectives (U.S. Department of Health and Human Services, 2000a).

The two indicators most relevant to the topic of childhood obesity are overweight and obesity and physical activity. In the late 1990s nearly 65%

of adolescents (in grades 9 through 12) were engaged in vigorous physical activity 3 or more days a week. The 2010 target is 85%. The baseline for the overweight and obesity indicator was 11%, which represented the percentage of youngsters between the ages of 6 and 19 (between 1988 and 1999) who were considered overweight and obese. The 2010 target is 5%.

Dietary Guidelines for Americans

The U.S. Department of Health and Human Services and the U.S. Department of Agriculture collaborate to furnish the *Dietary Guidelines for Americans, 2005*. This report also originated in 1980; however, the guidelines, which are revised every 5 years by an appointed expert advisory committee, are recommendations on the nutritional consumption and physical exercise that is considered best for Americans over the age of 2. The *Dietary Guidelines*, as they are often referred to, are the very blueprint for federal and nutrition programs that seek to reduce common diet-related diseases, such as hypertension and coronary heart disease. After the initial background and purpose discourse, the 23 scientifically based recommendations (with 18 key recommendations for specific population groups) are found in chapters titled "Adequate Nutrition Within Calorie Needs," "Weight Management," "Physical Activity," "Food Groups to Encourage," "Fats," "Carbohydrates," "Sodium and Potassium," "Alcoholic Beverages," and "Food Safety." In all, the current *Dietary Guidelines* "urge Americans to consume fewer calories, incorporate physical activity in their daily routine, and make smarter food choices" (Anspaugh et al., 2006, p. 210).

MyPyramid: Steps to a Healthier You

If *Dietary Guidelines* is the conceptual framework for this nation's health, then MyPyramid: Steps to a Healthier You (found at the USDA website, http://www.mypyramid.gov) is the functional medium to fulfill the outlined recommendations. Long before the inception of the nutritional pyramid that is so commonplace today, the USDA established four basic food groups— meat, dairy, grain, and fruits and vegetables—and encouraged Americans to consume from each group at every meal. There was no mention of moderation, proportion, and variety, primarily because medical science was in its infancy and research on conditions such as heart disease and diabetes, which are well known today, was meager. By 1992 the four food groups evolved into the food pyramid, which introduced proportions and layered the groups according to the number of servings that should be consumed in a given day. The bread, cereal, rice, and pasta group was at the base; the fruit group and vegetable group was on the second layer; following these were the milk, yogurt, and cheese group and meat, poultry, fish, dry beans, eggs, and nuts group on the third layer. On the remaining layer, the peak, was the fats, oils, and sweets group with "use sparingly" in parenthesis. The USDA revised the food pyramid again, and in 2004 introduced MyPyramid to complement the 2005 version of *Dietary Guidelines.*

MyPyramid is composed of colored bands that represent the food groups and oils. Each band is proportioned differently, according to the amount that should be eaten daily. Consider these visuals a nudge on limiting the consumption of foods loaded with fats, sugars, and salt. The grains, vegetables, fruits, and milk have wider bands, and the meats and beans and oils have narrower ones. Along the left side of the pyramid is a person climbing stairs, a reminder to balance diet with physical activity. (Figure 2.2 shows another version, MyPyramid for Kids). An added bonus of MyPyramid is a complete Web-based interactive system (www.mypyramid.gov) that allows consumers to type in their vitals to create their individual MyPyramid, which recommends the amount of foods to consume, stabilized with physical activity.

Let's Move

First Lady Michelle Obama showed interest in children's health when her husband, Barack Obama, was elected president. Within the year following his inauguration, she involved children in establishing a vegetable garden and a playground on the White House lawn. So there was little surprise when in February 2010 she officially announced that her campaign, Let's Move, would work to resolve the childhood obesity epidemic. Immediately thereafter, the president issued a memorandum to the heads of executive departments and agencies, calling for a task force on childhood obesity. In it the president wrote:

> My Administration is committed to redoubling our efforts to solve the problem of childhood obesity within a generation through a comprehensive approach that builds on effective strategies, engages families and communities, and mobilizes both public and private sector resources. . . . Therefore, I have set a goal to solve the problem of childhood obesity within a generation so that children born today will reach adulthood at a healthy weight. (The White House Office of the Press Secretary, 2010)

The task force was assigned to develop and implement an interagency plan with benchmarks and the outline of an action plan to reduce the childhood obesity rate to 5% by 2030. Within 90 days, the White House Task Force on Childhood Obesity Report to the President was released, with specific recommendations for early childhood; empowering parents and caregivers; healthy food in school; access to healthy, affordable food; and increasing physical activity.

FIGURE 2.2. MyPyramid for Kids

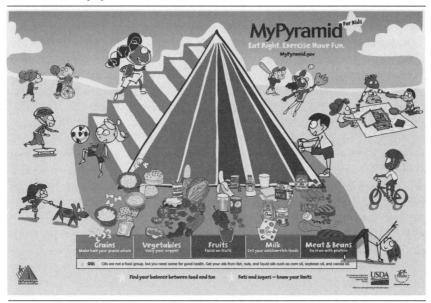

Source. U.S. Department of Agriculture (2005). *My pyramid for kids.* Retrieved May 18, 2010, from http://www.fns.usda.gov/tn/Mypyramid/mpk_poster.jpg.

Let's Move has a number of endeavors and activities under the groupings Healthy Choices, Healthier Schools, Physical Activity, and Access to Affordable Healthy Food. Healthy Choices is about informing parents and guiding them in how to plan for and make healthy choices that help their family to live healthier. The guiding principle herein is that children who observe their parents making healthier choices about diet and physical activity will follow suit. Federal agencies, specifically the Food and Drug Administration and the U.S. Department of Agriculture, in collaboration with the American Academy of Pediatrics, are assigned to empower consumers and engender behavior change through research, tool kits, and databases that map out best health practices.

The HealthierUS School Challenge program is found on the Let's Move website. The U.S. Department of Agriculture has been selected as the lead agency to disseminate information on healthy diets for children and collaborate with schools and their food suppliers to create nutritious meals. The Challenge specifically seeks to reduce the amount of sugar, fat, and salt in meals and snacks and increase the amount of whole grains and produce served at lunch. According to Let's Move (n.d.), the Challenge aims to establish "rigorous standards for schools' food quality, participation in meal programs, physical activity, and nutrition education—the key components that make for healthy and active kids—and provides recognition for schools that meet these standards."

The Physical Activity component is about increasing the opportunities for children to be physically active in and out school. Through Let's Move initiatives, communities will be empowered to create safe routes so that children can walk and bike to school; parks, playgrounds, and community centers where children can play; and sports, dance, and fitness programs that can motivate children and engage them in physical activity. As of this writing, this component of Let's Move was being formalized; in the interim, children and adults are encouraged to commit to physical fitness by way of the President's Challenge Program (discussed in the next section). The last component is about access to healthy food (or lack thereof), since there are people living in regions of this country who do not have easy access to affordable, healthy food. These regions are known as "food deserts" because the food that consumers can obtain is limited (e.g., convenience stores and bodegas are stocked with little to no fruits and vegetables) or of poor quality (e.g., fast-food establishments are abundant). Let's Move believes that this lack of access is one of the reasons why many children do not consume the recommended levels of whole grains, fruits and vegetables, dairy, and so forth. Let's Move seeks to wipe out food deserts with the support of the president and his administration. In fact, $400 million was appropriated in the fiscal year 2011 federal budget, through the Health Food Financing Initiative, to help underserved areas have healthier food options.

HealthierUS

HealthierUS is a comprehensive health initiative spawned by President George W. Bush's public health and wellness agenda. His agenda sought to encourage and support Americans to have a healthier lifestyle and healthier habits by accentuating four tenets:

- Be physically active every day
- Eat a nutritious diet
- Get preventive screenings and
- Make healthy choices.

(Despite President Bush's departure from office, the website and campaign are still operating.) In the mission to improve people's lives, the HealthierUS initiative also includes

- The HealthierUS website, which provides "credible, accurate information" for consumers seeking exercise and nutrition direction;

- Steps to a HealthierUS, which funds community-based programs proved to reduce the risk and burden of diseases largely attributed to excess weight. The 2004 federal budget earmarked $125 million for this endeavor. Since 2003, over $100 million has been awarded to 40 communities, including funding to the YMCA.
- An advisory committee to the president known as the President's Council on Fitness, Sports, and Nutrition. Its task, in collaboration with other public and private organizations, is to promote enjoyable, rewarding, and beneficial physical activity, fitness, and sports for all Americans regardless of ability. Its website, www.fitness.gov, offers downloadable publications, links to resources, and discourse on popular topics.
- The President's Challenge, which is sponsored by the President's Council on Fitness, Sports, and Nutrition. The challenge, found at www.presidentschallenge.org, is to engage 20 million Americans in physical activity on a daily basis. The program motivates users by offering awards (i.e., certificates, emblems, and medallions) to those who reach their defined goals, which are tracked through downloadable activity logs that are submitted at their completion.

Centers for Disease Control and Prevention: BAM!

The Centers for Disease Control and Prevention (CDC) is an expansive extension of the U.S. Department of Health and Human Services with numerous offices, centers, and initiatives that carry out the mission "to promote health and quality of life by preventing and controlling disease, injury, and disability." The CDC is the leading authority on health threats, including environmental health and injury prevention, infectious diseases, global health, and terrorism preparedness and response. The CDC website covers topics ranging from ABLES (Adult Blood Lead Epidemiology and Surveillance) to zoster (shingles); among them are obesity and overweight, but germane to this text is an enterprising program, BAM! Body and Mind.

BAM! is the interactive website (http://www.bam.gov/) for youth that features a range of developmentally appropriate topics shown in stylish graphics. The Food and Nutrition button will retrieve healthy recipes, ideas for the right snacks, and an interactive game called Dining Decisions allows players to select food items for their make-believe lunch tray. When players indicate that it is time to eat, the game describes how each item contributed to their overall health. The Physical Activity button offers site visitors the opportunity to create a calendar of physical activities, read activity cards that explain how to play specific sports and games, take a quiz on myths associated with physical activity, and use a profile determinant to ascertain the physical activities that are right for each site visitor. School personnel may find the button BAM! Classroom particularly helpful because of the array of downloadable activities and materials to use in the classroom.

United States Department of Agriculture: Eat Smart. Play Hard

The Food and Nutrition Services division of the USDA sponsors the interactive website Eat Smart. Play Hard. The campaign, launched in 2000, "encourages and teaches children, parents, and caregivers to eat healthy and be physically active every day" and "offers resources and tools to convey and reinforce healthy eating and lifestyle behaviors that are consistent with the *Dietary Guidelines for Americans* and the MyPyramid Food Guidance System."

There are three divisions at the home site (http://www.fns.usda.gov/eatsmartplayhard/): Kids, Parents, and Educators. The Kids link offers a village of icons that will retrieve resources such as activity sheets, PowerPoint slides, campaign songs and lyrics, posters and e-cards, and recipes, all of which employ the campaign spokesperson, Power Panther, and his nephew Slurp. The Parents button is more sophisticated. Site visitors will find recipes, menu-planning devices, physical activity ideas, and tracking cards. The Educators button displays a site index to access a bank of resources by topic, audience, and format.

CONCLUSION

In 2008, a government-funded study found that if the overweight and obesity trend continues as it has for the past 30 years, it is possible that by 2030, 86% of American adults could be overweight and nearly half could be obese (Wang, Beydoun, Liang, Caballero, & Kumanyika, 2008). And by 2048, nearly all adults in this nation could be at least mildly overweight. If this sobering news is not a wake-up call for large-scale social changes, then what is? This is the opportune time to help youth fully understand that health and wellness is about making better choices now and through life, which can lead to an improved quality of life. Clearly, telling them to eat less and move more is not enough. In this new century, parents, teachers, and youth-serving professionals are challenged to guide youth to take affirming control of their emotions, intellect, social and physical prowess, spiritual interest, and potential to directly or indirectly influence their activities and environment so that they lead meaningful, productive, satisfying, and contributing lives. A failure to meet the challenge puts the overall well-being (and longevity) of the populace at risk.

At this transition point, the discussion veers to two broad sections that with the combined background matter and practical information aim to nurture children's healthy eating practices and the pursuit of physical activity. In the next section, information about nutrition is presented as the foundation for the Ideas (found in Chapter 4), and also serves as a resource for teachers to use to raise children's awareness that specific behaviors contribute to health while others endanger it.

Part II

NURTURING HEALTHY DIETARY HABITS

CHAPTER 3

Snapshot on Nutrition

A recurring theme in this book is that healthy eating is key to well-being. Eating the right foods affects health in positive ways, primarily in feeling better and having more energy. But what exactly are the right foods to eat and why are they important in the daily diet? While *Jump Start Health!* is certainly not the definitive statement on nutrition, nor is it a comprehensive digest on the essential nutrients, it is imperative to address the components of a healthy dietary blueprint because eating smart suggests having some knowledge on the benefits of consuming specific foods. Therefore, this chapter discusses nutrition, which should be used to supplement *Jump Start Health!'s* principal focus, the Ideas that promote healthy eating (found in Chapter 4).

The following discussion covers foods whose consumption gives rise to good health. Its eight sections align with the food groups fundamental to MyPyramid:

- Grains
- Vegetables
- Fruits
- Milk
- Meats & Beans
- Oils
- Salt
- Sugar

GRAINS

Breads, cereals, and pastas are some foods that are commonly associated with grains like wheat, oats, rice, and corn. Some products are made from grains; others are made from whole grains. What exactly distinguishes the two? Food products made from whole grains, like whole wheat, brown rice, and whole oats, use the whole grain seed—the kernel—which includes the outer layer, the fiber-rich bran; the middle section, the endosperm; and the inner section, known as the nutrient-rich endosperm. In other words, the whole grain has not been refined. Refined foods that are made of grains have had the kernel cracked, and degrees of bran, germ, and endosperm have been separated out. In its most refined state, milled wheat grain has had the nutrient-rich components removed, resulting in white flour that is used to make white bread and pastas. This process is used in making white rice also. Ostensibly, consumers of whole-grain products benefit from the nutrients of the three components; thus MyPyramid promotes whole grain with the caption, "Make half your grains whole."

Whole grains and grains are considered great sources of energy. They are stocked with 14 rich nutrients, including the B vitamins thiamin, riboflavin, and niacin; vitamin E; selenium, which protects cells and benefits the central nervous system (Ward, 2005); iron, which supports the transport of oxygen in the blood; zinc; and magnesium, a mineral that builds bones and releases energy from muscles (Ward, 2005). Some refined grains are enriched with some of the lost nutrients and minerals, as well as folic acid, but these are not completely restored in the process. One cannot help but wonder why food manufacturers continue to refine the wondrous whole grain.

At one time refined grain was considered a luxury and was marketed to the upper classes as purer than whole-grain flour because it produced lighter and airier baked goods (Alleman, 1999). White flour, with its little amount of oil—the healthy oil had been removed—also keeps fresher longer. In time, white flour became accessible to the masses and a staple in kitchens nationwide. As Pitman and Kaufman (2000) point out, the traditional Western diet relies heavily on refined grain products.

The Grains food group appears in the orange band on the far left of the *MyPyramid*. One U.S. Department of Agriculture (2005c) publication adds that individuals with a 2,000-calorie diet should "eat at least 3 oz. of whole-grain cereals, breads, crackers, rice, or pasta every day" (p. 2). Health experts estimate that children between the ages of 9 and 13 who consume 1,600 to 1,800 calories a day need to eat five to six ounces of grains, while 14- to 18-year-olds who have an 1,800- to 2,200-calorie diet should eat six to seven ounces (University of Missouri, n.d.). The grain consumption recommendations also vary by gender and physical activity level. The best way to determine the actual consumption amounts is to visit MyPyramid.gov and enter the unique figures; the website will generate a personal plan.

The recommended ounces are high for a reason: They contribute to an overall positive effect on health and can help reduce the risk of chronic diseases such as coronary heart disease. Studies have found that consuming healthy doses of whole grains reduces the likelihood of developing type 2 diabetes and cancers of the mouth, stomach, colon, gall bladder, and ovaries (Willett & Skerrett, 2005). Moreover, health experts agree that eating the recommended whole grains can help one maintain a healthy weight. Unfortunately, most Americans eat less than one serving of whole grains a day (Healthgrain Project, 2008).

Whole grains are beneficial because of their rich nutrients, but their fiber content is just as important. Diets high in fiber help reduce the risk of developing acute diverticulitis (inflammation of the colon) and, because fiber is a natural laxative, help maintain regularity. This is welcome news considering that Americans spend over $725 million a year on laxatives and constipation is the leading gastrointestinal medical complaint, accounting for over 2 million physician visits a year (Willett & Skerrett, 2005). Fibrous foods—by way of whole grains—should also be favored because the body digests them slowly over a longer period of time, which means that it feels satisfied longer.

To check whether foods contain whole grains, read the ingredient list on the nutrition facts label. Whole grains, like wheat, rice, oats, and corn should appear as "whole." And, as important side note, keep to the recommended amount of grains needed for each day. A consumption of too many grains may lead to excess carbohydrates.

VEGETABLES

The Vegetables food group has its own color band (green) for good reason. Vegetables are impressive sources of nutrients and, when consumed as recommended, make for good health. The U.S. Department of Agriculture (2005c) currently encourages that we eat more and various kinds of vegetables than we are accustomed to. According to some research, Americans tend to eat a restricted number of vegetables: frozen potatoes, fresh potatoes, potato chips, iceberg lettuce, and canned tomatoes (Putnam, Allshouse, & Kantor, 2002). Recent studies have found that we are more likely to eat potatoes, lettuce, corn, artichokes, sweet potatoes, carrots, and cauliflower than any other vegetables (Ward, 2005). In terms of vegetable consumption:

- Only one child in five gets the recommended servings of vegetables a day (Centers for Disease Control, 2002);
- Less than a quarter of adolescents eat enough vegetables (Centers for Disease Control, 2008a);
- Nearly 27% of Americans eat vegetables three or more times per day (Centers for Disease Control, 2010a); and
- Children and adolescent vegetable consumption decreased by 32% and 42%, respectively, between 1997 and 2002 (California Pan-Ethnic Health Network, 2005).

Such findings may leave health officials a little worried because these figures fall considerably short of the *Healthy People 2010* health objective, which is to increase to 50% the percentage of persons (over 2 years old) who eat the minimum servings of three vegetables a day with at least a third being dark green or orange vegetables (Centers for Disease Control, 2007). As a prescription, think of the dark green (e.g., broccoli, collard greens, kale, turnip greens) and orange (e.g., carrots, pumpkin, sweet potatoes) vegetables in addition to the starchy vegetables (e.g., corn, green peas), dry beans and peas, and other vegetables (e.g., artichokes, asparagus, cabbage, cucumbers, okra) to maintain a balanced diet.

MyPyramid advocates varying one's vegetables because each kind of vegetable offers unique nutrients, and some are more nutritious than others, rendering more fiber than others. So to reap the maximum nutritional benefits of vegetables it is best to vary the types of vegetables eaten (Bounds et al., 2006). Each color provides its particular vitamins, minerals, and phytochemicals (plant nutrients that are neither vitamins nor minerals, but thousands of nutrients like lycopene, ellagic acid, carotenoids [beta-carotene], and isoflavones, believed to act as antioxidants that ward off diseases) (Ward, 2005).

Vegetables have many benefits. Sweet potatoes, beets, and winter squash, for example, are rich sources of potassium, which helps keep bodily fluid in check. Vegetables such as broccoli, collard greens, and Brussels sprouts are excellent sources of calcium for healthy teeth and bones. Vegetables also have few calories; are low in fat, sodium, and cholesterol; are filling; help satisfy daily fluid requirements; and when eaten as part of a reduced-calorie diet help maintain a healthy weight (Centers for Disease Control, 2007; National Institutes of Health, 2005). Moreover, as a natural laxative, their fiber can be counted on to contribute to regularity.

Studies have found that vegetables can contribute to cardiovascular and eye health and enhanced memory (Willett & Skerrett, 2005), as well as slow the effects of aging, help control weight, and boost energy levels (California Department of Health, n.d.). More important, eating the right vegetables keeps some cancers at bay, notably, mouth and throat, lung, stomach, bladder, colon and rectal, breast, and prostate (Willett & Skerrett, 2005). Nearly 1 in 10 cancers is attributed to insufficient consumption of vegetables (and fruit) (Corbin et al., 2008), and populations that eat large amounts of vegetables (and fruit) have lowered risks of developing cancer (Anspaugh et al., 2006). These kinds of findings were the impetus for the National Cancer Institute campaign "5 a Day," which promotes eating at least five vegetables and fruits a day.

The recommended servings of vegetables vary by age, gender, and physical activity level. For instance, 4- to 8-year-old youngsters should eat about 1½ cups; children between the ages of 9 and 13 who consume from 1,600 to

1,800 calories should eat 2 to 2½ cups, and youth 14 to 18 whose diet range is 1,800 to 2,200 calories should eat 2½ to 3 cups. These are minimum requirements, not goals to consider. After all, a unit of the recommended servings is small, often likened to half the size of a fist. And the opportunity to eat them is presented in a variety of mediums: from the freezer, the can, dried, juiced, or raw. (As a side note, some health experts argue that potatoes should not be included among the recommended servings because they do not offer the same health benefits as other vegetables [Willett & Skerrett, 2005]).

FRUITS

To the immediate right of the vegetables band is the fruits group colored in red with the caption "Focus on Fruit," which suggests that they should be eaten at meals or as snacks instead of the sugary, low-nutrient junk food. The recommended servings of fruit—generally 2 cups for a 2,000-calorie diet—can be eaten fresh, frozen, dried, juiced (although juices offer lower levels of fiber than raw fruit, and too much can cause diarrhea in young children), or from the can (dieticians are wary of added sugars found in canned products). For children, MyPyramid generally recommends 2 to 2½ cups for 9- to 13-year-olds on 1,600- to 1,800-calorie diets, and 2½ to 3 cups for those between 14 and 18 on 1,800 to 2,200 calories. As with vegetables, variety is key because each fruit contains unique nutrients. Eating the recommended servings of fruit keeps chronic diseases at bay as they, like vegetables, provide an array of vitamins, minerals, and phytochemicals that ward off toxins, as well as being good sources of fiber and water. Despite the value that fruits add to a diet, less than 15% of school children consume the recommended servings of fruit (U.S. Department of Agriculture, n.d., cited in Vail, 2004).

MILK

The Milk group, which includes various dairy products, has a blue color band with the expression "Get your calcium rich foods." MyPyramid recommends that youth between 9 and 18 years old get 3 cups of milk (or equivalent amounts of milk products) daily, and that youngsters between 2 and 8 years old consume about 2 cups (U.S. Department of Agriculture, 2005c). Less than a third of schoolchildren get the recommended amounts of milk (Gleason & Suitor, 2000). In fact, the number of youth who drink the recommended milk amounts has steadily declined over the past few decades. In 1978, youth were four times more likely to drink milk than soft drinks; 20 years later, they were only one and half times more likely to opt for milk over sodas and fruit drinks (Dalton, 2004). Astonishingly, production of soft drinks in the United States increased from about 100 (12 ounce) cans per person in the 1940s and 1950s to a whopping 600 cans per person in the 1990s (Gerrior, Putnam, & Bente, 1999; Jacobson, 2005).

Make no mistake about it: Youth have taken a strong liking to soft drinks, often reaching beyond the milk jug to the soda can. In *Underage and Overweight*, Frances Berg (2004) elaborates:

> Only one-half of teenagers drink milk today, compared with three-fourths in the 1970s. Teens who do drink milk consume only about 1.5 to 2 cups a day on average, not the 3 glasses recommended. . . . Teenage boys drink twice as much soda as milk. The typical teen boy drinks 20 ounces per day. One-fourth drink 2.5 or more cans of soda per day; one out of twenty drink 5 cans or more daily. Teenage girls are not far behind. The typical teen girl drinks 14 ounces per day. One-fourth drink 2 or more cans per day; one in twenty drink 3 cans or more. This is twice as much as only twenty years ago when the typical teen drank 9 ounces or ¾ of a can per day. (p. 123)

Because nutrient-rich milk and milk products are essential for bone health in growing youngsters, these figures have not gone unnoticed. The *Dietary Guidelines for Americans* has attributed low calcium intake to significant nutrient deficiencies (including potassium, magnesium, and vitamin A) in society, and the American Academy of Pediatrics (1999) has a policy statement on calcium requirements of infants, children, and adolescents, which urges pediatricians to recommend milk and dairy products as well as calcium-rich foods to help build bone mass. Clearly, adolescence is the time that growing bodies reach adult height (and continue to grow well into their mid-20s); ironically, though, calcium consumption declines during the teenage years (Berg, 2004). Alleman (1999) points out that nearly 9 out of 10 girls and almost 7 out of 10 boys between 12 and 19 years old do not get the recommended daily amount of calcium.

When it comes to milk and milk products, the *Dietary Guidelines for Americans* strongly recommends fat-free or low-fat products because they have less saturated fat, and higher fat milk (and milk products) consumed in excess can lead to weight gain. Moreover, if milk and milk products are not digested well because of the condition known as lactose intolerance, the *Dietary Guidelines* recommend the consumption of lactose-free products or calcium-fortified foods and beverages (U.S. Department of Health and Human Services, 2005a). The *Dietary Guidelines* elaborate:

> Those who avoid milk because of its lactose content may obtain all the nutrients provided by the milk group by using lactose-reduced or low-lactose milk prod-

ucts, taking small servings of milk several times a day, taking the enzyme lactase before consuming milk products, or eating other calcium-rich foods. (p. 9)

If milk cannot be digested, the U.S. Department of Health and Human Services (2007) encourages the consumption of other calcium-rich foods, namely, broccoli, mustard greens, kale, collard greens, and Brussels sprouts; great northern, navy, and black beans; and soy- and rice-based drinks.

In addition to having calcium, milk and milk products are great sources of other nutrients that make for good health and body maintenance (U.S. Department of Health and Human Services, 2005c). In fact, a diet composed of milk and milk products can lower the risk of developing osteoporosis (U.S. Department of Health and Human Services, 2005c), high blood pressure, and colon cancer (Gassenheimer, 2007). Milk is also a terrific source of at least 12 nutrients, among them iron, folate, potassium, magnesium, zinc, riboflavin, protein, and vitamin A, vitamin B12, and vitamin D (Hoeger & Hoeger, 2007). Ward (2005) summarizes the benefits of some of these vital nutrients:

- Protein provides the raw materials for building, repairing, and maintaining cells, tissues, and organs.
- Carbohydrates supply energy.
- Calcium builds bones and teeth and keeps them strong throughout your lifetime.
- Potassium helps maintain healthy blood pressure and normal muscle function.
- Vitamin D regulates levels of calcium and phosphorous, helping to build and maintain bones.
- Vitamin A keeps skin healthy, regulates the immune system, and helps your eyes see normally in the dark.
- Riboflavin assists in energy production for all the cells in your body.
- Niacin facilitates the normal function of enzymes in the body.
- Vitamin B12 works closely with folate to make red blood cells; plays a role in cell growth and division; and wards off nerve cell damage.
- Phosphorus collaborates with calcium to keep bones strong. (pp. 90–91)

Some studies suggest that consuming milk and milk products may also help control or reduce weight. Health experts have found that persons on high-calcium diets are less likely to gain weight or to have actually lost weight compared with those with low calcium intake. Hoeger and Hoeger (2007) explain,

Researchers believe that: calcium regulates fat storage inside the cell; calcium helps the body break down fat or causes fat cells to produce less fat; high calcium intake converts more calories into heat rather than fat; adequate calcium intake contributes to a decrease in intra-abdominal (visceral) fat. . . . Most likely, other nutrients found in dairy products may enhance the weight-regulating action of calcium. (p. 143)

Despite all these wonderful benefits, take heed of this caveat: Milk is the number one source of heart damaging saturated fat in children's diets; cheese is in second place (Center for Science in the Public Interest, 2005a). Milk and cheese are undoubtedly healthy, but in recommended doses—1 cup of low-fat or skim milk is a serving; 1½ ounces of low-fat or fat-free cheese, about the size of a single domino, is another. Americans simply are not used to that portion size, as cheese is seemingly on or in most foods, like burgers, fries, sandwiches, salads, potatoes, and tortilla chips. We consume three times as much cheese than 30 years ago (Center for Science in the Public Interest, 2008). Moreover, other dairy products, like cream cheese, cream, and butter, have little or no calcium and their calorie and saturated fat content can be quite high. Consuming them in excess—especially if they are made with whole milk—is health damaging. Incidentally, drinking 3 cups of whole milk, which has about 15 grams of saturated fat, quickly approaches the recommended 20-gram daily limit (Willett & Skerrett, 2005).

If this information does not impel consumers to ease away from dairy products and seek out healthier foods and beverages, perhaps this will: Studies have found that too many dairy products in a diet can increase the chances of developing ovarian and prostate cancer (Willett & Skerrett, 2005). Take it to heart: Consume milk and milk products as recommended and supplement your diet with calcium-rich foods and beverages.

MEAT AND BEANS

The purple color band is assigned to the Meat and Bean group. Do not let this rubric fool you; it encompasses all foods made from meat, poultry, fish (seafood), dry beans, eggs, nuts, and seeds (U.S. Department of Health and Human Services, 2005c). But why are all these foods lumped into one group? As heterogeneous as this group is, these foods all have a commonality: protein. Protein is critical for bone, muscle, cartilage, and skin health, and because the body cannot store the amino acids that protein supplies, the body needs it daily (Ward, 2005). Without a sufficient supply of protein, the body begins to suffer.

This is why MyPyramid recommends that children between 4 and 8 years old eat 3 to 4 ounces from this group each day, 9- and 13-year-olds (who consume anywhere from 1,600 to 1,800 calories daily) eat 5 ounces, while youth between 14 and 18 years old (who consume 1,800 to 2,200 calories) eat 5 to 6 ounces. And any adult who is on a 2,000-calorie diet should stick to 5½ ounces a day. For an idea of 1-ounce equivalents, consider this: One egg is 1 ounce, while a quarter cup of cooked beans or tofu, one tablespoon of peanut butter, and half an ounce of nuts or seeds is another (U.S. Department of Health and Human Services, 2005a).

Because some foods from this group can be high in fat, the phrase "Go lean with protein" is anchored to the rubric. The *Dietary Guidelines*, MyPyramid, and a host of others strongly recommend that meat and meat alternatives be lean (i.e., low in fat, which suggests that the main dish is trimmed of fat, the skin is removed, or is canned in water instead of oil), and that consumers vary their selection between meals (e.g., fish for lunch and chicken for dinner one day; a salad for lunch and lean beef for dinner the next). The American Heart Association (1997) urges that fish be eaten a couple of times a week, and the website MyPyramid.gov even recommends beans and peas and nuts and seeds as main dishes. It is important to point out that nuts and seeds, which contain healthy fats, should be substituted for—not added to—main dishes or snacks to make for the variety. This will help keep calorie amounts in balance. Moreover, foods that are baked, broiled, or grilled should be selected to keep fat and cholesterol intake low. In other words, keep fried foods to a minimum.

Foods from this group have many valuable nutrients, including protein (1 ounce of meat provides as much as 28 grams of protein), fatty acids, vitamin E, B vitamins (niacin, thiamin, riboflavin, and B6), and minerals such as iron, zinc, phosophorus, sulfur, copper, and magnesium (Alleman, 1999; Kirschmann, 2007; U.S. Department of Health and Human Services, 2005c). All these benefit the body in many ways. For instance, vitamin E protects cell membranes, thiamin helps normal function of the central nervous system, iron helps with formation of hemoglobin and myoglobin, and omega-3 fatty acids reduce the risk of coronary heart disease (Williams, 2007). Some studies, like the Bogalusa Heart Study, from Louisiana, found that children who eat meat are less likely to be nutrient deficient than those who do not eat much (or any) meat (Berg, 2004).

As a rule, keep red meat at arm's length because eating more than the recommended amounts can be unhealthy. Meats are main sources of fat, protein, and cholesterol and eaten in excess (especially saturated fat) can lead to weight gain, cardiovascular diseases, and cancer (Rizza, Go, McMahon, & Harrison, 2002). Hoeger and Hoeger (2007) explain:

> Nutritional guidelines discourage the excessive intake of protein. The daily protein intake from some people is almost twice the amount the human body needs. Too much animal protein apparently decreases blood enzymes that prevent precancerous cells from developing into tumors. According to the National Cancer Institute, eating substantial amounts of red meat may increase the risk of colorectal, pancreatic, breast, prostate, and renal cancer. (p. 333)

As a rule, to promote, rather than dimish, health, seek out some of the other foods in this group, namely skinless chicken, fish, and healthy doses of nuts and seeds.

OILS

The thinnest band—the yellow one—in MyPyramid is assigned to oils. While oils are not a food group, they are essential for good health. In fact, MyPyramid states, "We all need oil. Get your oils from fish, nuts, and liquid oils such as corn oil, soybean oil, and canola oil." Oils have many benefits. They can make food taste better—creamier, richer, crispier—they can keep you feeling full longer, and they supply vitamin E and fatty acids (Rizza et al., 2002). But because they are fats, they are high in calories (fat has 9 calories per gram, equivalent to 100 calories in just one tablespoon), and too much of the wrong kinds (e.g., saturated and trans) can lead to cardio-vascular disease.

To understand oils, let us explore fats. There are four different kinds of fats: saturated, trans, polyunsaturated, and monounsaturated. Saturated and trans are considered the "bad" fats because they increase low-density lipoproteins—LDL, "the bad cholesterol"—that can clog arteries (Bounds et al., 2006). Saturated fats, like butter, lard, margarine, and shortening, gener-ally do not melt at room temperature. They typically come from animals, but are sources from plants as well. Foods that are high in saturated fats include meat (like bacon and sausage), poultry, and whole milk products (like ice cream, cheese, and cream) and some oils like coconut, palm, and palm kernel. Your body produces all the saturated fat your body needs. Too much of it can cause the condition where the excess fatty substances (plaque) deposit them-selves on the inner linings of the arterial walls. This is known as atherosclero-sis and is the catalyst for a heart attack or stroke for many people.

Trans fats are interesting because they are not natural. They are manu-factured through a process known as hydrogenation. The hydrogenation process allows for liquid fat (e.g., corn, soy, and cottonseed oils) to trans-form into a semisoft (like margarine in a tub) or hard (like stick margarine) substance (Bauer, 2005). Hydrogenation allows for an extended shelf life (because the oil does not spoil), and the newly altered substance makes for a texture that appeals to many consumers (Kirschmann, 2007). Trans fats are hidden in many commercial treats like pastries, candies, granola bars, microwave popcorn, and crackers and in the fried foods prepared in restau-rants (Willett & Skerrett, 2005). Regrettably, about 80% of the trans fats consumed are found in products like these (U.S. Department of Health and

Human Services, 2005a). As Bauer (2005) points out, "If you ever read the ingredients on food products, you'll know that trans-fats are everywhere" (p. 38). In fact, trans fats may be more harmful than saturated fats. Sears, Sears, and Foy (2003) assert that these fats can possibly interfere with how the body uses the more nutritious fats. Many nutritionists, for good reason, encourage consumers to avoid trans fats and limit saturated fats to 14 to 20 grams a day, depending on a person's calorie intake (Gassenheimer, 2007). In light of the damage that trans fat can cause, many countries (e.g., Brazil, Denmark, and Switzerland), states (e.g., California), and cities (e.g., New York City, Philadelphia, Chicago, and San Francisco) are actively working toward enacting policies that ban or restrict the use of trans fats in foods, especially meals at restaurants.

That leaves the "good" unsaturated fats: polyunsaturated (e.g., safflower, soybean, and sunflower oils) and monounsaturated (e.g., olive and canola oils) fats, which are low in saturated fat and supply essential fatty acids. They come from plant products like vegetable oils, avocados, and nuts. In spite of the fact that some plants and seeds have their oils extracted by heat or are cold pressed, these oils remain in liquid form at room temperature. They are considered heart healthy because they help keep cholesterol levels at normal ranges (American Heart Association, 2006a; Ward, 2005). A diet of these fats has shown that these kinds of oils reduce heart and cardiovascular diseases. Anspaugh and colleagues (2006) explain:

> Although the diet of people in Mediterranean countries is higher in fat than that of Americans, the incidence of heart disease and stroke in those countries is much lower. The main difference is that the Mediterraean diet is high in monounsaturated fat, usually from the consumption of olive oil. This has prompted some scientists to suggest that Americans adopt this pattern of eating. (p. 174)

This oil yellow band is narrow for a reason: Oil and fat must be consumed sparingly. Too much (and also too little) fat is counterproductive to good health, which is why many health experts and organizations strongly recommend that fat consumption range from 20% and 35% of the total calories in a day. Bounds and colleagues (2006) stress, "Diets with excess fat have attributed to 30 to 40 percent of all cancers in men and 60 percent of all cancers in women, and have also been linked to cancer of the breast, colon, and prostate more frequently than any other dietary factor" (p. 127). For children from 2 to 3 years old, the percentage is higher, 30% to 35%; and for youth 4 to 18, 25% to 35% of calories.

SALT

Salt—40% sodium/60% chloride—has its benefits. In addition to serving as a preservative, it adds a unique flavor to foods that many people like. In small doses, the body needs sodium to regulate body fluids, maintain the right acid-base balance, help with digestion, aid in nerve transmission, contract muscles, and absorb nutrients (Bauer, 2005). Without enough sodium, the body become restless, fatigued, and weak (Anspaugh et al., 2006).

Despite these benefits, salt (the sodium part, actually) has garnered negative press over the past few years. Consuming too much of it can wreak havoc on health. And we consume too much of it. A teaspoon of salt contains about 2,300 milligrams of sodium, which the *Dietary Guidelines for Americans 2005* recommends for daily intake. This includes the consumption found hidden in processed and prepared foods, as well as intake from table salt. But the sodium intake of the average American is a whopping 3,735 milligrams. The average American man takes in about 3,100 to 4,700 milligrams of sodium each day, and his female counterpart consumes about 2,300 to 3,100 milligrams. On average, this is about 10 to 12 grams of salt (Williams, 2007). Most of the sodium comes from processed foods and those prepared at restaurants, not the salt shaker (U.S. Department of Health and Human Services, 2005b).

Excess salt in a diet can lead to hypertension, osteoporosis, and stomach cancer. When the sodium level is high in the body, the body retains water, which increases blood volume, which in turn increases heart pressure and makes the heart work harder (American Heart Association, 2006a); sodium removes calcium from bones and excretes it; and it irritates the stomach lining that causes cells to replicate, thereby increasing the risk of cancer cell initiation (Anspaugh et al., 2006). Some researchers believe that reducing salt consumption lessens the risk of hypertension. The Center for Science in the Public Interest (2005a) writes:

> Currently, 65 million Americans suffer from [hypertension], which increases the risk of heart disease and stroke. Together those diseases kill about 650,000 people annually. Sodium's contribution is major. The directors of the National Heart, Lung, and Blood Institute and two other experts on cardiovascular disease have estimated that reducing sodium levels in processed and restaurant foods by 50% would save 150,000 lives a year. (p. 1)

Some research suggests that salt restriction does not necessarily lead to dramatic reduction in blood pressure levels (Williams, 2007). However, the *Dietary Guidelines* and most health experts; physicians; and organizations, including the American Heart Association, to promote cardiovascular health, strongly recommend cutting back on sodium. While this may be difficult for some to do, most health experts agree that salt is an acquired taste and that the palate can be disciplined to welcome a less salty flavor. Most recently, the Institute of Medicine (2010) released a report, *Strategies to Reduce Sodium Intake in the United States,* which urges the Food and Drug Administration (FDA) to impose standards on the amount of salt added to processed food and prepared meals (Young, 2010). The FDA subsequently announced that the agency would establish an interagency group to review the recommendations set forth in the report (U.S. Department of Health & Human Services, 2010).

SUGAR

Americans eat a lot sugar. Two centuries ago, the average person consumed about 2 pounds of sugar a year. By 1970, that consumption figure increased to a whopping 123 pounds. Today, the average person eats an astonishing 156 pounds of sugar a year, about 3 pounds (or 6 cups) a week (Berg, 2004). Clearly, sugar is prevalent in this country, used liberally in many food products. It is found in foods where it is expected, like sweet snack items (cookies, cake, pie, ice cream, chocolates) and in breakfast cereals found on kitchen tables nationwide. Surprisingly, however, sugar is often a main ingredient in processed foods like spaghetti sauce, bread, ketchup, soups, and salad dressings.

Many health experts believe that sugar is pervasive in our diet because added sweeteners like brown sugar, raw sugar, corn syrup, glucose, honey, fruit juice concentrates, sorbitol, and molasses are forms of sugar, and chemistry-like words that end in –*ose* such as *fructose, maltose, sucrose,* and *lactose* are sugars. This is particularly concerning because sweeteners, while they satisfy the palate, provide calories with little to no nutritional value (commonly referred to as empty calories). Particularly worrisome is that forms of sugar may be listed separately on the ingredient list, yet when combined could contribute significantly to the whole product.

The caption that MyPyramid uses with sugar is "Know your limits," followed by "Don't sugarcoat it. Choose foods and beverages that do not have sugar and caloric sweeteners as one of the first ingredients" (U.S. Department of Agriculture, 2005c). This is valuable, and timely, advice because consumers who do not monitor their sugar intake can quickly pile on the calories (and the pounds). Because ingredients are listed in order of their proportion to the whole product (with the largest proportion appearing first), it is important to look for sugar and its position on the list. The closer sugar is to the top of the list, the higher its content; the closer to the end, the lower its content. Ironically, sugar-free, or sugarless, products may have some forms of sugar but no sucrose, and fat-free snacks can be high in sugars that make up for the flavor of the lost fat.

Of course sugary snacks and products fulfill a sweet tooth (otherwise the snack industry would fail to exist!), but they deplete the body of potential nutriments. Think about this:

- When you drink a 12-ounce can of orange soda, you consume about 150 calories and some caffeine. But when you eat an orange instead, you consume 80 calories, vitamins A and C, iron, calcium, 7 grams of fiber, and a gram of protein.
- When you eat a 2-ounce bar of milk chocolate, you consume 210 calories, 13 grams of fat, 24 grams of sugar, 1 gram of fiber, and 3 grams of protein. But eat a banana instead, and you eat 100 calories; 3 grams of fiber; 1 gram of protein, and calcium, potassium, magnesium, phosphorus, vitamin A, vitamin B6, and vitamin C.

Nutritionists recommend that people on a daily 2,000-calorie diet consume 10% of their calories from sugar, roughly 13 teaspoons. Today, however, the average person eats about 42 teaspoons of sugar in one day. Children from 1 to 3 years old consume 6 teaspoons of sugar a day; 4- to 6-year-olds eat about 13, and adolescents average more than 33 (Berg, 2004). With a teaspoon of sugar containing 15 calories (and a teaspoon of corn syrup 20), without heeding the MyPyramid advice, one could easily drown in sugar calories.

Wolfing down 10 or 12 teaspoons of sugar at one setting seems unimaginable, but this is the dreadful practice of many when they drink sugary sodas. In this country, sodas are intense contributors of sugar in our diet: one 12-ounce can of soda has about 11 teaspoons of sugar (165 calories); a 20-ounce can has about 16 teaspoons (320 calories), and a 32-ounce can has about 29 teaspoons (417 calories) (this varies by product). Drinking just one 12-ounce can of soda is enough to exceed the daily recommended sugar allowance (since other consumed foods that day will have sugar), and other popular beverages—such as Sunny Delight, Tampico, Snapple, and Tang—can have just as much sugar as does soda. Without doubt, these are tasty and can tempt most persons to drink too much. A guzzle of a 20-ounce sugary drink at breakfast, another at lunch, snack time, and dinner could amount to a staggering 1,280 calories, not only replacing nutritious foods but leading to weight gain. One 2-year Harvard study of 548 grade school children found that a daily serving of an extra sugar-sweetened beverage raises the risk of obesity by 60% (Tartamella, Herscher, & Woolston, 2004).

Further, consuming large doses of these beverages can erode tooth enamel, leading to tooth decay. With such news, it is no accident that many health advocates recommend keeping sugar consumption in check; as the National Institutes of Health (2004) advises, "Do not let sugary soda or other sweets crowd out healthy foods and beverages" (p. 2).

CONCLUSION

Eating the right foods is essential to health and well-being. Undoubtedly, eating right leads to improved body weight, more energy, and feeling better, not to mention that the consumption of nutritious foods keeps disabling diseases at bay. Because some foods are better than others and each has a nutritional value composed of essential vitamins and minerals, children and adults alike should be mindful of what they consume. Knowledge of the benefits of grains, vegetables, fruits, milk, meats and bean, oils, salt, and sugar can help children incorporate eating right into their daily lives, and it can enhance the very foundation for eating right for the rest of their lives. Now with this background on good dietary practices at hand, let's concentrate on the Ideas that are designed to provide this knowledge to youth and encourage them to assume habits that engender a better quality of life.

CHAPTER 4

Ideas to Promote Healthy Eating Habits

According to the U.S. Department of Agriculture (2005b), poor eating habits cause many of the public health problems in America. As discussed in earlier chapters, we eat more often, we eat larger portions, and we regularly eat nutrient-inferior products. We have a serious health problem on our hands because children emulate the unhealthy eating habits of adults and are gaining weight at an unprecedented record. Health experts agree that children do not consume enough of the foods that contribute positively to their health, which is worrisome because an unhealthy diet affects their wellness, growth and development, and readiness to learn (U.S. Department of Agriculture, 2000a). Many children do not recognize that they are making poor health-related decisions when they eat, and to heighten this problem, they do not realize that they are shaping the good habits they could practice for a lifetime. In all likelihood, poor eating habits increase their risk for mortality and the development of chronic, diet-related diseases (U.S. Department of Agriculture, 2005b). Children need to learn about making judicious health-related decisions, which include learning about the nutritional values of foods they should consume and behaviors that lend themselves to eating the right foods.

The Ideas presented in this chapter are designed to increase children's knowledge about nutrition and diet and to jump-start the habits they need to improve their health. The Ideas are presented in three sections:

- Assumptions Guiding the Ideas
- Background on the Ideas
- The 15 Ideas

ASSUMPTIONS GUIDING THE IDEAS

The driving force behind the 15 Ideas to promote healthy eating habits are found in seven key assumptions:

1. Americans have developed unhealthy eating patterns. In recent decades, there has been a shift in this country toward eating more convenient foods (i.e., processed and fast foods). Nestle (2002) notes, "The increased calories in American diets come from eating more food in general, but especially more of foods high in fat (meat, dairy, fried foods, grain dishes with added fat), sugar (soft drinks, juice drinks, desserts), and salt (snack foods)" (p. 10). Children and adults alike consistently fail to consume the federal nutritional recommendations.

2. Food is an important part of everyday life. Children need the right balance of nutrients to grow and develop into adolescence and adulthood. To that end, they need to know that a balanced diet is about what and how much to eat, and that the consumption of a variety of foods from the MyPyramid food groups is the very basis of a lifetime of good health. It is essential that children learn about the right amounts of whole grains, fruits, and vegetables, and choose low-fat or skim milk (and milk products) and selections of lean meats to consume. They also need to know the hazards associated with excessive consumption of trans and saturated fats, salt, and added sugar.

3. The decisions that children make about food affect their present and future health. When children have balanced diets that correspond to the MyPyramid recommendations and regularly choose foods that maximize the nutrients their growing bodies need, they will maintain a healthy weight, reduce the risk of acquiring the chronic diseases commonly associated with obesity (such as heart disease and diabetes), have the energy to enhance their learning, and feel better about their bodies and themselves. Conversely, eating a lot of random foods—not to mention fast and processed foods—is not only reprehensible; it is harmful to their health. To prevent obesity and the associated chronic diseases, children need healthy diets.

4. Many factors influence children's decisions about food. Parents, relatives, and other significant adults; children; and the media (e.g., commercials, ads, and product placements) are some of the external influences that children casually encounter yet make profound impressions on what and how often they eat. Through their interactions with and observations of people, children learn and are reinforced about health-related behaviors. Unfortunately, children make poor eating decisions because the people around them model poor eating decisions, not to mention that children

are bombarded with advertisements that promote nutrient-inferior foods. These very influences put children at risk for overweight and obesity and a range of health problems. Children need correct knowledge associated with making smart food choices and the skills to counter the consistent observation that people do not maintain diets consistent with the *Dietary Guidelines*.

5. The adage "You can't teach an old dog new tricks" is relevant to dietary habits. As most adults can attest, it is difficult to break old habits and build new ones, especially those associated with healthy eating. Most habits develop in childhood and continue well into adulthood, which makes it extremely important to introduce healthy eating habits in the early grades. Studies confirm that children who are overweight in the early grades continue to be overweight adolescents and adults. One National Institute of Child Health and Human Development (Nader et al., 2006) study found that children who were overweight in preschool were 60% more likely to be overweight at 12 years old than children who were never overweight, and children who were overweight in elementary school had an 80% chance of being overweight at age 12. While some may scoff at these kinds of findings and believe that claims of childhood obesity are nonsense, carrying excess weight as a youngster puts their health at risk. The Center for Science in the Public Interest (2003b) explains, "Those chronic diseases/conditions often take decades to develop and have their roots in childhood, when disease processes begin and eating habits are formed. Yet few children are eating in accordance with dietary guidelines, and the rates of childhood obesity and diabetes are rising rapidly" (p. 1). It is important to teach children the knowledge and skills associated with eating right because healthy habits can take years to develop.

6. Children are faced with making difficult decisions about food. They can choose the convenient and appetizing, which are often processed and fast foods (and nutrient inferior), as do many of the youngsters and adults in their association, or actively work at finding and choosing the healthier alternatives. They often choose less healthy food because they lack the knowledge and skills associated with healthy eating. In simple terms, they do not know any better and everyone eats this way. The classroom is the ideal location to learn about food and nutritional matter because they can practice and apply their acquired knowledge and tools with their peers under the guidance of an informed teacher. With the Ideas in *Jump Start Health!*, children begin to understand that the

health decisions they make affect their present and future health and well-being and make feasible changes to their diet.

7. Youngsters often have decisions made for them over what they eat. However, as they mature they develop their own tastes and preferences for food and beverages and begin to make choices for themselves. Children are consumers; while some may have little control over what they eat now, they will eventually become adult consumers with complete control over their lives. If we expect children to take increasing responsibility (and better care) of their health and wellness as they grow older, they need to be taught that they hold the potential to manage what and how much goes into their bodies.

BACKGROUND ON THE IDEAS

There are a number of resources available on the topic of childhood obesity, books such as *Save Your Child from the Fat Epidemic* (Alleman, 1999), *Underage and Overweight* (Berg, 2004), *Our Overweight Children* (Dalton, 2004), *The Overweight Child* (Pitman & Kaufman, 2000), *Dr. Sears' Lean Kids* (Sears, Sears, & Foy, 2003), and *Generation Extra Large* (Tartamella et al., 2004). These are all a worthwhile read and add considerably to the literature on childhood health, nutrition, and physical activity. However, readers must comb through the texts to determine how to implement the ideas that the authors offer. That is to say, these books are not practical enough for teachers and do not offer reproducibles that can be immediately used in the classroom.

There are two books that are similar to the spirit of *Jump Start Health!*: *Healthy Habits for Life* (Sesame Workshop, 2007) and *Eat Well and Keep Moving* (Cheung, Dart, Kalin, & Gormaker, 2007). The former includes a wonderful collection of activities, reproducibles, and a CD of songs, but these are designed for preschool youngsters. The latter, too, has reproducibles that can be adapted for children in the younger grades, but seem most appropriate for students in the upper elementary grades. *Healthy Start: Preschool Health Education, Healthy Hops*, and *Animal Trackers* (all published by Healthy Start LLC) are ideal for the preschool youngster because they include poems, songs, and physical activities, but offer no handouts or reproducibles. *Jump Start Health!* is the first of its kind (as of this writing) that offers a contextual framework (in Chapters 1, 2, 3 and 5), the Ideas, which are based on the National Health Education Standards, and has a range of reproducibles that can be immediately photocopied and used in the classroom. (Figure 4.1 includes the standards and a matrix for how the Ideas address them).

FIGURE 4.1. National Health Education Standards Addressed by Each Idea

Standards

1. Students will comprehend concepts related to health promotion and disease prevention to enhance health.
2. Students will analyze the influence of family, peers, culture, media, technology, and other factors on health behaviors.
3. Students will demonstrate the ability to access valid information and products and services to enhance health.
4. Students will demonstrate the ability to use interpersonal communication skills to enhance health and avoid or reduce health risks.
5. Students will demonstrate the ability to use decision-making skills to enhance health.
6. Students will demonstrate the ability to use goal-setting skills to enhance health.
7. Students will demonstrate the ability to practice health-enhancing behaviors and avoid or reduce health risks.
8. Students will demonstrate the ability to advocate for personal, family, and community health.

Jump Start Health! Ideas	National Health Education Standards							
	1	2	3	4	5	6	7	8
Idea 1 Energy Balance	✓			✓	✓		✓	
Idea 2 MyPyramid		✓	✓		✓			✓
Idea 3 Grains		✓	✓			✓	✓	
Idea 4 Vegetables and Fruits	✓		✓			✓	✓	✓
Idea 5 Milk	✓		✓				✓	✓
Idea 6 Meat and Beans		✓	✓		✓		✓	✓
Idea 7 Nutrition Facts Label			✓			✓	✓	
Idea 8 Snacks and Beverages	✓			✓	✓			
Idea 9 Portion Control	✓	✓	✓		✓		✓	
Idea 10 Moderation	✓	✓			✓		✓	
Idea 11 Averting Savory Temptations		✓		✓	✓		✓	
Idea 12 Influences of Advertising		✓			✓		✓	✓
Idea 13 Sugar and Salt	✓				✓		✓	✓
Idea 14 Meal Planning		✓		✓		✓		✓
Idea 15 Setting and Tracking Goals	✓			✓		✓		✓

Source: The Joint Committee on National Health Education Standards. (2007). *National Health Education Standards: Achieving excellence* (2nd ed.). Atlanta: American Cancer Society.

Each Idea has a rationale and is presented in a lesson plan format; and it culminates with activities for both guided and independent practices. Because the Ideas are designed for children in second through fifth grade, it is important that teachers make appropriate adjustments that reflect developmentally appropriate practice for their age group. The instructional delivery and content should be differentiated with respect to the social, emotional, and cognitive abilities of the target group. Adaptations and modifications will have to be made for English language learners and learners with special needs. In these instances, teachers will have to adjust the conditions of the lesson and respective assignments to meet their students' unique needs.

In the instructional delivery of the Ideas, teachers should employ their traditional classroom methods. Have the students work in pairs or in groups if this is a usual routine, or have them work independently if this is what the students are used to. In cases when there are instructional or delivery constraints (e.g., no technology available, limited time), carry out the Idea in the practice that has proved most effective for your students. Education experts consistently report that sound instructional practices include recalling students' prior knowledge; calling on every student and validating his or her responses, making the content meaningful by drawing examples from their own lives (as well as yours), integrating other content areas, enabling them to see connections among the content areas and real life, varying modes to support their learning (e.g., small group, independent, cooperative learning tasks, whole group, and peer instruction), showcasing their work, and supplementing the lessons with books for independent reading. Remember to ask the students a wide range of questions. In lieu of similar questions repeated throughout the Ideas in this chapter and Chapter 6, Figure 4.2 outlines basic questions modeled after Bloom's taxonomy. These can be easily adapted to reflect the content in each Idea.

While the Ideas are not meant to be exhaustive (or definitive on childhood health), the first three chapters in this book can be used to supplement the material. Moreover, each Idea includes a section titled "Tips," which offers additional ways to reinforce the instructional concepts. Consider these when the students need added direction or for those who have finished their work well before the others.

Understandably, some schools are better equipped with technology than others. For that reason, some of the Ideas include graphics that can be easily photocopied onto transparencies. However, the students will need access to the Internet, specifically the website MyPyramid.gov, where they will research the amount of foods they should eat. Encourage the students to bookmark the website so that they can return to it easily and complete Reproducible 3.2, which is used in a number of the Ideas. In some instances the

FIGURE 4.2. Bloom's Taxonomy and Action Verbs to Consider in Questions

Level	Key words	Prompts	Example
Knowledge: Recall data or information.	define, describe, identify, know, label, list, match, name, outline, recall, recognize, reproduce, select, state	Where is . . . What did . . . Who was . . . When did . . . How many . . . Locate it in the story . . . Point to the . . .	*Name as many milk products as you can. Will you point to the fruit? Say and spell tofu. Circle all the vegetables.*
Comprehension: Understand the meaning, translation, interpolation, and interpretation of instructions and problems.	comprehend, convert, defend, distinguish, estimate, explain, extend, generalize, give examples, infer, interpret, paraphrase, predict, rewrite, summarize, translate	Tell me in your own words . . . What does it mean . . . Give me an example of . . . Describe what . . . Illustrate the part of the story that . . . Make a map of . . . What is the main idea of . . .	*What is a grain? Add the calories of a pudding cup to the calories of a cookie. Who can summarize what we just learned?*
Application: Use a concept in a new situation or unprompted use of an abstraction.	apply, change, compute, adapt, construct, demonstrate, discover, manipulate, modify, operate, predict, prepare, produce, relate, show, solve, use	What would happen to you if . . . Would you have done the same as . . . If you were there, would you . . . How would you solve the problem . . . In the library, find information about . . .	*How would you change this breakfast plan to include more fruit? Demonstrate one way to resist a savory treat. If you have too many large portions, then what might happen?*

FIGURE 4.2. Continued

Level	Key words	Prompts	Example
Analysis: Separate material or concepts into component parts so that its organizational structure may be understood.	analyze, break down, compare, contrast, diagram, deconstruct, differentiate, discriminate, distinguish, identify, illustrate, infer, outline, relate, select, separate	What things would you have used . . . What other ways could . . . What things are similar/different? What part of this story was the most exciting? What things couldn't have happened in real life? What kind of person is . . . What caused _____ to act the way he/she did?	*Compare the beans and the grains. Which product does not belong in this group? Classify an influence according to internal or external.*
Synthesis: Build a structure or pattern from diverse elements. Put parts together to form a whole, with emphasis on creating a new meaning or structure.	categorize, combine, compile, compose, create, devise, design, explain, generate, modify, organize, plan rearranged, reconstruct, relate, reorganize, review, rewrite, summarize, tell, write	What would it be like if . . . What would it be like to live . . . Design a . . . Pretend you are a . . . What would have happened if . . . Why/why not? Use your imagination to draw a picture of . . . Add a new item on your own . . . Tell/write a different ending . . .	*Can you think of a way to reduce your sugar intake? How can we improve the chances of meeting our goals? What do you predict will happen if you drink soda for breakfast, lunch, and dinner?*
Evaluation: Make judgments about the value of ideas or materials.	Appraise, compare, conclude, contrast, criticize, critique, defend, describe, discriminate, evaluate, explain, interpret, justify, relate, summarize, support	Would you recommend this book? Why or why not? Select the best . . . Why is it the best? What do you think will happen to . . . Why do you think that? Could this story really have happened? Which character would you most like to meet? Was _____ good or bad? Why? Did you like the story? Why?	*What are some reasons to choose water over soda? What are the most important ideas? Why is this important?*

Source: Fisher, D., & Frey, N. (2007). *Checking for understanding: Formative assessment techniques for your classroom*. Alexandria, VA: ASCD. Reprinted with permission.

Ideas require that teachers show students examples of food. While magazine and newspaper photos will do (actual foods are even better), a Google image search will retrieve rare and unusual pictures. Nutritiondata.com is a valuable website that furnishes the nutrition facts on raw foods as well as generic and name-brand packaged products.

While teaching the Ideas, be sensitive to the fact that many children will likely live in homes where their parents or caregivers do not support healthy eating habits. In fact, it will prove difficult for some students to alter their diets if they live in households where the families regularly buy economical foods that tend to be nutrient inferior to those the *Dietary Guidelines* recommends; are rooted in their cultural heritage and regularly eat their ethnic foods, which in excessive consumption may be harmful to health; and are fixed in their ways and do not know how to cultivate a healthy diet or do not want to. As a result, some children have very little control over what they eat.

That said, it is important to have them genuinely reflect on the knowledge that is being imparted, on their current situations, and how they can gradually introduce healthy eating to their families in the face of their existing situation. (National Health Education Standard 8 pertains to teaching students health advocacy skills. The nature of the standard is to help students develop and hone their skills to promote health to others). One way to accomplish this is to invite them to journal after each Idea. Specifically, the students can respond to the following:

- "How does _____ matter to me?" (e.g., How does moderation matter to me?)
- "What did I learn about myself?"
- "What are some problems I encounter in applying this in my life?"
- "What are some ways I can promote _____ at home with my family?" (e.g., "What are some ways I can promote moderation at home with my family?)
- Questions I have . . .
- Connections I have made . . .

These questions afford students the opportunity to think deeply about how to introduce change at home. Students can use these to record their reactions and to conceive plans to promote healthy eating habits, which teachers can then gather and respond to with additional suggestions.

In all, the Ideas are about improving children's lives. The Ideas seek to impart the principles of the *Dietary Guidelines* and MyPyramid by way of consistent messages that there is pleasure and benefit in a healthy diet. At present, children are underwhelmed with what is considered good eating practices. They need reliable information and guidance to attain a diet that meets the federal recommendations. The Ideas are tools that will empower them to make a change that affects their health now and will do so throughout their lives.

THE 15 IDEAS

The 15 Ideas comprise the following categories: Energy Balance, MyPyramid, Grains, Vegetables and Fruits, Milk, Meats and Beans, Nutrition Facts Label, Snacks and Beverages, Portion Control, Moderation, Averting Savory Temptations, Influences of Advertising, Sugar and Salt, Meal Planning, and Setting and Tracking Goals. The reproducibles, which accompany each Idea, can be used in varied ways (i.e., to motivate the students, as a step in the instruction, or as an activity). Each reproducible is numbered consecutively (e.g., 2.3 corresponds to Idea 2 and is the third reproducible) and can be downloaded from the Teachers College Press website (http://www. teacherscollegepress.com, under "Free Downloads").

IDEA 1: ENERGY BALANCE

Rationale

One of the factors contributing to the childhood obesity epidemic is that youth today consume too much food and too many beverages and do not engage in enough physical activity. Some health experts have noted that even 100 extra calories a day can make for significant weight gain in a year (Hill, Wyatt, Reed, & Peters, 2003). This Idea is designed to set the foundation for youth to practice balancing their energy "in" with energy "out" so that they understand that what they consume should not significantly exceed what they burn off. It is critical to teach youth this information early in their lives because by the time they are adults they are too set in their ways (Hoeger & Hoeger, 2007). The *Dietary Guidelines* (U.S. Department of Health and Human Services, 2005b) and *Healthy People 2010* (U.S. Department of Health and Human Services, 2000a) both address the importance of balance. The sooner youth learn about energy balance, the better the chances are for them to practice eating less and moving more.

Objectives

After learning about energy balance, the students will

- Evaluate whether there is energy balance in certain scenarios
- Compose a list of physical activities to balance their energy "in"

Download and use Reproducibles 1.1–1.8 for this Idea.

To Motivate the Students

Begin by asking the students how many know how to ride a bicycle. Spark a short discussion with questions about when they started to ride a bike, where they bike, and how often they bike. Follow by asking what it takes to ride a bike well and safely. Emphasize that without balance, they are doomed to fall. Then ask if any of them have ever played on a seesaw. Mention that a seesaw is a mechanism for recreation that requires balance. That is, in order for children to enjoy the ride up and down, a balance must exist between the child at each end. Ask the students to predict the unfortunate outcome of the child who is at one end of the plank and the child at the other end who is considerably bigger and heavier. Clarify that without balance, the back-and-forth movement that is intended for the seesaw to work will abruptly end. Underscore that balance in these two activities is important and that balance is also critical to their own health.

Frame the Instruction

Inform the students that they will be learning about the importance of balance to their health. You can accomplish this by saying something to the effect, "Today, we will discuss the idea of balance and why it is important to the health of our bodies. You will learn that the amount of food you eat should balance with the amount of physical activity or exercise you have in a day and that the decisions you make determine whether you have balance, which can have long-term effects on your personal health."

Step by Step

1. If a scale is available, use it to demonstrate balance with assorted small objects. Use Reproducible 1.1 to show the students the concept of a scale. Ask the students whether they have ever seen a scale, how they believe a scale works, and why scales are used in society. After garnering their responses, ask them to define balance. Explain that there are many definitions of balance, but the one in mind for this lesson is associated with the notion of equal or even. Use some of the language the children used from the examples, adding that one definition of balance is about being or having equal amounts. Using the scale or Reproducible 1.1, point out how the scale is not balanced when one side is heavier than other.

2. Mention that balance is part of everyday life. Provide examples from your own life that require balance (e.g., balancing a checkbook, balancing time to prepare lessons with time devoted to your family and friends), and ask them to contemplate how they use balance at

home, at school, and in organized sports. Using these questions, ask them to predict what happens when they do not practice balance:

- "What would happen if you spent more time with some friends than others?"
- "What would happen if you spent all your time playing with no time devoted to studying or doing homework?"
- "What would happen if you promised to buy something that cost more than you had?"

Emphasize that when balance is not practiced in life, the results can be dreadful. Mention that consumers have to maintain a good balance in the foods they eat for good health.

3. Introduce the term *calorie*. Ask the students if they have ever heard this word and what they think it means. Explain that *calorie* has an elaborate definition they will learn later, but for now a calorie is a unit that holds energy-producing value. Mention that foods and beverages are composed of calories. At this point, bring in various packages of foods and beverages and reveal their calorie count. Or use Reproducible 1.2 to show some examples of foods and their calories, such as water (none), a banana (about 95), cola (240 for 20 ounces), a medium-size chocolate chip cookie (about 80), and so forth. Tell the students that every time they consume food or beverages, the calories add up. At this point, mention that when a person is engaged in physical activity or exercise, calories are burned. Ask the students to predict what happens if too many calories are consumed and not enough are burned, and alternate with what happens if too many calories are burned.

4. Define energy balance. Energy "in" is by way of calories through food and beverages. Energy "out" is expending calories through physical activity and exercise. Use Reproducible 1.3 to show the students that energy "in" should balance with energy "out" for good health. Explain that this is called energy balance.

5. Introduce MyPyramid for Kids (Reproducible 1.4). Mention that you will discuss this illustration in later activities, but for the time being ask them to reflect on what is depicted on the image. Point out that this image is provided by the federal government to guide the public to balance energy "in" with energy "out." Ask the students to explain how the image accomplishes this. The appropriate response should resemble that the food groups from which we should eat are complemented with pictures of children engaged in physical activity. Emphasize that energy balance is good for health.

6. Mention that good "energy balance" begins with making the right decisions about food and physical activity. Explain that the decisions they make (i.e., their behavior) affect their health. Identify some examples of unhealthy behavior such as not brushing teeth or eating too much sugar, which can lead to tooth decay, and smoking, which is harmful to the lungs. Ask the students to identify some poor health behaviors and alternate these with positive behaviors that affect health. Add that the decisions they make about food and physical activity affect their current and future health.

Activities

Guided. Have the children work in pairs to cut out the deck of cards (found in Reproducible 1.5; 1.6 is blank). Point out that one set of cards has pictures of foods and snacks on them with "ENERGY IN" printed on the back, and the other set has pictures of activities on one side and EN-ERGY OUT printed on the back side. Have the students divide the cards according to their respective group (the "In's" on one side and the "Out's" on the other) and spread them accordingly. One student will spin the spin-ner (Reproducible 1.7; attach a spinner commonly found at teacher supply stores) two times: once to determine the number of "IN" cards to turn over and the other for the respective number of "OUT" cards to flip. Based on the cards the students turn over, they can evaluate whether there was more energy in than energy out and justify their answer. The students can play rounds of cards as often as time permits. The children can verbalize their responses, or if a goal is to have them develop the skill of making lists or work on their penmanship, for instance, they can write their responses. As you walk around assessing their performance, acknowledge the dialogues they are having and resolve their challenges.

Independent. Pass out double-sided copies of Reproducible 1.8, "Bal-ance for Good Health." Instruct the students to fold and cut where indi-cated. Ask the students to lift the first tab, Energy "IN," and list the foods they plan to eat that day or the day after. Students lift the second tab, Energy "OUT," and write how they intend to balance the energy "in" with activi-ties that require them to expend their energy.

Conclusion

Call on students to share their responses they wrote on their "Balance for Good Health" reproducible. As a review, have the students explain how knowing about energy balance is important to their health.

Tips

- The students can flip over all of the "IN" and "OUT" cards and identify good balances
- The students make their own cards to add to the card game
- Have the students contribute to a bulletin board titled "Ways to Balance Our Health"

IDEA 2: MYPYRAMID

Rationale

Part of the childhood obesity problem is that youth today eat too much of the nutrient inferior foods and not enough of the nutrient rich. According to one study, only 2% of children meet the federal recommendations of eating foods from all the individual food groups (Action for Healthy Kids, 2005b). And one child in five eats five servings of fruit and vegetables each day and drinks three or more glasses of milk (Strock, Cottrell, Abang, & Buschbacher, 2005). These grim statistics and others show that many youth today lack healthy, balanced diets. The *Dietary Guidelines* (U.S. Department of Health and Human Services, 2005b) clearly encourages Americans to make wiser food choices and recommends the consumption of "a variety of nutrient-dense foods and beverages within and among the basic food groups" (p. vii). MyPyramid was developed as a food guidance system to help Americans fulfill the recommendations in the *Dietary Guidelines*. MyPyramid is important for children and adults alike because the sooner they use it as a reference for choosing the right foods to consume every day, the sooner their health is improved. Improved health and diet has the potential to prevent the illnesses and disease commonly associated with excess weight.

Objectives

After learning about MyPyramid, the students will

- Classify foods into the respective food groups found on MyPyramid
- Create their own MyPyramid advertisement

Download and use Reproducibles 1.4 and 2.1–2.3 for this Idea.

To Motivate the Students

Recall students' prior knowledge on energy balance. Remind them that they have to be conscientious about the foods and beverages they consume.

Excite the students by asking them to imagine a party for a special friend, sibling, or relative. Ask them to suggest the foods they would bring. Write all the students' responses on the board, classifying them into the food groups (grains, vegetables, fruits, milk, and meat and beans), which can be written ahead of the activity. Mention that the federal government has designed MyPyramid for public health and that it not only stresses a balance of energy "in" with energy "out" (as they learned in Idea 1), it guides consumers to eat from individual food groups each day. Have the students contemplate what would happen if no guide existed and how MyPyramid could be used ahead of time to plan their meals and other celebrations.

Frame the Instruction

Inform the students that they will be learning more about the components of MyPyramid. Mention that by the end of the activity they will be able to identify its characteristics and use them as valid sources of health information to improve their health. Add that MyPyramid may transform into a different representation within their lifetime, but that it will continue to be a reliable source to guide their food and drink consumption.

Step by Step

1. Reintroduce MyPyramid (Reproducible 1.4) from Idea 1. Have the students make note of the different elements that are depicted throughout the illustration. Ask them to identify what they see. Some of the elements the students point out can be clustered into three categories: the food groups (e.g., foods found in any of the vertical bands, such as grapes, bread, or milk), the slogans (e.g., "Go lean with protein"), and the physical activities (e.g., girl walking her dog or boy riding a bike). Elaborate on what is evident in the illustration: There are six color bands, some of the bands are wider than others, there appears to be a classification system of foods, the widest band is the grains, the narrowest band is the oil, a slogan appears to accompany the individual groups and two additional slogans are found at the base of the pyramid, and children are engaged in physical activity.

2. Point out that the six different color bands represent individual groups: grains, vegetables, fruits, milk, meats and beans, and oils. Provide examples from each group to enhance their understanding:

   - Grains: brown rice, oatmeal, popcorn, bread, crackers, pasta, cereals, couscous
   - Vegetables: carrots, spinach, broccoli, corn, eggplant, asparagus,
   - Fruits: apples, grapes, bananas, strawberries, oranges, peaches
   - Milk: milk, yogurt, cheese, ice cream, pudding (made from milk)

- Meats and beans: beef, ham, lamb, pork, chicken, turkey, eggs, fish and shellfish, nuts and seeds, dry beans and peas
- Oils: canola oil, corn oil, olive oil, sunflower oil, safflower oil

If possible, visit the MyPyramid.gov homepage and navigate to the Related Topics sidebar for a thorough list of examples. Underscore that all the food groups play an important role in their health and no group is better or more important than the other. Add that foods within each band play a significant role in their health:

- Grains: provide energy, benefit the central nervous system, enhance bowel movements, support blood circulation
- Vegetables and fruits: contribute to cardiovascular health, good for eye health, slow the effects of aging
- Milk: contributes to bones and teeth health, helps regulate blood pressure
- Meat and beans: Build muscles, reduce the risk of heart disease

Indicate that they will later learn about each of these individual food groups.

3. Explain that MyPyramid is composed of other images that depict variety, moderation, proportionality, and activity, which may not be readily apparent to the students. Define these terms in developmentally appropriate language. For *variety*, add that MyPyramid guides consumers to eat foods from each of the groups because different foods offer unique vitamins, minerals, and nutrients, which help the body in different ways. Emphasize that to protect their current and future health they should strive to eat a variety of foods from the individual groups every day so that their bodies get the nutrients they need. After all, eating one type of food consistently does not provide the nutrients their growing bodies need. Some health experts promote, "Every color, every day" to help youth remember to eat foods from all the groups.

For *moderation,* mention that some bands are wider than others, which suggests that foods from these groups have greater nutritional value. Some children may have a difficult time detecting the implication that the tapering of the bands suggest that some foods within the individual group should be consumed more often (those found at the base) than others (those found at the tip). For example, within the milk group, the image of low-fat yogurt would be located near the base because it should be consumed more often than ice cream, which would likely be near the tip.

For *proportionality*, explain that the different band widths also suggest how much food they should select from each group. While they are not exact proportions, consumers should look at these as a guide to select more plant foods to eat, and fewer meats.

Activity is more apparent to youth because there are a number of illustrations depicting youth engaged in physical activity. There is a child climbing the stairs of the pyramid, which also serves to remind youth about the importance of daily exercise.

4. Ask the students to identify familiar catchy commercial slogans and to explain their purpose. Point out that MyPyramid also has a number of slogans to remind and inspire consumers to follow the federal guidelines. These include the following:

"Make half your grains whole," "Vary your veggies," "Focus on fruits," "Get your calcium-rich foods," "Go lean with protein," "Find your balance between food and fun," and "Fats and sugars—know your limits." Explain that they will later learn the meaning of each of these.

Activities

Guided. To reinforce the respective food groups found on MyPyramid, have the students play a few rounds of the game MyPyramid Bingo, which is found as Reproducible 2.1. Distribute a copy to each student and have them write the name of each food group in each column. Have them start with the grains on the far left column and write the other groups accordingly. (Remind students that while oil is among those bands found on MyPyramid, it is not a food group but is essential in one's diet). If you like, have the students color the columns according to the colors represented on MyPyramid. Use Reproducible 2.2 to display the list of foods from the respective categories. Instruct the students to copy any of the foods onto their bingo card within the respective columns. Encourage them to mix the order. Using a photocopy of Reproducible 2.2, cut up the words and put them in a container. Begin the game by calling out the foods (and their respective categories) that you select out of the container. If you pull out "Grains/Toast," for instance, students who have written that food on their grains column can cross it off their cards. A winning card is one that has five foods in a row or in a diagonal.

Independent. Distribute copies of Reproducible 2.3, MyPyramid Ad. Explain that MyPyramid has many slogans and catchy phrases to inspire children to balance what they eat with physical activity. Point out some of the phrases such as "Eat Right, Exercise. Have Fun," "Find your balance between food and fun," and so forth. Instruct the students to come up with their own ad or slogan to motivate children across the nation to pursue

MyPyramid recommendations. The only conditions of the assignment are that they have to use the pyramid, have to include physical activity, and cannot use the slogans already characterized on MyPyramid.

Conclusion

Have the students show their ads to the class. Follow with questions such as

- "Why is it important to follow MyPyramid recommendations?"
- "What do you predict will happen if more Americans begin to follow the suggestions?"
- "Can you think of other ways to inspire people to follow MyPyramid suggestions?"
- "How might we improve MyPyramid or spread the news about about it?"

Tips

- Have the students design a school- or community-wide campaign promoting MyPyramid
- Have the students design a complete meal that includes foods from the individual groups (younger students could cut out pictures of foods from magazines and classify them according to the five groups)

IDEA 3: GRAINS

Rationale

One of the MyPyramid food groups is grains; when consumed daily as recommended grains contribute significantly to diet. Grains are beneficial because they provide an array of nutrients for the body: vitamins, minerals, carbohydrates, and fiber. Yet many youth today do not eat enough grains, let alone the more nutrient-rich whole grains. Recent studies found that children consume about one serving or less of whole grains a day. Because whole grains are packed with nutrients that reduce the risk of chronic diseases (including coronary heart disease) and the wholesome fiber that can prevent them from gaining weight, it is important that children learn about grains so that they can begin to choose them as part of their daily diet.

Objectives

After learning about the benefits of whole grains and grains, the students will

- Create an alphabet page with a corresponding grain or grains product
- Assemble grains and grains products into two categories

Download and use Reproducibles 3.1–3.3 for this Idea.

To Motivate the Students

Show the students various packages of foods made from grains, such as cereals, bread, crackers, macaroni, and oatmeal. Have them contemplate what they have in common. Then, call on some students to read the first few ingredients on the labels. Record the responses from the Grains food group on the board. Then mention that their commonality is that all the foods are made from grains, one of the food groups found on MyPyramid. Ask if they remember the slogan associated with the Grains group. Confirm that MyPyramid encourages them to "make half your grains whole" and show them foods from this group, especially products (or packages thereof) like rice, corn, and popcorn. Record these on the board. Ask a few students to report what they ate the day before, and as they do, write on the board the food products they consumed that were likely from the Grains food group.

Frame the Instruction

To recall their prior knowledge, ask the students to mention what they remember about the grains food group found on MyPyramid (from Idea 1 and 2). Compliment them for their responses and mention that they will be learning about the importance of selecting grains as part of their daily diet. Specifically mention that they will learn what grains are, the difference between whole grains and refined grains, and how to determine the amount of grains they need to eat every day.

Step by Step

1. Show the students additional grain products that they may not be familiar with, such as couscous, brown rice, English muffins, corn and flour tortillas, and hominy grits. If packages are not available, consider a Google image search, which should retrieve pictures of grains that can easily be copied and pasted onto a PowerPoint (or color printed and adhered to a poster board). Based on the examples that the students have seen thus far, ask them to develop a definition of grains. After the students have constructed their own definition, emphasize that a grain is a seed from food plants like wheat, rice, corn, oats, rye, or millet.
2. Tell them that grains provide the body with energy; are low in fat (which they will earn about later); and supply an array of vitamins, minerals, and carbohydrates. Explain that there is a difference between

whole grains and refined grains. Whole grains generally have more nutrients than refined grains because they have not been milled (the process of stripping away the outer layer). Ask students to define *whole* so that they have a perspective for the whole grain. Verify that *whole* means "full, undivided, intact, not broken apart," and associate the definition with whole grain. Explain that the entire grain seed, sometimes referred to as the kernel, still has all the elements of the bran (the outer layer), germ (inner part), and endosperm (middle part) and that they are beneficial for health.

3. Use Reproducible 3.1 to show students the kernel's bran, germ, and endosperm. Explain that some manufacturers mill (refine or crack) the kernel—a process that removes the fiber and other nutrients—to make the texture of food products finer (e.g., a lighter, airier snack cake or white bread), and sometimes they enrich the grains with nutrients. Tell the students that in order for the grain to be considered whole, it must still have all its natural elements. Generally, anything made from white flour comes from refined grains. Demonstrate some examples of whole grains, such as brown rice, oatmeal, wild rice, buckwheat, whole wheat breads, crackers, pasta, and tortillas. Again, images from an Internet search will retrieve examples that can be shown to the students.

4. Point out that whole grains are particularly important because of the natural fiber found in the kernel. Fiber is particularly beneficial because it relieves constipation (keeps consumers regular); leaves consumers feeling full (satisfied) longer, which curbs the appetite and the urge to snack or eat more; and protects the body against certain diseases. MyPyramid encourages consumers to eat more whole grains to benefit from the kernel's original nutrients, especially fiber. Despite some refined grains being enriched with nutrients, often fiber is not added back into the final product. Add that later students will learn more about nutrition facts labels, which disclose the amount of fiber a product has and whether the ingredients include whole grains. Show them an example of a food nutrition label and call attention to the fiber content feature. Explain that the amount of fiber in a food product often indicates the amount of whole grains it has.

5. Quantify the whole grains and grains they need for the day. According to MyPyramid, youth should eat about 5 to 6 ounces of grains a day, half of which should include whole grains. Introduce the MyPyramid website (http://www.mypyramid.gov/index.html) where they can figure out exactly what portion of grains they need according to their age, gender, and how active they are. At this point, have them visit the site, open the webpage "MyPyramid Plan," and using their personal data, type in their information. (It will be helpful to measure the students' height and weight ahead of time). If the need warrants, demonstrate

this process using a student or two as an example. The interactive site will display their unique daily diet plan. Distribute copies of Reproducible 3.2 and have the students write in the amount of foods that are recommended, and note an example or two of grains. The students will use this Reproducible for Idea 4. (Generally, children 9 to 13 years old need about 5 to 6 ounces, and youth between the ages of 14 and 18 should have about 6 to 7 ounces). Mention that as they age they should gradually increase the amount of whole-grain products they consume.

6.   Have them open the Grains' "Tip" link, which will display grains as meal and snack items. Additionally, a "What counts as an ounce?" link can be found on a sidebar that will exhibit 1-ounce examples of grains. Examples such as a slice of toast or bread, five crackers, a cup of cereal, 3 cups of popcorn, a mini-bagel, and half an English muffin all count as an ounce. Another link on that grains page—"Click here to see the chart"—will retrieve a list of 1-ounce foods. Announce that they will visit the website again for later activities.

7.   Mention that grains are good because the vitamin and minerals they offer keep the heart healthy, protect cells from pollutants, and protect the body from diseases such as diabetes, heart disease, cancer, and gastrointestinal problems.

Activities

Guided. Have the students make a class alphabet book of grains. Assign each student a letter, have them identify a whole grain, grain, or grain product that starts with that assigned letter, and draw a picture for its respective page. If students have a difficult time finding a grain or grain product, they can use introductory articles or adjectives. The student with the letter *A* for example, can have "A mini-bagel." The student with the letter *D* can use "Delicious whole wheat crackers." Students can get creative for the more difficult letters like *X* (e.g., eXquisite buckwheat) and *Z* (e.g., Zesty wild rice).

Independent. Distribute two-sided copies of Reproducible 3.3 and display examples of grain products (taken from the MyPyramid.gov website or from an Internet search). Have the students cut and fold the reproducible accordingly and list under the respective tabs the grain products they have tried and those they intend to try.

Conclusion

As the students are working independently, assemble the class alphabet book of grains. When they are finished, read it with the class, and then call on some students to report on the grain products they intend to try.

Tips

- Bring in grains that the students may not be familiar with and have them touch and smell them
- Have the students compare and contrast actual foods made from grains and whole grains (e.g., crackers, breads, tortillas), conduct a taste test, and make a graph according to their preferences

IDEA 4: VEGETABLES AND FRUITS

Rationale

The next two bands found on MyPyramid represent the individual food groups Vegetables and Fruits, respectively. Vegetables and fruits provide many nutrients and fiber that contribute to a healthy diet when consumed as recommended. They are naturally potent, as they keep blood pressure at healthy levels; help keep chronic diseases at bay; are good sources of dietary fiber, keeping consumers feeling full longer; enhance vision health and memory function; and lower the risk of acquiring certain cancers. Unfortunately, most youth today tend to fall short of the recommended vegetable and fruit allowance. Research finds that only one in five youngsters eats the recommended servings of vegetables and fruits each day. This Idea is particularly important to youth because they *can* learn to eat more vegetables and fruits, and hence benefit from the proven potency that the respective vitamins, minerals, and fiber provide.

Objectives

After learning about the benefits of vegetables and fruits, the students will

- Compose a banner promoting the respective serving size of a vegetable and a fruit
- Construct two postcards—one for a vegetable and one for a fruit—and record the respective serving size

Download and use Reproducibles 1.4, 3.2, and 4.1 for this Idea.

To Motivate the Students

Tell the students that they will be playing a quick game, called Name As Many as You Can. Divide the class into groups of four. Hand each group a double-sided copy of Reproducible 4.1. Using a timer, give the groups 2 or 3 minutes (depending on the age group) to list as many vegetables as they can. When time is up, determine the group that thinks they have the most vegetables (some children may believe that some foods are vegetables, when in fact they are not). Make a t-chart (i.e., a graphic organizer with two columns that enables students to compare ideas) on the board and on the left of it write the vegetables the students have named. Announce the winning team with the most vegetables and compliment their contributions. Have the students repeat the process for fruits. Write the fruits on the right of the t-chart and declare the winning team.

Frame the Instruction

Ask the students to deduce the topic of this strategy based on the game they have just played, and have them recall what they remember about the two individual food groups, Vegetables and Fruits. Demonstrate MyPyramid again (Reproducible 1.4) and have them articulate additional observations they have about the two food groups. Inform them that they will learn about the importance of vegetable and fruit consumption and how much they should eat daily.

Step by Step

1. Mention that the Vegetable and Fruit bands found on MyPyramid indicate two separate food groups. Tell them that the slogan "Vary your veggies," is associated with the Vegetables band, which encourages consumers to eat a variety of vegetables. Point out that the *Dietary Guidelines* complements MyPyramid and recommends, "Consume a sufficient amount of fruits and vegetables while staying within energy needs," and "Choose a variety of fruits and vegetables each day. In particular, select from all five vegetable subgroups (dark green, orange, legumes, starchy vegetables, and other vegetables) several times a week." Explain that color reveals that each vegetable (and fruit) has a unique blend of vitamins and minerals. While consumers should eat different kinds of vegetables, health experts and nutritionists believe that dark green and orange vegetables are particularly beneficial.

2. Demonstrate examples of vegetables. There are a number of ways to do this: Consider an Internet search to retrieve images to compile into a PowerPoint, cut out pictures from magazines, find books on vegetables, take digital photos of vegetables found at your local grocer, or bring in actual vegetables. Consider these for the examples:
   - Dark green: spinach, broccoli, kale, watercress, beet greens, mustard greens
   - Orange: carrots, sweet potatoes, pumpkin, winter squash
   - Other: tomatoes, green beans, celery, cabbage, onions, mushrooms, white potatoes, corn, green peas

Emphasize that there are many ways to eat vegetables—fresh, cooked, from the can, frozen, dried, and juiced—all of which count toward meeting the daily recommendations.

3. Explain that eating vegetables keeps the body healthy, as they provide vitamins, minerals and other nutrients that ward off chronic diseases, reduce the risk of cancer and stroke, maintain a healthy blood pressure, benefit eye health and memory function, help cell growth throughout the body; and provide fiber to aid regularity. Comment that studies have found that people who consume more vegetables and fruits as part of their diet are less likely to develop heart disease; stroke; type 2 diabetes; and cancers of the mouth, stomach, and colon and rectum. Add that vegetables also contribute to their fluid requirements because they are composed largely of water (e.g., lettuce has 95% water, carrots have 87%), and they are sources of carbohydrates that provide energy. All of these beneficial effects may seem foreign to children because these diseases are commonly associated with adults, so underscore that regularly eating vegetables will give them the nutrients and energy to play and exercise, concentrate in school, and keep common illnesses at bay.

4. Assert that youth between the ages of 9 and 13 years old should consume about 2 to 2½ cups, and 14- and 18-year-olds should eat 2½ to 3 cups of vegetables a day. Allow time for the students to compare their data from Reproducible 3.2 to the actual amount of vegetables they need to consume each day. If time is available, allow for students to visit www.mypyramid.gov. Instruct them to open the link "MyPyramid Plan," enter their personal data again, and click the "Tip" link, located on each student's personal plan. On that web page will be the helpful link "What counts as cup?" The link lists examples of a cup of vegetables. While the students write examples of fruit on Reproducible 3.2, show the students an actual 1-cup measurement.

5. Turn the students' attention to fruits. Emphasize that Fruits is a separate food group with its own slogan, "Focus on fruits." Add that MyPyramid advises, "Eat them at meals, and at snack time, too. Choose fresh, frozen, canned, or dried, and go easy on the fruit juice." Many children are drawn to fruits because of their natural sweet taste, so one way to interest students in fruit is to ask them to name some of their favorite fruits. Point out that they should vary the fruit they eat because, just like vegetables, fruits have their own unique blend of nutrients. Advise the students that because fruit juices often have a lot of calories (and often heaps of sugar and less fiber than the actual fruit); students are better off eating fruit.

6. Use some of the suggestions found in Idea 1 above to demonstrate examples of fruit, and transition to a period that allows the students to bring to mind the exact amount of fruit they should eat per day. In general, children should eat 1½ to 2 cups of fruit a day. If time is lacking, the link "How much is needed?" will retrieve a chart that specifies how much fruit children should eat. The "Tip" link will deliver users to additional links: "What's in the Fruit Group?" has a range of examples for the children to note, and "What counts as cup?" includes the dimensions of fruit that count as ½ cup and 1 cup. Ask the students to name some fruits on their Reproducible 3.2. Again, an actual measuring cup would be a useful tool to reinforce students' understanding and recognition of "cup."

7. Underscore that fruits offer an array of nutrients with proven health benefits similar to those found among vegetables.

Activities

Guided. Divide the students into small groups and instruct them to make a banner. Explain that a banner is a flexible sign or flag that bears a motto or slogan that can be hung over a street, in a storefront or entryway, or in the hallway of a building. Tell them that one side of the banner will promote "Vary your veggies" with a simple reminder about the serving size of a vegetable, and the back will be similar, but should publicize the "Focus on fruits" slogan and the serving size of a fruit. Ask the students to first identify the vegetable and fruit they want promoted. Then a group member can visit MyPyramid.gov and navigate through the "Tips" link to "What counts as a cup?" for the vegetables and fruits. (For convenience and to save time later, tab this link or create it as a favorite). After the student has acquired the information, the group should come up with phrases for their vegetable and fruit. Assist the students with an Internet search for the serving sizes of vegetables and fruits not found on the MyPyramid.gov website.

Independent. Mention that students will make two postcards: one for the Vegetables food group and one for the Fruits. One side of the postcard should include a drawing of a vegetable of their choice; the back should include the amount of one serving. For the second postcard, the students repeat the process for the fruit. Allow them time to use the MyPyramid.gov website to retrieve the information on serving sizes. The students are likely to need assistance with an Internet search if they cannot locate the information on the MyPyramid.gov homepage.

Conclusion

Collect the postcards and play a quick game with the whole group that requires them to guess at the serving sizes of their pictures you show.

Follow with questions such as:

- "Now that we have studied three food groups, what can conclusions can you make about a healthy diet?"
- "What do you predict will happen if you do not eat the recommended servings vegetables and fruit?"
- "How can we get more people to eat the recommended servings vegetables and fruit?"

Tips

- Use the student-made postcards at a learning center where early finishers can guess at the serving sizes
- Have the students conduct an Internet search to create an exhaustive list of vegetables and fruit and their serving sizes

---

IDEA 5: MILK

Rationale

Milk has received a lot of publicity over the past few years, for good reason. Milk and milk products are critical to bone health because of the calcium they provide to growing youngsters. Adults and youth alike may recognize the heavily marketed milk mustache and "Got milk?" campaign and others may recall the jingle "Milk: It does a body good." Despite these widespread efforts, however, youth—teens especially—are not consuming the recommended servings. Some have reported that less than one child out of three consumes enough milk (Gleason & Suitor, 2000), while only half of all teens drink milk (and those who do drink less than the recommended amounts) (Berg, 2004). Many youth today opt for nutrient-poor sodas over milk at a time in their lives when their bodies need calcium-rich foods to build bone mass. This may explain why the *Dietary Guidelines for Americans* (U.S. Department of Health and Human Services, 2005b) recommends, "Children 2 to 8 years should consume 2 cups per day of fat-free or low-fat milk or equivalent milk products. Children 9 years of age and older should consume 3 cups per day of fat-free or low-fat milk or equivalent milk products" (p. x). This strategy is particularly important for children so that they can begin to understand the healthy amounts and sorts of milk and milk products they should consume for their growth and development.

Objectives

After learning about the benefits of milk and milk products, the students will

- Assemble a collage of milk, milk products, and other calcium-rich products and evaluate phrases that are appropriate for the images
- Select a magazine picture and incorporate a phrase that makes a healthy recommendation

Download and use Reproducibles 1.4 and 3.2 for this Idea.

To Motivate the Students

To spark students' interest in milk, have them solve a riddle, which can be accomplished as a whole class, in small groups, or individually. Reveal these riddles:

- What kind of dairy cow doesn't provide any milk at all? (An udder failure.)
- When do you milk a dairy cow? (When you're in the moo-d.)
- What happens to dairy cows after they've been in an earthquake? (They provide milk shakes.)
- What mows lawns and provides heaps of milk a day? (A lawn moo-er.)

Compliment students who answered these riddles, and explain the answers to those who were unsuccessful. Ask them to contemplate what the riddles had in common. Verify that they were all based on milk and mention that there are many products made from it, such as cheese, yogurt, cottage cheese, and ice cream.

Frame the Instruction

Inform the students that they will be learning about milk and milk products. Before showing them MyPyramid (Reproducible 1.4) again, ask them to recall what they remember from the Milk food group. Show them MyPyramid and have them point out any additional observations specific to the Milk food group. Mention that they will learn why milk and milk products are important for their health, how much milk they should consume daily, and why they should choose low-fat and fat-free milk and milk products.

Step by Step

1. Explain that the slogan "Get your calcium rich foods" is associated with the Milk food group, and underscore that milk and milk products are important for health because of the calcium that contributes significantly to bone maintenance and growth. Tell them that milk and milk products offer 12 valuable nutrients, including potassium, vitamins A and D, and protein. Mention that MyPyramid strongly encourages milk and milk product consumption because there are too

many youth who choose to drink soda and eat nutrient-poor foods, which makes them vulnerable to an inadequate share of essential nutrients. Emphasize that milk and milk products are much better alternatives because they not only improve bone mass, they lower the risk of low bone mass (i.e., osteoporosis, which afflicts 28 million Americans), keep teeth strong and healthy, help keep blood pressure at healthy levels, keeps skin healthy, and supply energy. Because some children may have a difficult time finding the relevance of drinking milk to prevent adult-onset diseases, underscore that when they regularly drink milk they make their teeth and bones stronger and help their bodies grown into adulthood.

2. Mention there are various ways to consume milk: in the form of cheese, yogurt, frozen yogurt, and ice cream; foods made with milk like pudding and milk in cereal; and flavored milk drinks. Show the students a measured cup, and ask them to recall without looking at their MyPyramid Plan (Reproducible 3.2) how much milk they think they need (in cups) a day. Write some of their responses on the board and verify that youth need up to 3 cups of milk and milk products a day. Have them review their personal data on Reproducible 3.2, or if time permits, allow them the opportunity to visit the MyPyramid Plan web page (see Ideas 3 and 4 for how to access the link) to retrieve the exact amounts students need based on their personnel information. The link within the milk food group, "What counts as one cup?" will orient them to amounts, common portions, and 1-cup equivalents (e.g., one scoop of ice cream is equivalent to 1/3 cup of milk).

3. Inform the students that there is a caveat associated with milk and milk products: Because whole milk is composed of saturated fat that can clog arteries, too much of it and products made from it can be damaging to health. (Incidentally, cream cheese, cream, and butter have very little calcium and they are high in saturated fat and calories). Some speculate that healthy aspects of whole-milk products come at a high price, which is why it is important to teach the students to consume milk that is skim, low fat or fat free (and products made thereof). If they drink whole milk, let them know that they can gradually transition to skim milk. They can choose the 2% milk, then after some time try the 1%, and then skim. They can also advise their caregivers to buy and serve them smaller portions of cheese and yogurt that are low fat or fat free. Emphasize that 1 cup of cheese is about the size of two 9-volt batteries, and one slice of cheese is about ½ cup. Warn them that some yogurts have a lot of sugar, which means a lot more calories.

4. Explain that because of these caveats and because some youth cannot consume milk or milk products, as they are lactose intolerant (their

bodies cannot digest the sugar in milk), there are nonmilk options, primarily calcium-rich foods like calcium-fortified drinks (e.g., orange juice) and cereals, soy- and rice-based drinks, lactose-free products, tofu, sardines, spinach, and broccoli. List these on the board.

Activities

Guided. The students will collaborate in small teams to make a collage of milk, milk products, and other calcium-rich foods. Divide the students into small groups; provide them a large sheet of paper (either poster board or 11 x 17 inches) and assorted popular magazines. Instruct them to cut out five (this can vary according to time constraints) pictures of milk and milk products as well as nonmilk calcium-rich products. While they are engaged in the activity write the following on the board:

- "Make sure it is low fat or fat free"
- "1 cup will be fine"
- "2 cups will do"
- "One slice is enough"
- "Have you tried a healthy alternative?"
- "Don't forget the two-9-volt-battery rule"
- "That can hurt you: Scale back"
- "Right on"

After the students have assembled the collage, have them write out an appropriate phrase or two somewhere near each picture.

Independent. Using the assorted magazines, instruct the students to find one picture of a milk, milk product or calcium-rich alternative and paste it onto a single sheet of paper. (The students can draw pictures if the resources are unavailable). Then ask them to select a phrase appropriate (or write one of their own) for their product and attach it somewhere near their image.

Conclusion

While the students are working, tape string or thin rope from one end of the classroom to another and use some clothespins to hang their work as an exhibit for all the students to see. Ask them to look at their work carefully and to articulate the most interesting facts they learned about milk. Ask them to articulate how they might ask their caregivers for low-fat or fat-free milk or milk products.

Tips

- Bring in packages of milk and milk products and show the students the differences in the amount of calories and fat between whole, low-fat, and fat-free milk and milk products. (While they may not yet be familiar with fat at this point, this comparison will provide them the basis that whole milk has more fat).

- Bring in a can of soda and a cup of milk, have the students compare the nutrients in each, and make generalizations about their contributions to their health.

IDEA 6: MEAT AND BEANS

Rationale

The Meat and Beans band is the last of the MyPyramid food groups. (Oil is a band on the pyramid but is not considered a food group). The slogan associated with Meat and Beans recommends eating all kinds of foods in this group and adds that lean portions are ideal. There is a wide selection of meats, poultry, fish, and dry beans that are rich sources of protein and nutrients; however, some foods are high in calories and saturated fats that, consumed in excess, lead to weight gain and can damage the heart. Americans presently consume too much animal protein. Hoeger and Hoeger (2007) explain, "Nutritional guidelines discourage the excessive intake of protein. The daily protein intake from some people is almost twice the amount the human body needs. Too much animal protein apparently decreases blood enzymes that prevent precancerous cells from developing into tumors. According to the National Cancer Institute, eating substantial amounts of red meat may increase the risk of colorectal, pancreatic, breast, prostate, and renal cancer" (p. 334). Here, students learn that meats are important to their diet, but smaller portions and leaner selections benefit them the most.

Objectives

After learning about the benefits of foods from the Meat and Beans group, the students will

- Recommend the replacement of a meat item with a healthier alternative
- Propose five protein alternatives to a meat of their choice

Download and use Reproducibles 1.4, 6.1, and 6.2 for this Idea.

To Motivate the Students

Play a guessing game with the students. Show the students a picture of peanuts and pinto beans and have them guess what they have in common. If a student has not correctly guessed that they belong to the Meat and Beans food group, keep them guessing as you gradually show them additional pictures in the following order: an egg, chickpeas, fish, tofu, a piece of chicken, a pecan, shrimp, and a steak. Confirm that as different as these foods are, they are all common foods found in the MyPyramid food group Meat and Beans, which is the last of the food groups. Mention that "Oils" has a band on the MyPyramid, but is not a food group.

Frame the Instruction

Show the students MyPyramid for Kids (Reproducible 1.4) and point out that the Meat and Beans food group has six subgroups: meats, which can be divided into meats, game, and organs (e.g., liver, giblets); poultry; eggs; dry beans and peas; nuts and seeds; and fish, which can be divided into finfish, shellfish, and canned fish. Write these items on the board. Point out that the slogan "Go lean with protein" is associated with the Meat food group. Ask them to infer what this slogan may mean, and emphasize that they will learn that this food group has a variety of choices and associated health benefits when foods selected from this group are lean.

Step by Step

1. Mention that the last of the food groups has a band that is the narrowest of the five, which is symbolic. (Again, underscore that oil, which is the narrowest band of all, is not a food group). Have them deliberate what the smaller width suggests, and explain that people need less from this food group and are reminded not to eat excessively from it. Explain that research shows that Americans already eat too much from this food group, putting their health at risk. The American Heart Association and the American Cancer Society strongly recommend that consumers eat less red meat because despite its inherent nutrients, too much increases cholesterol to alarming levels that can harm the heart.

2. Visit www.MyPyramid.gov to access what foods are in the subgroups. This can be accomplished by entering personal data onto the MyPyramid Plan link. A screen appears that reveals the amounts of foods to consume. The "Tips" link found at the Meat and Beans bar will feature "What's in the Meats & Beans group?" Demonstrate some of these foods, especially those that children may not find familiar, like veal, bison, venison, giblets, chickpeas, falafel, lentils, and tempeh. (An Internet image search will retrieve pictures of these foods that can be easily assembled into a PowerPoint or printed for their inquiry). Show the students the exhaustive list that MyPyramid provides or as an alternative, have the children think of as many foods they believe fall within the Meat and Beans groups and list them correctly in the respective subgroups.

3. Mention some of the health benefits associated with foods from this group. The foods offer assorted nutrients that produce energy, maintain the central nervous system, enhance red blood cells, and help build tissue. These include amino acids, antioxidants, iron, magnesium, phosphorous, protein, sulfur, vitamin A, B vitamins, vitamin E, and zinc. (Mention the nutrients that are developmentally appropriate for the age group). Emphasize that these foods offer heavy doses of protein that can leave people satisfied longer, which helps curb the craving for between-meal snacks. According to MyPyramid, children between the ages of 2 and 8 should have up to 4 ounces, 9- to 13-year-olds should have about 5 ounces, and older youth (14- to 18-year-olds) should have about 5 to 6 ounces. Emphasize that these amounts are not cups, as in the other food groups, but ounces. Ask the students to review their personal data on Reproducible 1.4 and to enter examples of foods from this group onto the respective box. If a measuring cup is available, show the students the amount of an ounce. They will be surprised to see how little it is! If available, show the following items as representations of amounts: a deck of cards (2–3 ounces); 9-volt battery (1 ounce); and a computer mouse (½ cup of beans).

4. Explain that "Go lean with protein" suggests selecting portions that have little or no fat. The recommendation is intended to encourage the public to cut back on consumption of particular meats that contain high amounts of saturated fat, which can cause long-term health problems. Encourage the students to ask their caregivers for smaller pieces of red meat and to regularly choose other foods from this group.

Activities

Guided. Divide the students in pairs. Distribute double-sided copies of Reproducible 6.1 to each pair. Ask them to imagine that their parents have asked their guidance in planning the main dish for dinner. Using the list of foods found in the Meat and Beans group seen on the back side of the reproducible, have the students decide on one alternative to (and a reasonable portion size for) steak, barbeque ribs, wieners, roast beef, and fajitas.

Independent. Have the students complete Reproducible 6.2, Protein Alternative Stars. Distribute the reproducible and instruct them to write one of these foods in the center of the star: fajitas, bologna, salami, pork chops, and ham. Then, using the same list of foods from the guided activity, have them choose five food alternatives (from the Meat and Beans group) and write one for each arm of the star.

Conclusion

Select some students to unveil their stars to the class. Follow with reflective questions such as:

- "Did _____ choose wise alternatives? Why or why not?"
- "Why is it important to know to go lean?"
- "Why do you think it's so difficult to go lean?"
- "What can we do get more people to go lean?"

Tips

- Visit the websites of the American Heart Association and the American Cancer Society to retrieve their statements and recommendations on eating healthy amounts of meats
- Take a poll on the class's favorite meat item (e.g., hamburger, hot dog, baloney) and conduct Internet research on its common serving size and contrast that with the recommended amount for healthy consumption

---

IDEA 7: NUTRITION FACTS LABEL

Rationale

The Nutrition Facts label is a convenient tool for consumers who want to eat and drink nutritious food. The United States Department of Agriculture (USDA) mandates that a Nutrition Facts label be printed on the packages of most foods (there are exemptions), putting at consumers' fingertips the information needed to account for the amount of calories, fat, carbohydrates, sodium, and other nutrients found in a single serving; the label also discloses the ingredients. In short, the Nutrition Facts label answers, "What are the nutrients in this food? And if I eat a single serving, how much of this contributes to my overall daily requirements?" With the awareness that Nutrition Facts labels bring, consumers can shop and compare similar products from different manufacturers and select those that offer the most nutrients and fewest calories, fat, cholesterol, and salt. Williams (2007) found that carefully reading food labels can make a difference in diet. Some individuals changed their behavior to decrease their fat intake, while others used the labels to reduce the amount of sodium in their diet. This strategy is important because the more familiar that youth are with the Nutrition Facts label, the likelier they are to use it throughout their lives for planning a healthy, balanced diet.

Objectives

After learning about the Nutrition Facts label, the students will

- Compare and contrast the nutritional values of similar products
- Compare and contrast the nutritional values of different products

Download and use Reproducible 7.1 for this Idea.

To Motivate the Students

Select some small novelty toys to place in a shoe or small box. A rubber ball, a toy car, toy jacks, an action figure, Green Army Men soldiers, and a paddle ball are some examples to include. Fasten the box closed so that the items cannot be seen and the box can be shaken. Pass the box around from student to student and have them guess at its contents. Compliment those who guess at some of the items correctly, and reassure the students who did not that it is nearly impossible to guess at the contents simply by shaking it. Casually mention that the box is available for sale, but it can only be opened after it is purchased. Ask if this condition influences their judgment (and eagerness) to buy it. Next, attach a stick-on note to the box that lists the contents. Have a student read the list, and then confirm that these are the items. Ask if they are more inclined to purchase the box now that they know its contents. Have them deliberate how a label can be helpful to a consumer. Affirm that labels can be valuable, informational tools that contribute to the decision to buy the food item. Use some examples of labels and their purposes, such as on files and on most items available for commercial purchase. Explain that the federal government mandates that packaged foods bear a label of contents so that consumers know their exact ingredients and nutrients, which can influence their decision to buy it.

Frame the Instruction

Tell the students that they will be learning about the Nutrition Facts labels, which appeared on food packages in 1994 after the passage of the Nutrition Labeling and Education Act of 1990. Clarify that not all foods are required to have a Nutrition Facts label. Foods prepared in restaurants, in hospitals, on airplanes, and at other public venues are exempt, and so are fresh meat, fish, fruit, and vegetables. Ask the students to think about why knowing the nutritional information of individual packaged foods is important to their health. After listening to their responses, confirm that knowing the nutrients and ingredients in commercially made and packaged foods can help consumers structure a diet that includes a generous selection of the healthy foods and a limited one of the nutrient poor. Tell them that they will

learn about the components of the Nutrition Facts label so that they learn
how to read and use them in deciding what is and is not healthy to consume.

Step by Step

1. A day or two before using this lesson plan, assign the students to bring
    a Nutrition Facts label from a packaged food of their choosing. Allow
    them a few minutes to examine their labels, and have them report on
    their observations. Write their responses on the board if warranted.
    Explain that the Nutrition Facts label is composed of universal
    components that impart nutritional information about the contents of
    packaged foods. As the function of each component is described, have
    the students follow along with their own label. Explain:

    - Title—"Nutrition Facts" is printed in bold letters, which is
      important because it draws the consumer's attention to the
      nutrients contained in the packaged food.
    - Serving size—the amount of food considered a serving, such
      as 2 cookies, 1 tablespoon, 1 cup, 1 packet, and so forth.
      Note that serving sizes may be smaller or larger than what is
      regularly consumed. Warn them that if they eat twice or three
      times the serving size, the amounts and the percentage of daily
      values have to be multiplied accordingly. So, if a package of
      cookies has a serving size of 2 with 250 calories and 4 cookies
      are eaten, 500 calories have been consumed and all the other
      nutrients are doubled. This component is particularly beneficial
      because similar products from different manufacturers—like
      cookies—have different serving sizes, which makes it ideal for
      comparing the calories, fat, and nutrients. One manufacturer,
      for instance, could offer 5 vanilla cookies at 200 calories for
      a single serving, while another may have 10 vanilla cookies
      at 200 calories for a single serving. Federal standards restrict
      manufacturers from having serving sizes that are unreasonably
      small so that good nutrition claims can be made.
    - Servings per container—how many servings there are in the
      entire package. Explain that packages often have more than
      one serving. Larger packages generally have more servings.
    - Calories and calories from fat—the number of calories,
      which can come from fat, protein, or carbohydrates, in a
      single serving. Mention that more calories that are regularly
      consumed without a balance of exercise can lead to weight
      gain. This information allows consumers to compare whether
      the product is worth eating because they may be able to find

an alternative to a product that is high in calories and low in nutrients (e.g., a small bran muffin of 150 calories, low in fat and high in fiber, can be healthier substitute for a 325-calorie cupcake high in fat, cholesterol, sugar, and sodium and with no fiber or vitamins)

- Percentage daily value—the amount that contributes to what should be consumed in one day. It is based on 2,000- and 2,500-calorie diets (for adults) and varies according to age and size. This percentage helps consumers determine how much of the food contributes to the daily requirements and indicates whether the serving has high or low amounts of nutrients. Foods with figures lower than 5% daily value are considered low amounts of nutrients, and figures higher than 20% daily value are considered high. Consider percentage of daily value as a gauge for what is being consumed relative to what is required for each day. As an example, if an orange beverage provides 10% daily value vitamin C, then consumption of the drink has contributed 10% vitamin C required for the day.

2. Mention that the following nutrients are for single servings:

- Total fat—the total amount of all the different fats (in grams). Limit these because an excessive consumption of fat can lead to weight gain and increases the risk of developing heart disease, high blood pressure, and certain cancers.
- Saturated fat—the amount of saturated fat. While some saturated fats are beneficial, consumption of these should be kept to a minimum because they too contribute to heart disease.
- Trans fat—the amount of trans fat. Choose foods that have lower amounts of trans fat because excess consumption increases the risk of heart disease.
- Cholesterol, sodium, and potassium—measured in milligrams, these reveal the amount of cholesterol, sodium (salt), and potassium.
- Total carbohydrate—the amount of carbohydrates (measured in grams). Two types of carbohydrates are listed—fiber and sugar.
- Dietary fiber—the amount of fiber. Students should strive for higher amounts of fiber: five percent or less is considered low, 20% or higher is considered high.

- Sugar—the amount of sugar (measured in grams). There is no corresponding percentage daily value, but the amounts can be used to compare the amount of sugar in one food product with another. Sugar is addressed again in Idea 13.
- Protein—the amount of protein (measured in grams)
- Vitamin A and vitamin C—the percentage amounts of these vitamins provided in percent of the daily value. Nutrients such as calcium, iron, and vitamin D may be listed here as well. Mention that consumers should strive to reach 100% of the daily value for fiber, vitamins, calcium, iron, and other key nutrients.
- The footnote—indicates the percentage daily values, based on 2,000- and 2,500-calorie diets for all consumers.
- Because the diseases commonly associated with a poor diet often do not manifest until adulthood, many children will have a difficult time believing that they can become afflicted with such diseases or are prone to common illnesses when they eat nutrient-inferior foods. Thus, it is important to stress that when they have poor dietary habits, their health is at risk for common illnesses that can keep them from doing activities they enjoy.

3. While reviewing these components, ask individual students to identify the serving size, the number of servings in the package, the number of calories, the amount of fat, and so forth, associated with their respective Nutrition Facts label. Confirm that 5% or less is low and over 20% or more is high. Emphasize that they should use the Nutrition Facts label to seek out lower amounts of fats and cholesterol, because in excess these can lead to weight gain and harm the body, and aim for higher amounts of fiber, vitamins, and other nutrients printed in this area.

4. Underscore that a Nutrition Facts label is a convenient resource that helps consumers make smart, informed decisions about the foods and beverages they eat and drink. Before the Nutrition Facts label appeared, consumers needed to guess at how nutritional a product was. The labels can guide them to make healthy decisions as they comparison shop, plan for a meal, and cook (when they are able to). The bottom line: Nutrition Facts labels help consumers decide whether to buy a packaged food, based on the nutrients that are offered (or lacking). Ask the students to refer to the labels on all the packaged foods they or their parents purchase, especially the snacks and beverages, which are often nutrient poor.

Activities

Guided. Instruct the students to report on how much of their product they would generally eat. Explain that the serving size is a gentle reminder not to eat too much of the product (i.e., their portions should not be excessive) because the nutrients consumed are magnified when they do. Using their label, ask them to identify what their serving size is, and estimate if they would have eaten the same amounts as the suggested serving size, more, or less. To pairs of students, distribute Reproducible 7.1, which invites them to jointly compare and contrast nutritional values of similar products and answer the questions.

Independent. Bring in, photocopy, or retrieve through an Internet search Nutrition Facts labels that individual students can compare. Some example include similar cereals from different manufacturers; soda, orange juice, and milk; a slice of bread and a bagel; popcorn and chips; a candy bar and strawberries; and mozzarella cheese and carrots. The purpose is to reinforce the understanding that when the students have options the Nutrition Facts label can help them make healthier choices. To that end, ask that they compare and contrast their foods' serving sizes; calorie contents; and the amount of total fat, cholesterol, dietary fiber, sugars, protein, and other nutrients and their respective percentage daily value. Then have them identify the healthier product based on these findings.

Conclusion

Have the students report their findings on the healthier products. Follow with questions, such as

- "What is the most interesting aspect you learned about the Nutrition Facts labels?"
- "What will you do with the knowledge you now have about the labels?"
- "Why do you suppose that the labels are a relatively recent occurrence?"
- "What relationships can you draw between energy balance, MyPyramid, and the Nutrition Facts labels?"

Tips

- Have the students visit the website Nutritiondata.com and look up the Nutrition Facts labels on common vegetables and fruits and think about their healthy nutrients
- Assign the students to write a critique to the manufacturer of their favorite snack reporting what they found on the Nutrition Facts label

IDEA 8: SNACKS AND BEVERAGES

Rationale

Snacks and beverages are a large part of children's diets. Current data suggest that most children consume about two snacks a day, which is about 600 calories (Berg, 2004; Center for Science in the Public Interest, 2003a). And when it comes to selecting a beverage, soda seems to be the drink of choice. More than half of all children consume soda daily, which displaces healthier beverage options. Considering that 1 can of regular soda averages between 150 to 200 calories and 9 to 11 teaspoons of sugar, it is no surprise that children who regularly drink sodas are more likely to become overweight than their counterparts who do not (Center for Science in the Public Interest, 2003b). Snacks and beverages can help children meet their daily nutritional recommendations and receive an energy boost they need between meals, but they can also lead to poor health—and weight gain—when they are nutrient poor, high in calories, and consumed excessively. This strategy is important for children because it teaches them to explore and consume a variety of snacks and consider beverages other than sodas. When children learn to eat snacks and drink beverages that are consistent with the MyPyramid recommendations, they establish a lifelong habit of choosing those that contribute positively to their diet.

Objectives

After learning about healthy snacks and beverages, the students will

- Recommend a healthier alternative to a snack and beverage
- Create bumper stickers that announce healthier substitutes for nutrient-poor snacks and beverages

Download and use Reproducibles 8.1–8.3 for this Idea.

To Motivate the Students

Write the food groups on the board and ask the students to ponder their favorite snacks and beverages. Record their responses on the board under the respective food groups. Point out the food groups that are well represented, and underscore those that are not. Explain that MyPyramid encourages the regular consumption of a variety of foods so that the body gets as many different nutrients as possible, and that the spirit of variety applies to snacks and beverages as well. Invite the students to identify the snacks and beverages they believe are excessively high in calories, sugar, fat, or salt. Emphasize that consuming nutrient-poor snacks in large portions or too frequently throughout the day can lead to a host of problems.

Frame the Instruction

State that healthy snacks and beverages contribute positively to a healthy diet. Mention that this lesson explores why snacks and beverages are important and describes those that should be consumed most often. Explain that an awareness of healthy snacks and beverages that meets MyPyramid recommendations engenders a likelihood that they will consume them.

Step by Step

1. Explain that eating healthy means that snacking—eating between meals—is acceptable. In fact, snacking provides energy that the body needs between meals, especially those spaced four or more hours apart. Without that source of energy, people begin to lose focus and start feeling tired or sluggish. Mention that snacks are not intended to make someone feel full; they should provide just enough energy to tide the person over to the next meal. After all, snacks and beverages contribute to a full day's calorie needs. Acknowledge that they should seek out snacks that are between 100 to 150 calories and are nutritious. The calories can easily add up from high-calorie snacks, which can lead to a few extra pounds in a year's time. Conversely, consuming low-calorie snacks—just trimming off 100 calories a day each year—can lead to weight loss. For these reasons, mention that it is worthwhile to consider these questions when they are about to reach for a snack: "Am I really hungry?" And "Do I really want a snack?" (Rizza, Go, McMahon, & Harrison, 2002).

2. Remind the students that because variety is important, they should aim for snacks from all the MyPyramid food groups. Encourage them to look for and consume low-fat or fat-free snacks (that fulfill the MyPyramid recommendations) and are high in fiber and protein (because they keep consumers feeling full longer). Define *low fat* (i.e., 3 grams of fat or less) and *fat free* (i.e., no fat) for them. Snacks that are excessively fattening, sugary, and salty are generally high in calories and low in nutrients and should be eaten in moderation. (Reese's Peanut Butter Cups 1.6 oz. size package, for instance, has 232 calories and 14 grams of fat).

3. Tell the students that they should check the nutritional contents of snacks by reading the Nutrition Facts labels. Tell them that some snack foods are often marketed as "good for you" or "a healthy alternative," yet they are high in fat, sugar, and salt. Some examples include granola bars, chips, and trail mix. Then mention some examples of healthy snacks: pretzels; baked chips (potato or tortilla); microwave popcorn; bread sticks; fig bars; ginger snaps; graham crackers; animal crackers; raw, frozen, canned, or dried fruit and vegetables; applesauce; rice

cakes; whole-grain crackers; half a bagel; frozen yogurt (low fat or fat free); yogurt (low fat or fat free); fruit sorbet; 100% fruit juice popsicle; and tomato juice. Underscore that small amounts (according to MyPyramid portion recommendations) are best because the bigger the snack size, the more calories. Mention that there are times, understandably, when they will crave treats and will want to splurge on ice cream, chips, candy, and other foods that are not healthy, and in those situations it is smart to consume small, measured amounts.

4. Because drinks can add substantially to calories, advise students that water and low-fat or fat-free milk are wonderful choices for beverages. Water is the ideal thirst quencher because it is virtually free of calories, fat, cholesterol, and sugar. Further, water is a natural appetite suppressant that helps maintain regularity, keeps muscles toned, helps keep the body hydrated and cool, and helps the organs function. As of now, there is no prescription on how much water should be consumed. The amount varies according to one's activity level, diet, and size, but most experts advise drinking enough so that urine is clear (Roizen & Oz, 2007). Drinking low-fat or fat-free milk will help meet the recommended allowance that adds calcium to the diet needed for bone health. One-hundred-percent fruit juices are fine in small quantities because they can fulfill the recommended fruit servings. (Incidentally, the Nutrition Facts label should list 100% fruit juice in the ingredients. Fruit drinks, as opposed to 100% fruit juices, are generally made with water and sugar and offer very little fruit juice. Even though many fruit drinks are fortified with vitamins, they rarely offer the nutrients that 100% fruit juices do). Tell students that consumers should refrain from the sugary fruit drinks and sodas that offer few nutrients. Forewarn the students about cream-based beverages like milk shakes (a large one from McDonald's has 1,010 calories) and cold drinks (a large Dunkin' Donuts Coolatta has 820 calories), which can add substantially to the daily calorie count.

5. Convey how you understand how palatable and available sodas are, but counter that regular consumption of nondiet sodas contributes poorly to their diet. Inform them that nondiet sodas have from 150 to 200 calories and about 9 to 11 teaspoons of sugar and offer very few nutrients. Gather some Nutrition Facts labels of popular sodas and demonstrate their nutritional content. Underscore that, in effect, when they choose to drink sodas they lose out on nutrients that other beverages offer. Add that health experts believe that consumers miss out on calcium when they drink sodas instead of milk, which puts them at risk for osteoporosis, not to mention that heavy doses of sugar can lead to tooth decay. Because children are likely to have a difficult time

understanding the long-term effects of osteoporosis, explain that bones that do not have sufficient calcium over time become thin and brittle and can break more easily, which can devastate the quality of life.

6. Note that planning for snacks is a good idea because they can put some thought into seeking or buying healthier snacks. Emphasize that families are often too busy to think about healthier snacks and beverages at the times they want them, and hence will be tempted to select those that are convenient and savory (but nutrient poor). But snacks that have been planned for and made readily available ensure that they get the nutrients they need. They can, for example, buy healthy prepackaged foods, divide veggies into baggies, or plan exactly when they will consume foods from specific food groups (e.g., a snack from the Milk group in the morning and a small piece of fruit in the afternoon).

Activities

Guided. Group the students in pairs and distribute Reproducibles 8.1 and 8.2. The students cut Reproducible 8.1 into a deck of cards; Reproducible 8.2 remains the playing board. As each student takes a turn drawing a card from the deck he or she reads the snack or beverage printed on the card and proclaims, "Instead of _____, I'm going to eat the less healthy (snack or beverage) _____" and places the card over the healthier alternative. The students continue playing until they have filled the board with the cards or time is up.

Independent. Distribute Reproducible 8.3, which illustrates the two blank bumper stickers. Instruct the students to make one bumper sticker for snacks and another for beverages. The students complete the phrase "I used to reach for_____, but now I reach for _____!" for each with the intended goal of enabling them to change their behavior and choose healthier snacks and beverages.

Conclusion

Invite the students to share their bumper stickers. Ask other students to recommend some reasonable snack and beverage substitutes.

Tips

- Gather some vegetables and fruits and have the students take a taste test to determine a favored snack
- Instruct the students to compose a list of healthy snacks that are 100 calories each
- Compare the nutrients of skim milk, a soda, 100% fruit juice, and a popular juice

IDEA 9: PORTION CONTROL

Rationale

Portion sizes are much larger today than just 20 years ago. Most consumers fail to recognize that their portion sizes at any given meal are larger than recommended serving sizes. Having this distorted impression of portion sizes leads many to consume more calories, fat, cholesterol, sodium, and sugar. Large portions are most evident at restaurants and fast-food eateries that seek to attract customers by offering a value with larger portions. It can cost cents to get larger portions by way of a "Biggie," "Super Size," "King Size," "Value Meal," "Supreme," or "Colossal." But as noted earlier, excessive consumption of foods and beverages can lead to weight gain, putting consumers at risk for future health problems. Young children may not be familiar with serving sizes and are likely to assume that the portions provided to them are standard and consume them without question. Research has found that children overeat when they are served larger portions (Dalton, 2004). Without understanding portion control, children could consume excessive amounts of foods and beverages for years before discerning the source of their weight gain. This strategy teaches children to control their portions by scaling back on the amount they consume to sizes that approximate the MyPyramid recommendations.

Objectives

After learning the difference between portion size and serving size, the students will

- Compare the portion sizes of foods they typically eat with the actual serving size
- Distinguish common objects that represent the serving sizes of foods

Download and use Reproducibles 9.1 and 9.2 for this Idea.

To Motivate the Students

Demonstrate a Nutrition Facts label and quickly review the different elements (based on the information from Idea 7). Highlight the serving size and ask a student to explain—to the best of his or her knowledge—what that is. Next, ask the students to think about the portion sizes of meals and snacks that they eat at home, in restaurants, and in the school cafeteria. Inform them that what they eat at one sitting may be significantly larger than the recommended serving size.

Frame the Instruction

Explain that a healthy diet is not exclusively about eating a variety of foods; it is also about eating moderate amounts. Emphasize that they have control over the portion sizes they consume for a meal, snack, or beverage, and in this lesson they will learn about the elements commonly associated with portion control.

Step by Step

1. Explain that there is a difference between serving size and portion size. Serving size is a specified size of food recommended for consumers; portion size is the amount that is consumed at a given time. Mention that studies confirm that portion sizes for many foods have increased over time and that consumers have a tendency to eat much larger portions than the recommended serving size. A single serving of a food often exceeds the actual serving size in multiples. Typically, a medium order of fries, for instance, is equal to four of MyPyramid's 1-ounce recommendation. Ask the students to speculate what happens when larger portions are consistently consumed.

2. Confirm that *portion distortion* refers to the idea that large portion sizes are mistaken for serving sizes. In other words, consumers presume that the amounts they eat are the correct amounts to maintain healthy weight. Elaborate that the term *portion distortion* is fitting because consumers often have a distorted belief that the portions they are served are the recommended size, when in fact they are inflated versions of the recommended serving size. Consequently, they often underestimate how much they eat or drink and how many calories, fat, and other nutrients they consume at a given time. Remind them that too much energy "in" that is not balanced with exercise or physical activity can lead to a larger waistline and future health problems.

3. Mention that portion sizes are typically larger at restaurants, sometimes two to three times larger than the recommended serving size. Explain that a restaurant entrée can provide a half day's worth of calories, fat, and nutrients. Add that marketing campaigns such as Biggie, Super Size, King Size, Value Meal, Supreme, and Colossal, which advertise larger portions for cents more, tend to be popular because most consumers believe that there is value associated with more food. In short, consumers demand more for their money because they are value driven. But what most consumers fail to realize is that larger portion sizes also mean more fat, calories, sodium, and cholesterol. As an example, the McDonald's Super Size

Extra Value Meal, which is composed of a Quarter Pounder with cheese, supersize fries, and a supersize nondiet drink, has about 1,550 calories. Underscore that when consumers scale back on their portion sizes they limit calories, fat, and other nutrients.

4. Define *portion control*, which is reducing portion sizes so that they approximate the serving sizes that MyPyramid recommends or are a moderate size. Inform the students that MyPyramid and Nutrition Facts labels can help them evaluate their portion sizes. A habit they can develop is locating the serving size on the Nutrition Facts label and measuring it out on their dish or in their bowl. This is beneficial for three reasons: They can compare the serving size with the portion they would have been inclined to eat; they are reminded that second helpings contribute more to the daily calorie and nutrient count; and if they are still hungry after the first helping, they can elect for seconds of vegetables, salads, or grain-based sides instead of foods that are high in calories and fat.

5. Encourage them to become visually familiar with the serving sizes of foods they eat most often (Thompson & Shanley, 2004). Reasonably, they could learn the serving sizes of cereal, macaroni and cheese, peanut butter, fruit juice, and other foods. Explain that health experts agree that consumers eat the portions that are served to them, even when they are large.

6. Assert that everyday objects can be used to estimate the serving sizes of food they are about to eat:

   - Mention that food the size of a baseball counts as 1 cup. So, an apple the size of a baseball is 1 cup. A cup of raw vegetables, a cup of yogurt, and a cup of dry cereal are all about the size of a baseball.
   - Half a baseball is a ½ cup of cooked rice or pasta.
   - An egg is about a ¼ cup of raisins.
   - A small computer mouse is about a ½ cup of fruit, a ½ cup of vegetables, and a ½ cup of beans.
   - A deck of cards represents a ½ cup of fries (about 10) and 2 to 3 ounces of meat, poultry, or fish.
   - Two dominoes are about 1½ ounces.
   - Four stacked dice are about 1 ounce of cheese.
   - A tennis ball is about a ½ cup.
   - A Ping-Pong ball is about 2 tablespoons of butter.
   - Two 9-volt batteries are about 1½ ounces of cheese.
   - One 9-volt battery is about 1 ounce of peanut butter.
   - A CD is about a 1 ounce slice of bread.

Activities

Guided. For this whole-group activity, the students need their own copy of Reproducible 9.1. Gather the packages of foods popular among children, like cookies, potato chips, cereal, chocolate milk, and chocolate candies. Have the students list these foods on the far-left column of the reproducible. Announce each food item and have the students guess at how many/much they would typically have and write their anticipated amount in the adjacent column. Then, reveal the serving size, and have the students write whether they had more than, less than, or the actual serving size. For instance, for cookies, show the students an Oreo cookies package. Ask how many they would generally have in one setting. Then reveal the serving size and ask them to note if they ate more than, less than, or the actual serving size. Proceed accordingly. If packages are not available, visit www.nutritiondata. com to access a search engine of nutrition facts.

Independent. Have the students complete Reproducible 9.2, which is composed of common objects and their measures. Instruct the students to search the foods they have at home (or at a grocery store) and examine the Nutrition Facts labels for serving sizes and list the foods under the respective object.

Conclusion

Ask the students to share what they learned and report on the serving size they were most surprised to discover. Ask them to suggest a practice they could start to keep their portions moderately sized. When the students return with the completed homework, have them share their findings and reveal the serving sizes they found most surprising.

Tips

- Have the students write a letter to restaurant or a fast-food chain asking for the creation of a meal that is composed of smaller portions
- Assign the students a food such as a salty snack (chips, pretzels, or popcorn), sweets (cookies, packaged pastry, or candies), or popular drinks (sodas or juices) and have each student find the serving size of the most popular brands

---

IDEA 10: MODERATION

Rationale

MyPyramid is composed of important principles, three of which, balance, variety, and proportion, have been addressed in this book. Moderation is another. Children need to learn about moderation because too much of any food is never that good for health. In this context, moderation is about limiting the savory indulgences that are typically nutrient poor and avoiding extremes by way of (1) regular consumption of nutrient-poor foods (e.g., eating pizza 5 days a week) and (2) excessive consumption of foods at one setting (e.g., eating three snack cakes at a given time). Arguably, one of the factors contributing to the obesity crisis is that children and adults alike do not practice moderation and regularly yield to their cravings and overindulge in supersize portions. This strategy teaches children that the foods they enjoy do not have to be eliminated from their diets; they can be included on occasion and in limited amounts. The students also learn how to counter the tendencies that interfere with the practice of moderation in daily life.

Objectives

After learning the principle of moderation as it relates to food consumption, the students will

- Evaluate whether a serving of food is excessive or in moderation
- Determine when portions of foods are excessive and when they are fine in moderation

Download and use Reproducibles 1.4, 10.1, and 10.2 for this Idea.

To Motivate the Students

Retrieve a picture of Aristotle from the Internet. Show the students his picture and provide some general biographical information about him (e.g., a Greek philosopher, lived from 384 BC to 322 BC, wrote on many subjects). Mention that even though he lived over 2,300 years ago, he imparted wisdom that applies in contemporary society. In fact, his insight is relevant to healthy eating today because of his notion about moderation: He believed that too much of a "good thing" can have harmful effects. Ask the students to contemplate this notion and how it applies to healthy eating. Invite the students to share their own experiences of having too much of a "good thing."

Frame the Discussion

Tell the students they will be learning about one of the MyPyramid principles, moderation. Explain that moderation can be a difficult habit to maintain, but as a rule of thumb it can make for good health. Ask them to bear in mind the notion that more of something is not always better.

Step by Step

1. Show the students the MyPyramid for Kids image (Reproducible 1.4). Remind them that each food group has a color band that is wider at

the base than at the top, rendering the triangle image. Explain that this tapering was not created by whim; it represents the MyPyramid principle of moderation. Ask the students if they have ever heard the word *moderation* and invite them to define it as best as they can. Affirm that MyPyramid explicitly defines *moderation* this way: "Moderation is represented by the narrowing of each food group from bottom to top. The wider base stands for foods with little or no solid fats or added sugars. These would be selected more often. The narrower top area stands for foods containing more added sugars and solid fats. The more active you are, the more of these foods can fit into your diet" (U.S. Department of Agriculture, 2005a, p. 1). Reinforce that the healthier foods, the ones that should be consumed more often, are figuratively at the base, the not-so healthy foods, the ones that are considered nutrient poor but hold a place in the food group, are at the top and should be consumed on occasion. Review that when people are active, they have more energy "out," which enables them to have more energy "in," empowering them with the flexibility to eat more food.

2. Tell the students that *moderation* suggests a reasonable consumption of foods that are high in calories, fats, sugars, and salt. Moderation in this context means consumers can eat what they crave (1) occasionally and (2) in limited amounts. Define *frequently*, *occasionally*, *limited*, and *excessive*. Explain that a healthy diet is one that has limits on nutrient-poor foods. Use pizza, snack cakes, nondiet sodas, potato chips, and a chocolate candy bar as examples of moderate and excessive consumptions:

- A cheese pizza is fine in moderation, a slice once a week or two. Eating six slices of pizza at a given time is excessive, as is three slices of pizza every day for lunch.
- A snack cake is fine in moderation: one prepackaged portion once every other day. Eating four servings at one setting is excessive, as is eating one between every meal.
- Nondiet sodas are fine in moderation: half a cup every other day. Drinking a 12-ounce can with each meal is excessive, as is a supersize fountain drink consumed at one setting.
- Potato chips are fine in moderation: consume the recommended serving size every other day. Eating half a family-size bag at one setting is excessive, as is eating large servings between each meal.
- A chocolate candy bar is fine in moderation: one standard size every two weeks or one or two mini versions a week. Eating a candy bar a day, or eating two at one setting, is excessive.

Other examples of excessive consumption can be the combination of foods. For instance, a breakfast composed of two eggs, two sausages, five strips of bacon, a 12-stack of pancakes, and 12 ounces of a nondiet drink is also excessive, as is a supersize meal with supersize drink and dessert. Have the students describe moderate and excessive amounts of macaroni and cheese, cookies, fruit drinks, trail mix, and pie. Ask them to contemplate the repercussions (i.e., the effects on their bodies, on their development and growth, on their physical ability, and on the future of their health) of eating what they crave (generally the nutrient-poor foods) frequently and in excessive amounts.

3. Tell the students that consumers have tendencies that counter moderation. (The tendencies were cultivated from the discussion on causes of cravings found in the Mellin and Johnson (2005) book, *Just for Kids!*). An awareness of these tendencies will help students make moderation a practice.

- Tendency 1: Bad habits. It is often difficult to start moderation because consumers are used to eating nutrient-poor foods. Some may be in the bad habit of drinking sodas with every meal; eating a pastry or two as an after-school snack; eating ice cream as a dessert for every lunch; eating while watching TV; or eating out every Tuesday, Friday, Saturday, and Sunday.
- Tendency 2: Emotions. Consumers often eat nutrient-poor foods because of their emotional state. Some may eat pastries or large servings of ice cream because they are excited and happy. Others may eat high-calorie, high-fat foods when they are sad because it makes them feel better. And others reach for nutrient-poor food because it minimizes their stress.
- Tendency 3: Deprivation. Consumers often feel that they have not eaten their favorite foods for an extended time, so they will eat excessive amounts at one setting when they encounter it. Many consumers will gorge on ice cream, chips, and candy because they believe they do not eat them regularly.
- Tendency 4: Hunger. Consumers will often eat excessive amounts of nutrient-poor foods because they are hungry. Because their meals are poorly planned, with intervals between them too long, they become hungry and will consume foods they crave and that are most convenient. Hungry consumers tend to eat large amounts of food.
- Tendency 5: Reminders. Consumers may eat nutrient-poor foods because they are bombarded with advertisements on TV, in magazines, and at stores, and they witness their friends and

family members delighting in tasty treats. For many, it becomes very difficult to ignore the constant reminder of foods waiting to be savored.

4. Emphasize that they can develop the practice of moderation. To counter these tendencies, the students can

- Plan for regular meals and snacks (planning is addressed in Idea 14);
- Stick to a list of all the healthy foods that can be eaten generously to avoid reaching for the nutrient-poor foods;
- Allow for foods they crave in reasonable portions (reference Idea 9);
- Consume foods they crave infrequently, which will vary according to the respective nutritional contributions; and
- Make a list of all the activities they can do when they are happy, sad, or stressed that do not involve eating nutrient-poor foods and beverages.

Activities

Guided. Divide the students into pairs. Distribute Reproducible 10.1 to each pair and have them evaluate when a serving is excessive or in moderation.

Independent. Distribute double-sided photocopies of Reproducible 10.2. Instruct the students to cut and fold accordingly. Two examples are printed on the tabs: pancakes and orange juice. The students determine when each is excessive and recommend moderate prescriptions, which can be found directly on Nutrition Facts labels, among the MyPyramid recommendations (www.MyPyramid.gov), or by way of an Internet search. For the remaining tabs, have the students find three food items at home and identify excessive and moderate amounts.

Conclusion

Have the students demonstrate their work from Reproducible 10.1. Thereafter, invite the students to compose a classroom definition of *moderation, excessive, occasionally,* and *limit.* When the students return with their completed Reproducible 10.2, review moderation and have them present their findings of foods from home.

Tips

- Bring in packages of popular foods and have the students report excessive amounts and determine amounts in moderation

- Have the students make a list of all the popular foods they should be careful to consume in moderation
- Make a collage of foods that should be especially consumed in moderation and create a catchy title that captures the sentiment of moderation

---

IDEA 11: AVERTING SAVORY TEMPTATIONS

Rationale

Understandably, hunger drives consumers to eat. However, a wide range of internal (e.g., emotional) and external (e.g., social and environmental) stimuli influence consumers to eat when they are not hungry. Considering that food is often offered as a sign of hospitality and love (think of all those chocolates that are exchanged during Valentine's Day!) and is universal at parties and celebrations, it is often difficult to resist delectable foods and treats. The habit of eating when one is not hungry would not be so troublesome if the foods were healthy, but too often they are nutrient poor, loaded with fat and sugar. Because food is readily available in this country and is central to social situations, before too long the habit of eating when not hungry is fixed. This is disturbing because such a habit amounts to added calories in the day, and if these are not balanced with physical activity, the consequence is weight gain. Children need the skills to avert temptation so that they do not spend a lifetime with a habit that increases their likelihood of becoming overweight or obese.

Objectives

After learning strategies to avert savory temptations, the students will

- Analyze and propose alternatives for a situation when they ate and were not hungry
- Create signs that remind them to resist eating when they are not hungry

Download and use Reproducible 11.1 for this Idea.

To Motivate the Students

Ask the students to contemplate the question, "When do I eat?" Record their responses (e.g., "When I get home." "When I go out." "For lunch." "At parties." "At the movies." "Because I want to." "Because someone gives it to me." "Because it looks and smells good.") on the board. Mention how you noticed that there are different circumstances that stimulate them to eat (circle the similar circumstances). Sometimes they eat because they are authentically hungry; sometimes they eat because they are served food; sometimes they eat because they are at a party; and sometimes they eat because the food looks good. Ask them to ponder the notion that it is not good practice to eat when one is not hungry. Invite the students to share their thoughts.

Frame the Instruction

Inform the students that they will be learning strategies designed to help them resist the temptation to eat when they are not hungry. Mention that will learn about reflective self-talk and how to handle moments when they are served food and they are not hungry.

Step by Step

1. Review the notion of tendencies (from Idea 10) that counter moderation: bad habits, emotions, deprivation, hunger, and reminders. Explain that as consumers we generally eat because we are hungry. There are times, however, when many of us are not hungry and eat nevertheless because food is offered to us, we are at a party or celebration and everyone is eating, food is available, or we want to eat. Underscore that it is generally not good practice to eat when one is not hungry (especially if the food is nutrient poor) because all foods that are consumed throughout the day are energy "in" and the calories can quickly accumulate if there is no balance with energy "out." Emphasize that they may develop the habit of expecting food wherever they are and eating it even though they are not even hungry.

2. Mention that using reflective self-talk can help counter the temptation to eat when they are not hungry and foods are within reach. Explain that reflective self-talk is internal conversation that one uses to help motivate and encourage oneself in specific situations. Teach the students these two questions to ask themselves during tempting situations (e.g., a bowl of small candies is put before them, a friend offers a snack cake, or everyone is enjoying a large piece of chocolate cake):

    "Am I hungry?" Explain that if the answer is no, they can walk away and return later when they are. If it is food that they are offered and the answer is no, teach them to say, "No, thank you. I'm not hungry now, but maybe later." Note that if the answer is yes, they should remember to eat reasonable portions, and think about physical activities that they can do later for more energy "out."

    "Do I really want to eat it?" Report that if the answer is "no," they can walk away and return later when they are. If it is food that they are offered and the answer is no, they can say, "No, thank you. I'm not hungry now, but maybe later." If their answer is yes, they should eat a reasonable portion, and plan for physical activities that can be done for more energy "out."

3. Acknowledge that there are other methods to avert temptation. If foods are in the pantry, cabinets, or refrigerator, suggest that they avoid those areas until a specific time or until they are authentically hungry. They can also collaborate with their parents to put the nutrient-inferior goodies in an inconvenient location where they can visit in moderation. They can also make a list of all the alternatives they can eat instead of the treats (e.g., two pieces of fruit instead of a snack cake), or simply wait for the time when they are hungry to return. If the students are going to a celebration and they anticipate that there will be plenty of food, planning ahead is a good idea, too. For instance, if they know that cake will be served, the students can plan to eat healthy food before eating a small piece. Or if they expect a bag of delectable treats as a parting gift, they can plan to eat one or two candies and save the rest for a later time.

Activities

Guided. Divide the students in pairs and distribute back-and-front copies of Reproducible 11.1. Have the students sit across from each other and instruct them to complete "Times I ate but was not hungry" one at a time. Then, have them turn over the reproducible and offer their partner advice under the statement, "I could have . . ."

Independent. Pass out blank sheets of paper and instruct the students to create signs to post in their personal spaces that remind them of the strategies that can help them avert temptation.

Conclusion

Review the strategies to avert temptation, and invite the students to share their signs with the class.

Tips

- Have the students role-play being offered food and averting the temptation to say yes. Situations may include being offered a slice of cake at a party; fresh sugar cookies the neighbor just baked; a dish their favorite relative made; popcorn, candy, nachos, and a tall drink that friends at the movies just offered to pay for; and a box of chocolates that a relative sent as a gift.
- Have the students make a list of healthy alternatives to savory treats
- Have the students research the calorie, fat, and nutritional contents of savory temptations such as cake, pie, candy, smoothie, cookies, chips, cheesecake, brownies, and donuts

IDEA 12: INFLUENCES OF ADVERTISING

Rationale

Many food manufacturers spend billions of dollars advertising their products to young consumers. Their efforts to attract children's attention and foster brand loyalty do not go unrewarded. One study found that 2- to 5-year-olds are aware of six leading brands: Cheerios, McDonald's, Pop-Tarts, Coke, Disney, and Barbie (McNeal, 2003, cited in California Pan-Ethnic Health Network, 2005). As expected, many of the products are processed and convenience foods and sodas, which are largely nutrient inferior. In 2008 alone, McDonald's spent $1.2 billion in advertising, Coca-Cola spent $752 million, while the manufacturers of M&M's (Mars, Inc.) and Oreos (Kraft) spent nearly $103 and $57 million, respectively (Advertising Age, 2009). In comparison, advertising costs associated with vegetables and fruit are a pittance. The bottom line is that children are bombarded with advertisements that promote the consumption of nutrient-poor foods, which is worrisome because their cognitive abilities are immature, rendering them vulnerable to exaggerated claims, hip graphics and fashionable spokespersons. This strategy seeks to increase children's awareness of the powerful influence ads and commercials can have helping them make decisions irrespective of their persuasions.

Objectives

After learning about the influences that ads can have, the students will

- Identify the attractive features of an ad and recommend changes informing consumers about its nutritional contents

Download and use Reproducible 12.1 for this Idea.

To Motivate the Students

Show the students general advertisements about inedible products. The initial ads can be aimed at adults so that they understand that ads are designed for the general public, but eventually transition to ads for products that they are familiar with, like toys, games, and sports equipment. Show them ads for places of entertainment, such as vacation destinations and theme parks. As you demonstrate the ads designed for children, ask (1) if they would buy the product and (2) what about the ad leads them to believe that the product is something they need or should have. Invite the students to share their favorite commercials and what they remember the most from them. If they can recall, ask a few students to sing a commercial jingle or utter an expression closely associated with a product.

Frame the Instruction

Tell the students that they will be learning about the intentions advertisers have and the means they use to influence consumers' decisions to buy their products.

Step by Step

1. Explain that advertisements are everywhere: on TV, on the Internet, on billboards, in magazines, and in newspapers. Ask the students to identify other areas where they have seen ads (school stadiums, grocery carts, cars, traveling billboards, and movies). Mention that advertisements—which include commercials—are designed to sell products and that in a year's time, children see about 40,000 TV commercials alone. Underscore that ads are powerful because they seek to influence consumers to believe they need the product, that it is better than similar products, that it tastes good, that life is easier with it, or that it will improve physical appearance. In short, advertisers lead consumers to believe that the product will improve life when it is purchased.

2. Report that food manufacturers spend millions of dollars trying to attract, persuade, and entertain consumers. They use many fashionable effects, including hip sounds, modern graphics, popular music, attractive actors, or cute characters and enlist celebrities, athletes, and professionals (e.g., "As a doctor, I recommend . . .") to make the product enticing. Their goal is to sell a lot of it to make a profit, so they aim to make their product as attractive as possible, which leads many consumers to buy the product. Stress that food manufacturers do not intentionally seek to make the public unhealthy; they simply want consumers to buy their products. Continual promotion of a product by way of catchy jingles and repeated phrases reminds consumers of its qualities, and in time they seek it out. This is known as "brand loyalty." Explain that advertisers have two objectives when they market products to children: They want children (1) to spend their allowance on the product or beg their parents to buy it and (2) be brand loyal well into their adult lives.

3. Tell the students that advertisements promote products that are processed, generally nutrient inferior (high in calories, fat, sugar, and sodium), but tasty nonetheless. Emphasize that because the product is in a commercial or ad does not imply that it is healthy or good for consumers despite all the attractive nuances hovering around it. In fact, advertisers of nutrient-poor processed foods leave out important details, like their product is high in calories, fat, and sugar. Show the students more ads and have them point out the aspects of the ads that

lead them to believe that they are trying to be influenced (e.g., the presence of slender people, cool colors, and attractive graphics).

Activities

Guided. Clip ads from magazines and give one each to small groups of students. Distribute Reproducible 12.1 and instruct the students to answer the questions accordingly.

Independent. Distribute another copy of Reproducible 12.1 to each student and instruct them to complete it with a different food.

Conclusion

Invite the students to share the findings from their food ads and demonstrate the changes they recommend so that the ad is more informational.

Tips

- Demonstrate various commercials from the Internet or TV and point out the features that advertisers use to influence consumers
- Have the students make ads for MyPyramid food groups
- Have the students write a letter to manufacturers asking how they use their profits to promote healthier lifestyles

IDEA 13: SUGAR AND SALT

Rationale

The nation as a whole consumes too much sugar and salt. Nearly 200 years ago, the average American ate about 2 pounds of sugar a year. Today, that figure is estimated at 152 pounds, which is about 6 cups of sugar a week and 42.5 teaspoons a day (New Hampshire Department of Health and Human Services, 2007). Considering that health experts recommend 13 teaspoons a day, it should come as no surprise that the waists of Americans are expanding at record speed. The news on salt consumption is no better. In fact, the *Dietary Guidelines* (U.S. Department of Health and Human Services, 2005b) devotes a whole chapter to salt (sodium), summarizing the problem neatly: "Nearly all Americans consume substantially more salt than they need" (p. 39). Particularly concerning is that salt intake is positively correlated with high blood pressure: The higher the salt intake, the higher the blood pressure (U.S. Department of Health and Human Services, 2005b). The National Heart, Lung and Blood Institute and others assert that reducing salt in restaurant and processed foods in half would save nearly 150,000 lives a year (Center for Science in the Public Interest, 2005b). Because these deceptively harmless white granules (and their forms) can be health destructive, it is important that youth learn to moderate their intake.

Objectives

After learning about the nutritional qualities of sugar and salt, the students will

- Assess the sugar content of a candy and recommend healthy, reasonable alternatives
- Identify the sodium contents of 10 food products

Download and use Reproducible 1.4, 13.1, and 13.2 for this Idea.

To Motivate the Students

Show the students pictures of various sugar holders and salt shakers. Ask the students to identify what they are, and ask them to report how many times in a day and in a week they (and their family members) use them to add sugar and salt to dishes. Explain that sugar and salt are naturally occurring in many foods, but all too often excessive amounts are added to many of the foods we eat. Emphasize that too much sugar and salt in a diet can lead to a range of health problems.

Frame the Instruction

Mention that the students will learn more about sugar and salt. Explain that you will first address sugar, proceed to salt, and discuss the importance of moderating their daily consumption.

Step by Step

1. Explain that sugar is found in natural foods like fruits, vegetables, milk, and grains; in many processed foods; and in unexpected products like soup, ketchup, and salad dressing. Show the students MyPyramid for Kids (Reproducible 1.4) and draw their attention to two slogans found near the base of the image. One slogan is "Find your balance between food and fun," and the other is "Fats and sugars—know your limits." Ask them to contemplate what the latter slogan means. Reinforce that "knowing your limits" suggests that consumers should be informed about the extent of sugar amounts they should consume per day.

2. Mention that a widely distributed MyPyramid brochure further encourages, "Don't sugarcoat it. Choose food and beverages that do not have sugar and caloric sweeteners as one of the first ingredients." Ask them to deliberate why it is not a good idea to consume a lot of sugary foods. Continue reading the MyPyramid statement "Added sugars contribute calories with few, if any, nutrients." Reinforce that it is not good practice to regularly consume foods that are high in sugar

because they (and forms of them) supply empty calories (i.e., calories that offer few nutrients), and too much consumption of sugary foods displaces the allowance for healthier nutrients, leads to weight gain, and can cause tooth decay. Sugary foods in moderation are fine.

3. Tell them that nutritionists believe that 13 teaspoons of sugar a day is a healthy allowance. They can determine how much sugar their foods have by checking the respective Nutrition Facts label for the sugar (and sodium) content. The contents are measured in grams, and there are about 5 grams of sugar in 1 teaspoon. Inform them that sugar has different forms, and hence can be listed under different names. Write these names on the board: high fructose corn syrup, sucrose, glucose, fructose, lactose, maltose, brown sugar, honey, and molasses. Emphasize that these ingredients are similar to sugar in that they make products tastier, but offer few nutrients. Using a variety of Nutrition Facts labels, point out some of the different forms of sugar listed in the ingredient lists. Subsequently, ask a student or two to find other names (for sugar) in the ingredient list.

4. Indicate that they also have to moderate their salt intake. Salt is composed of two components: sodium and chloride. It is the sodium that consumers have to closely monitor. Explain that our bodies need salt (sodium) to function, but too much causes the body to retain fluids, which makes the heart work harder. This process increases blood pressure, and a consistent high blood pressure damages the heart. Health experts agree that consumers need a 10th of a teaspoon a day, but most people get 5 to 18 times that amount. The *Dietary Guidelines* recommends a daily dose of no more than 2,300 milligrams. Underscore that they should aim for 480 milligrams or less of sodium per serving. Some foods are sold as "no salt added" and "low sodium," which suggests that the products have less than 140 milligrams of sodium per serving. Scientists have found that reducing salt intake to 1 teaspoon (2,300 milligrams) a day reduces the risk of high blood pressure. Incidentally, most of the salt that people consume is not from the table shaker, but from what is already found in foods. About 75% of salt is from foods that are processed or served at restaurants; only 6% is added in home cooking. Underscore that it is always a good idea to read the Nutrition Facts label and check on the amount of sodium found in foods.

Activities

Guided. Divide the students into pairs. Distribute double-sided copies of Reproducible 13.1 to each pair. Instruct the students to cut and fold them accordingly. On the left side—the "Instead of this . . ."—have the students write three favorite candies. Have them locate (by Internet) the Nutrition Facts labels of each to determine the amount of sugar the candies have. Then, have them find healthy and reasonable alternatives to the candies (such as vegetables and fruits) and write these in under the tab "Eat this!"

Independent. Distribute copies of Reproducible 13.2 to each student. Instruct them to follow the directions for finding the sodium content of 10 products.

Conclusion

Invite the students to share their healthy alternatives to sugary foods. Ask them which foods they were surprised to learn had the most sugar and which had the least. When the students return with the completed Reproducible 13.2, have them share their findings with the class.

Tips

- Provide the students with various Nutrition Facts labels and instruct them to find as many forms of sugar in the ingredient list as they can
- Demonstrate 11 grams of sugar so that the students can see how much sugar they are consuming whenever they drink a 12-ounce can of soda
- Provide the students with various Nutrition Facts labels and have them convert the milligrams of sugar to teaspoons

---

IDEA 14: MEAL PLANNING

Rationale

Meal planning is essential to helping youth consume a variety of foods and practice proportionality and moderation. The very nature of a plan is that of a guide that ensures that intentions are fulfilled. A plan helps keep to the target goal—and in the case of diet—to consume more nutritious foods and less of the nutrient poor. Without a plan for daily meals and snacks, youth are likely to choose and consume any number of foods that are regularly (and readily) available, succumb to impulse eating, and perceive no inherent threat in eating out frequently. Without a plan, it is a good bet that youth will stray from healthy eating and lose out on valuable nutrients their growing bodies need. This strategy reinforces that youth have control over what and how much they eat and that eating—despite the fundamental, simple, and causal impression it radiates—is cardinal to health and should be planned for. The students are expected to indirectly learn that planning for healthy meals and snacks is a smart habit to practice throughout their lives.

Objectives

After learning about meal planning, the students will

- Work in pairs to develop a 1-day meal plan
- Plan a 1-day meal that includes a variety of healthy foods

Download and use Reproducible 3.2, 14.1, and 14.2 for this Idea.

To Motivate the Students

Ask the students if they have ever been on a camping trip and, if so, to report what made the trip successful. Invite them to imagine that they are going on a 3-day camping trip that includes swimming, boating, fishing, and hiking. Ask them to think of all the items they will need to enjoy the trip and survive sweltering sunshine, chilly evenings, and mosquitoes. (Tell them not to worry about the food or beverages because they will be provided by park officials). Record their responses on the board, clustering similar items and encouraging students to think of all the personal effects and equipment they will need. Have them contemplate why planning for this trip is important, and ask the students to share their thoughts. Reinforce that planning for the trip will allow them to partake in the camping activities without having to waste time deciding if they have what they need or to miss out on activities because they left behind crucial supplies. Explain that planning empowers them because they can decide how to focus their time and energy, since they are prepared with what they need. Moreover, planning is worthwhile because it leads to the likelihood of a successful trip. Emphasize that similar to planning for a trip, planning for meals is valuable because it guides consumers to eat and drink healthier foods.

Frame the Instruction

Inform the students that they will be learning about the value of meal planning. Indicate that many of the aspects to be discussed have been addressed in previous lessons, but now they will apply their knowledge to plans for actual meals.

Step by Step

1. Provide students with a number of reasons why meal planning is important, such as

   - A plan helps consumers work toward the target goal of eating healthy (i.e., consumers are more likely to stray from a healthy diet when there is no plan);

- A plan increases the likelihood that consumers do not eat too much or too little;
- A plan increases the likelihood that their favorite treats are enjoyed in moderation;
- A plan saves time at the grocery store because they do not waste time figuring out what foods to buy;
- Planning increases consumers' awareness about healthy foods, making them likelier to include a variety of foods in their meals and snacks; and
- With no plan, when consumers are busy and rushed, they are likelier to eat foods that are nutrient inferior.

2. Ask the students to take out their MyPyramid Plan (Reproducible 3.2), which they completed throughout Ideas 3–6, and have them determine their calorie food pattern. (These will vary according to each student's size, height, weight, and physical activity level). Tell them that this amount of calories is the daily benchmark that they should aim for and that the excess calories they consume can be expended through physical activity. Remind them that too few calories will make them undernourished, and too many calories (not balanced with physical activity) can lead to weight gain. Reinforce that they can take charge of what they eat, how much or little they eat, and how often they eat. Have them contemplate the amounts of foods they should consume from each food group. Call on some students to share their daily recommendations.

3. Tell the students that meal planning is not about what they plan to eat for a day or 2; instead, it is about what and how they eat over extended periods and, ultimately, throughout their lives. They can start with short plans (i.e., a day or 2) and progress to weeklong menus. Remind them of the MyPyramid principles: variety, proportionality, and moderation. Mention that when planning for meals and snacks, they should include a variety of foods from each group. Revisit the idea of proportionality: Encourage them to look for and eat more whole grains; dark and leafy greens; colorful vegetables and fruits; foods that provide calcium; and lean selections of red meat, poultry, and fish. Emphasize that they should try all kinds of foods. After all, some of the healthier foods may not look appetizing, but they are rich in vitamins and minerals and taste good. Last, remind the students to consider moderation. They should learn to practice eating desserts, sugary treats, and foods that are laden with calories and fat in moderation or in small portions.

4. Have them contemplate what they could eat for breakfast, lunch, and dinner. Explain that breakfast is important because it provides

consumers with the energy to be productive at school. Breakfast also helps control their appetites so that they are not starved by lunchtime, and hence devour a heap of food then. While there is a wide range of foods that students can eat for breakfast, encourage them to ask their parents to serve them a complementary combination of whole-grain cereals and breads, low-fat yogurt, skim milk, pieces of fruit, and small glasses of 100% fruit juice. There are myriad options for lunch and dinner, but underscore that foods that are baked, steamed, grilled, broiled, or roasted are healthy alternatives to fried foods, which tend to have a lot of fat. (The students may need these cooking concepts explained). All the while, emphasize the importance of reasonable portion sizes and eating the food amounts outlined on their respective MyPyramid Plan (Reproducible 3.2).

5. Review the topic of healthy snacks. Affirm that snacking is important because it regulates appetite. Explain that snacks are not meals intended to fill them up but instead function to resolve their appetite and supply them with energy until the next meal. Ergo, snacks should be small (around 100 calories). Have the students review some healthy snacks from Idea 8 (pretzels; baked chips [potato or tortilla]; microwave popcorn; bread sticks; fig bars; ginger snaps; graham crackers; animal crackers; raw, frozen, canned, or dried fruit and vegetables; applesauce; rice cakes; whole-grain crackers; half a bagel; frozen yogurt [low fat or fat free]; yogurt [low fat or fat free]; fruit sorbet; 100% fruit juice popsicle; tomato juice) that can fulfill the recommended amounts from the food groups. Reinforce that processed sugary and salty snacks should be limited, as they are nutrient inferior to healthier, whole foods. Explain that processed snacks are popular because they are conveniently packaged, which makes for easy storage. In the best interest of their health, suggest that the students ask their parents to buy small baggies and divide fruits and vegetables (such carrots and celery sticks) into reasonable portions that can be enjoyed later.

6. Mention that many families frequently eat out as a change from home cooking or in celebration of a special occasion. Underscore that in recent times, the number of Americans eating out has drastically increased because restaurants are convenient and offer affordable menu items. Caution them that while eating out seems harmless to health, the foods served at restaurants are generally large and high in calories and saturated fat and low in nutrients. Indeed, supersized meals offer more than value; they offer a whopping amount of calories, fat, and sodium. Explain that eating out is fine in moderation, and have them consider these suggestions that can counter not-so-healthy restaurant menu items: Look for healthier foods or ask the

wait staff to recommend healthier options; choose a small salad (with dressing on the side) over fried side dishes; eat small portions and take the remainder home; share an entrée; select water over a large soft drink (with free refills); skip dessert (or share); eat slowly; skip the breads or chips that are often served before meals; pass on fried foods, and instead select baked, steamed, grilled, broiled, or roasted dishes; and choose a vegetable plate.

7. Distribute copies of Reproducible 14.1, Healthy Diet Tips (which are taken from www.SmallStep.gov), and read the tips with the students. Explain that they can apply some of these to their daily meals and snacks, and track how effective they are in their diet.

Activities

Guided. Divide the students into pairs, grouping those who have similar calorie food patterns on their respective MyPyramid Plan (Reproducible 3.2). Distribute copies of Reproducible 14.2 to each pair and instruct them to plan a 1-day meal with their partner. To assist with their meal planning, allow the students to use the list of foods found on the back of Reproducible 14.2, MyPyramid.gov, and assorted resources (e.g., the Internet, books).

Independent. Distribute another copy of Reproducible 14.2 to each student and instruct them to use their MyPyramid Plan (Reproducible 3.2) to plan an actual meal for a day. Encourage them to plan the meals for 2, 3, or 4 days. Emphasize that they should include foods they like and those they are willing try. To assist with their meal planning, the students can use the list of foods found on the back of the reproducible, MyPyramid.gov, and assorted resources (e.g., the Internet, books).

Conclusion

Ask the students to share their meal plans with the class and identify the foods they intend to try. When the students return to school in later days, have them report how closely they (and their families) fulfilled the meal plan and have them explain what they found most interesting about adhering to the plan.

Tips

- Have the students make a collage of magazine pictures (or their own drawings) for a healthy meal on a given day. Sequence some of the collages together and have the students analyze whether the meals are healthy if actually consumed.
- Divide the students into pairs and instruct them to interview one another, asking what they consumed the day before. Have

the students provide suggestions (perhaps using some of the tips found on Reproducible 14.1) of how the meals could have been healthier.

IDEA 15: MAKING AND TRACKING GOALS

Rationale

Constructive goals are essential because they help youth aspire to and work toward an improved life. In terms of health, goals are instrumental in helping them adjust their eating and physical activity habits, which can contribute positively toward their development. Many health experts agree that people are likelier to make lifestyle changes when they have goals. In this Idea, students learn that writing down their health goals make them official (Corbin et al., 2008) and motivates them to engender behavioral change (Hoeger & Hoeger, 2007). The students also learn that with formal health goals they are likelier to plan for healthy eating and to monitor their behavior and progress. What better way to track behavior than to keep a journal? The students learn that keeping a journal is a reasonable way to help them manage their eating (and later physical activity) behaviors. Students who are consistent in their journal writing will have self-reported data to analyze and hence revise their goals accordingly. In short, working toward and accomplishing goals lead to healthy habits.

Objectives

After learning about the benefits of making and tracking goals, the students will

- Contemplate, identify, and share three healthy eating goals they would like fulfill
- Analyze their weeklong journal entries and revise their healthy eating goals if necessary

Download and use Reproducible 1.4 and 15.1 for this Idea.

To Motivate the Students

Indicate some of the goals you have for the students (e.g., for the week, the semester, and the year) and that you have a target that you are working toward on their behalf. Explain that their parents have direct (e.g., saving for their college education, helping them with homework so that they get good grades) and indirect (e.g., keeping them well fed and clothed, helping them be prepared for school) goals for them as well. Invite the students to share some of the goals they have for themselves. Based on this discussion, have them define goals. As you write their definition on the board, ask the students to contemplate why goal-setting is important in life.

Frame the Instruction

Affirm that most people have short- and long-term goals. Show the students the MyPyramid for Kids (Reproducible 1.4) and ask the students to identify some goals they perceive the children (on the illustration) have. Explain that in this lesson the students are going to learn how keeping a "healthy eating" journal can help them achieve their goals.

Step by Step

1. Explain that reasonable, constructive goals are important in life because they provide youth a terminal point to aspire to and work toward, which often leads to an improved life or lifestyle. In terms of health, goals are instrumental in helping youth adjust their eating (and physical activity) habits that can contribute positively toward their development. Health goals are essential because when achieved they evolve into healthy habits. Discuss the difference between goals that are materialistic (e.g., "I'll save my allowance for that new toy"), constructive (e.g., "I'll eat more vegetables"), and destructive (e.g. "I'll steal his lunch money from him"). Stress that constructive goals enhance wellness, not depress it.

2. Tell the students that writing down health goals formalizes the goals. Written health goals are concrete and official, which reduces the risk of forgetting about them. Moreover, the students can measure their goals when they are written. Explain that there are five key points in constructing written goals; the acronym SMART can guide them in writing their health goals (Corbin et al., 2008).

3. Write SMART vertically on the board, and beside each letter, write what it represents. The *S* stands for *specific*. Relay that the students should make specific health goals, rather than vague or general ones (e.g., "I will eat better" or "I will drink more water"). The students should aim for details, such as "I will eat an apple a day" or "I will drink a glass of water with every meal." *M* stands for *measureable*. The goals should be written so that the students can effortlessly assess whether they have reached their goal (e.g., "Yes, I ate an apple a day" or "No, I was offered soda with most meals and could not resist"). *A* is for *attainability*. The goal should be reasonable. "I will never eat cookies again," or "I will only drink soda on special occasions," are ambitious goals that are likely insurmountable. Instead, "I will eat cookies in 150 calorie portions," and "I will reduce my soda drinking to 3 days a week" are more attainable. Remind the students that they can revise their goals after they have had some time to assess their

progress. *R* stands for *realistic*. As with attainable, the goal should never be too easy and trivial (e.g., "I'll drink a glass of water every other day") or too difficult to fulfill (e.g., "I will only eat sugary snacks on my birthday"). Last, *T* stands for *timely*. The goals should convey the relevance of working toward a goal that is meaningful in the present. Ask students to assess their current situations to form relevant goals. Individual students know their lifestyles best and the goals they have should be based on this assessment.

4. Discuss that keeping a "healthy eating" journal or diary can help them track their behaviors and monitor their progress toward fulfilling their goals. Inform the students they will be making a weeklong journal so that they can document what they eat and drink. Tell them that if they write in the journal daily, they will have self-reported data they can use to analyze and adjust their goals accordingly. From their entry data, they can recognize trends, for instance, of when they eat too much and when they lose opportunities to eat healthier foods. They can also appraise the contexts that influence them to eat (e.g., at parties, at friends' houses, and on errands) and isolate the times (e.g., while watching TV, while playing video games, or when bored) that they are most vulnerable to eating too much or eating too few nutrient-rich foods. Emphasize that they can use their data to tailor their goals or create new ones that lend themselves to healthier eating habits. Or more important, they can tune in to their behaviors and adjust them accordingly.

5. Affirm that a "healthy eating" journal can also be used for planning their meals. An analysis of their journal entries will reveal the foods that are eaten too often and those that are eaten infrequently. The students can use this information to plan (and shop) for future meals that incorporate food and beverages in the spirit of variety, proportionality, and moderation. In that the journal acts, to some extent, as a planning guide, emphasize that goals are likelier fulfilled when they have a plan. Refer to the discussion on Idea 14.

6. Mention that a fulfilled goal in this context is a positive change or the genesis of healthy behavior and deserves a mild celebration. Ask the student to brainstorm the number of ways they can celebrate their triumph, a celebration that does not include food. Such celebrations reinforce that working toward and accomplishing a goal lead to healthy habits.

Activities

Guided. Divide the students into pairs. Instruct each student to contemplate, identify, and share with his or her partner three healthy eating goals he or she would like to fulfill. Ask each partner to check the other partner's goals and provide feedback on how SMART his or her goals are. Have the students modify their goals and check them accordingly.

Independent. Distribute copies of Reproducible 15.1, "My Healthy Eating Journal" and instruct the students to assemble it. On the front page, ask that they make note of the week and write their three goals, which they modified in the guided activity. Instruct the children to write what they eat for a whole week, making note of the food and beverages they consume for each meal, each day, including snacks. At the end of the week, ask the students if they met their goals and to revise those that were unreasonable. Continue to distribute copies of Reproducible 15.1 for subsequent weeks and have the students contemplate what works in terms of meeting the goals, what does not, and what are some behaviors they can make to engender a positive change.

Conclusion

Ask the students for nominations for one healthy eating goal for the class and write these on the board. Have the class vote on one, evaluate how SMART it is, and brainstorm how to track their progress in fulfilling the goal. When the students return after a week of tracking their progress, have them share their results. Ask for those who were successful and for those who need to revise their goals, and invite some to share what they learned about the process and their eating behaviors.

Tips

- More advanced students can visit www.mypyramidtracker.gov/, which is an electronic journal-like interactive tool that allows users to enter the foods they eat each day and track their progress for up to a year. The site has the capacity to analyze the data and reveal how their consumption compares with the *Dietary Guidelines*.
- Have the students make a list of what helps them meet their goals.

Part III

PROMOTING REGULAR PHYSICAL ACTIVITY

CHAPTER 5

Snapshot on Physical Activity

It is nearly impossible to discuss issues of health, well-being, and body weight without mention of physical activity. In fact, a person climbing the stairs of MyPyramid (and a child running up the steps of MyPyramid for Kids) is depicted on the left side of the model to emphasize the importance of regular physical activity. Some even speculate that the steps symbolize the pace consumers can take—no matter the momentum—to fit physical activity in their daily lives (U.S. Department of Health and Human Services, n.d.). Nonetheless, physical activity is central to the energy balance equation as it keeps body weight balanced: The consumption of too much food and beverages (i.e., energy "in" the body) and not enough physical activity (i.e., energy "out" of the body) leads to excess weight, yet the right balance of calorie intake with physical activity makes for healthy body weight. Without doubt, youth and adults alike should aim for the right balance for overall health.

Now that healthy dietary practices have been addressed and can be promoted by way of the Ideas, let's carefully judge the role and benefits of physical activity in everyday life. After this background matter has been addressed, the discussion can then turn to the Ideas that are specific to physical activity. This chapter explores physical activity in six sections:

- Mounting Support for Physical Activity
- The Trouble with a Physically Inactive Nation
- Benefits of Regular Physical Activity
- Contrast Between Physical Activity, Exercise, and Physical Fitness
- Fulfilling the Physical Activity Recommendations
- Physical Activity and Exercise at School

MOUNTING SUPPORT FOR PHYSICAL ACTIVITY

The message that physical activity contributes to good health, improves physical functioning, and increases longevity is nothing new (Bauer, 2005). As far back as 400 BC Hippocrates wrote, "Eating alone will not keep man well; he must also exercise" (cited in Bauer, 2005, p. 169). And in his work, Plato affirmed, "Lack of activity destroys the good condition of every human being while movement and methodical physical exercise save and preserve it" (cited in Williams, 2007, p. 5). While this counsel is still relevant today, bear in mind that for centuries civilizations have been engaged in seemingly perpetual physical activity. Our bodies were unmistakably created for movement, considering that in the not-too-distant past, humans were using the physical body for survival: to seek out or build shelter, to hunt for food, for labor, and as a means of transportation. The body *had* to keep moving in order for it to survive.

As society has become more industrialized, however, our bodies have become more sedentary. Ideally, we should burn the energy we consume, but modern conveniences make that difficult and unlikely. We have jobs that require little physical activity, we drive when we can, and we take escalators and elevators rather than use the stairs. And today's children and youth are more physically inactive and unfit than their parents and grandparents were at their age. According to the Youth Risk Behavior Surveillance 2007 report, only three quarters of youth nationwide participated in any kind of physical activity in the span of a week for an hour or more that caused their heart rate to increase or made them breathe hard (Centers for Disease Control, 2008c).

Interestingly enough, it is by no coincidence that childhood obesity levels have increased in the past few decades, as have the number and range of entertaining technological and media devices (Sears et al., 2003). Television with a wide-range of premium cable channels, computers and the Internet, and popular video games can entice any youth away from physical activity.

Growing evidence suggests that as children become older, they become less active. A report to President Bill Clinton from the secretary of health and human services and the secretary of education asserted, "Available data indicate that young children are among the most active of all segments of the population, but physical activity levels begin to decline as children approach their teenage years and continue to decline throughout adolescence" (U.S. Department of Health and Human Services, 2000b, p. 10). Consider this: Seventy percent of 12-year-olds report that they regularly engage in physical activity, but of 21-year-old adults, only 42% of men and 30% of women report that they are vigorously active (Smith, 1999). The Youth Risk Behavior Surveillance 2007 report indicates that in terms of meeting the recommended levels of physical activity, high school freshmen (38.1%) did so more than sophomores (34.8%), juniors (34.8%), and seniors (29.5%) (Centers for Disease Control, 2008c). Furthermore, the report mentions that the prevalence of not participating in an hour or more of physical activity on any given day was higher among sophomores (24%), juniors (26.2%), and seniors (28.9%) than freshmen (21.5), and the prevalence of attending PE classes was higher among freshmen (66.8%) than sophomores (56.8%), juniors (45.1%), and seniors (41.5%). (As a side note, the report does not describe the degree of participation in physical activity while in PE. Reasonably, a student could be in PE class for a whole hour and never engage in any form of physical activity). Tartamella and colleagues (2004) observe:

> From preschool on, kids became gradually less active, partly because the brain's pleasure centers that reward kids for exercise gradually start disappearing. Seven-year-olds run around less than five-year olds, and by the time kids become teenagers, their brains are seeking out other types of satisfaction. (p. 119)

Girls are especially vulnerable to a sedentary lifestyle as they mature. One University of Pittsburgh study tracked nearly 2000 9- and 10-year-old girls for 10 years. The researchers found that the girls' activity levels fell dramatically by the time they were in their teens. When the girls were 14 to 15 years old they all reported at least some regular physical activity. But by ages 16 and 17, 55% of African American girls and 30% of White girls reported zero physical activity (Tartamella et al., 2004). According to the Youth Risk Behavior Surveillance 2007, only 20% of high school senior girls meet the recommended levels of physical activity, compared with 38.7% of senior boys.

These kinds of statistics suggest a grim notion: If children are less physically active as they age and there are more children becoming sedentary at younger ages, society could very well witness an even larger generation that is grossly inactive. This alone justifies crusades to motivate children to become physically active, which was not always the case. In the mid-1970s, Terris (1975) warned in the *American Journal of Public Health*, "Physical fitness and physical education have no respected place in the American public health movement" (p. 1040). His observation expressed a credible concern because up until this time no national campaign existed to increase physical activity among children and adults alike (Berg, 2004). But by 1980 the federal government had taken notice, and the U.S. Department of Health and Human Services added physical activity to *Healthy People*. The initiative sought to increase the percentage of adults exercising vigorously to 60% (from 11%), but the public fell considerably short of the goal and the percentage was later adjusted to 15% (Berg, 2004).

The absolute national wake-up call on physical activity came in a 259-page report issued in 1996 by the surgeon general, titled, *Physical Activity and Health*. Many hailed it a beacon because it was the first comprehensive investigation on the benefits of physical activity. The report underscored that a lack of regular physical activity contributed to poor health, and conversely, routine exercise contributed to well-being and prevented premature death, illness, and disability. The report clearly revealed the benefits for children and adolescence:

- Helps build and maintain healthy bones, muscles, and joints;
- Helps control weight, build lean muscle, and reduce fat;
- Prevents or delays the development of high blood pressure and helps reduce blood pressure in some adolescence with hypertension;
- Reduces feelings of depression and anxiety. (U.S. Department of Health and Human Services, 2000b, p. 7)

The report stated that sedentary behaviors were more prevalent among particular populations, specifically women, African Americans, Hispanic Americans, older adults, the less affluent, and the less well educated (Hoeger & Hoeger, 2007). In a call to action, Americans were encouraged to engage in moderate physical activity for at least 30 minutes a day on most days of the week. At the time, only 25% of Americans were getting that much exercise in their leisure time and another 25% were not active at all.

In 2000, to strengthen the government's support for better health, physical activity, and fitness among children and youth, President Clinton asked that the Department of Health and Human Services and the Department of Education collaborate with health experts and report on strategies to increase physical activity among the general population. In his directive, President Clinton wrote, "By identifying effective new steps and strengthening public-private partnerships, we will advance our efforts to prepare the nation's young people for lifelong physical fitness" (cited in U.S. Department of Health and Human Services, 2000b, p. 6). The secretaries from the respective departments produced the 2000 report *Promoting Better Health for Young People Through Physical Activity and Sports*. Since then, the federal government has taken an active role in promoting regular physical activity, which is most evident in the two previously mentioned national guidelines:

1. *Dietary Guidelines for Americans*. As a means to actualize good health, the *Dietary Guidelines* encourages everyone to aim for fitness. The key recommendations specifically mention the following:

   - Engage in regular physical activity and reduce sedentary activities to promote health, psychological well-being, and a healthy body weight.
   - Achieve physical fitness by including cardiovascular conditioning, stretching exercises for flexibility, and resistance exercises or calisthenics for muscle strength and endurance.

- (for children and adolescents) Engage in at least 60 minutes of physical activity on most, preferably all, days of the week. (U.S. Department of Health and Human Services, 2005c, p. 20)

2. *Healthy People 2010*. Physical activity is one of the leading health indicators (goals) for the country. Like the *Dietary Guidelines*, this report asserts that how routine physical activity enhances well-being and that it prevents premature death. It advises that children and youth need exercise for skeletal development and optimal bone mass. The indicators specify the following:

- Increase the proportion of adolescents who engage in vigorous physical activity that promotes cardiorespiratory fitness 3 or more days per week for 20 more minutes per occasion.
- Increase the proportion of adults who engage regularly, preferably daily, in moderate physical activity for at least 30 minutes per day. (U.S. Department of Health & Human Services, 2000a, p. 26)

THE TROUBLE WITH A PHYSICALLY INACTIVE NATION

Despite these grand-scale initiatives, the nation is still largely sedentary and unfit. In the *New York Times* best seller *You: The Owner's Manual*, Roizen and Oz (2005) note that in the span of 30 years (1966 to 1996) the number of Americans who engaged in regular physical activity decreased by 1% every year. Why? Berg (2004) suggests that our society is overwhelmed with messages about food—not to mention that modern conveniences and entertaining media engender a sedentary lifestyle—and underwhelmed with messages about being physical active. Nearly half of American adults do not exercise enough to reap the health benefits, about a quarter are not active in their leisure time, and 16% are completely inactive (Centers for Disease Control, 2008b; Hoeger & Hoeger, 2007). This suggests that about 80% of the adult population is not active enough or not active at all. Among those in the 12- to 21-year-old category, about half report that they are regularly vigorously physically active, a quarter mention that they engage in light to moderate physical activity (e.g., walking and cycling) nearly every day, and 14% state that they are not physically active (U.S. Department of Health and Human Services, 2003b). Based on these sorts of numbers, Beckman (2001) estimates that the population of physically inactive Americans exceeds the combined total of those who smoke, have high blood pressure, and have high cholesterol levels. Physical inactivity comes in close second to tobacco usage as the greatest threat to public health.

This fact is alarming because just as a consistently poor diet unleashes a range of health problems, so too can a sedentary lifestyle. To publicly spread the notion that there is a direct relationship with physical inactivity and chronic, preventable diseases, Frank Booth (2001), a professor of physiology at the University of Missouri–Columbia, and a team of leading physiologists coined the term sedentary death syndrome, or SeDS. They outlined 35 medical conditions that are exacerbated by physical inactivity, namely, "arthritis pain, arrhythmias, breast cancer, colon cancer, congestive heart failure, depression, gallstone disease, heart attack, hypertension, obesity, osteoporosis, peripheral vascular disease, respiratory problems, Type 2 diabetes, sleep apnea and stroke." Because many of these conditions do not manifest until adulthood, it is important to underscore that a physically inactive lifestyle harms children too. A lack of regular physical activity puts children at risk for diabetes, sleep disorders, asthma, and cardiovascular problems (Berkey, Rockett, Gillman, & Colditz, 2003), not to mention the stigma associated with being overweight, which can lead to psychological distress over low self-esteem, a negative body image, and other issues.

Physical inactivity is considered a major risk factor for cardiovascular diseases. Since 1992 the American Heart Association has considered inactivity as critical a risk factor for cardiovascular disease as high blood cholesterol, high blood pressure, and cigarette smoking (Bounds et al., 2006). Studies have shown that compared with their physically active counterparts, sedentary persons have about 2 times the risk of having a fatal heart attack when other factors (e.g., smoking and cholesterol) are equal (Rizza et al., 2002). Two published literature reviews on physical inactivity and its effect on heart disease have found that a sedentary lifestyle increases the risk for coronary heart disease by 1.5 to 2.4 times, and physically inactive persons have a 90% greater risk of developing coronary heart disease (Anspaugh et al., 2006). Some health experts worry that individuals' increasingly sedentary lifestyles threaten the medical strides this nation has made in the past century on average life expectancy.

Of the sedentary population, children and youth are seemingly the most vulnerable because they are likely to experience health problems at earlier ages and live with them throughout their lives. Tartamella and colleagues (2004) elaborate:

> Inactivity is especially hard on young bodies. Children who don't exercise may develop complications such as high blood pressure, high cholesterol, or insulin resistance (a precursor to diabetes) before they're old enough to get a driver's license. . . . Whether a child is fat or thin, sitting on her bottom all day is un-

questionably hazardous to her health; in fact, some experts believe that inactivity is even more dangerous than obesity. (p. 116)

BENEFITS OF REGULAR PHYSICAL ACTIVITY

In light of the egregious news on this nation's sedentary ways, the benefits of regular physical activity should be promoted often. The advantages of doing so are twofold: adults will become motivated to adjust the way they live, and youngsters will develop the lifelong habit of exercising. Regular physical activity has many substantial benefits, especially when balanced with a healthy diet. Regular exercise

- Helps reduce the risk of developing heart diseases. Daily physical activity causes the blood in the body to circulate smoothly. Exercise increases the amount of blood cells that generate higher oxygen levels, which carry more oxygen and other nutrients to organs and tissues; widen and condition blood vessels, which boosts circulation and lowers blood pressure; makes the heart pump more efficiently (i.e., stronger and less often); benefits cholesterol levels, namely increases the good cholesterol (HDL) and decreases the bad (LDL), which reduces the chances of plaque buildup in the arteries. Research has found that physically active persons can reduce the risk of coronary heart and cardiovascular diseases by as much as 50% (American College of Sports Medicine, 2006). In short, a daily dose of exercise helps the heart work more efficiently and protects the body from diseases that can lead to stroke, heart attack, aneurisms, and glaucoma. Coronary artery disease claims the lives of 2,000 Americans every day (Reisser, 2006).
- Helps reduce the chances of developing colon and breast cancer. Studies have found that a physically active lifestyle decreases the chances of developing colon cancer, the third most common cancer among men and women, killing nearly 55,000 Americans every year (Reisser, 2006). Health experts have found that engaging in vigorous physical activity in adolescence can help reduce the risk of breast cancer in adulthood.
- Helps reduce the risk of type 2 diabetes. A physically active body keeps the risk of adult-onset (i.e., type 2) diabetes to a minimum and helps reduce the need for diabetic medication. The Diabetes Prevention Program found that adults could reduce their chances of developing diabetes by as much as 58% (over a 3-year period)

by being moderately physically active and losing 5% to 7% of their body weight (Reisser, 2006). One University of Southern California study of Latino boys revealed that those who exercised experienced improved insulin sensitivity, despite no additional weight loss, while 60% of their sedentary counterparts had worse insulin sensitivity at the end of the study (Shaibi et al., 2006). These are critical findings, considering that poor insulin sensitivity leads to the development of type 2 diabetes (National Institutes of Health, 2007b).

- Helps maintain physical ability. Exercise is good for the body because it builds muscle and bones and makes for healthier joints, which leads to greater body strength. A toned body is one with increased flexibility, fitness, posture, balance, and coordination, not to mention a potent cardiorespiratory system that makes breathing easier.

- Helps maintain healthy body weight. Physical activity increases metabolism and burns calories (and body fat) making it easier to manage weight. A daily workout combined with daily activity helps keep the unhealthy weight off reducing needless strain on the body.

- Helps manage stress and improves self esteem. Daily exercise not only benefits the physical body, it works wonders on a person's emotional well-being. Regular physical activity is known to stimulate areas of the brain that boost feelings of happiness, as well as contribute to one's feeling better by reducing stress, anxiety, depression, and fatigue. (Exercise is also associated with better, restful sleep). In the "Good Health News" section of the August 2008 issue of *Good Housekeeping*, readers were given a glimpse of a 20,000-person study on the emotional benefits of physical activity. The news piece, humorously titled "Sweep Those Blues Away," delivered this timely message:

> [A] British health survey reveals that any kind of activity can lift your spirits. Researchers also noted how little activity it took to make a difference—just one to three 20-minute sessions a week reduced the chances of suffering from distress such as depression. The biggest impact came from doing *anything*—apparently even mopping—for at least 20 minutes every day. "Daily activity knocked down the distress score by more than half," says Mark Hamer, Ph.D., of University College London. (p. 38)

Health experts also find that exercise leaves people with feelings associated with accomplishment, productivity, and enthusiasm about further exercising. People with a fit body are more likely to feel better about their appearance, which can lead to stronger self-confidence.

- Helps youth perform better in school. In addition to the benefits of exercise on emotional health (e.g., lower stress levels, increased endurance), research finds mounting evidence that physically active children have increased concentration, reduced disruptive behaviors, and improved grades (Michigan Department of Education, 2001). Controlled studies found that exposing children to physical education improved (or left unchanged) their academic test scores (Shephard, Volle, Lavallee, LaBarre, Jequier, & Rajic, 1984; Dwyer, Coonan, Leitch, Hetzel, & Baghurst, 1983). One study found that youth with high fitness scores by way of a physical education scale known as FITNESSGRAM had the highest SAT-9 test scores (Shephard, 1997). Teachers and parents alike will be delighted to know that a positive causal relationship exists between movement and attention, spatial perception, and memory (Symons, Cinelli, James, & Groff, 1997; Gardner, 1993; Greenfield, 1995, cited in Michigan Department of Education, 2001).
- Engenders skills associated with collaboration and cooperation. Youth who are physically active by way of sports can learn lifelong skills associated with teamwork and sportsmanship. There are many opportunities in sports for youth and adults alike to refine their patience and social and leadership skills (U.S. Department of Health and Human Services, 2006b).

Because of these health benefits, regular physical activity is seemingly the very tool for living longer. Indeed, many studies have found that people who are physically active have lower rates of premature mortality than those who are sedentary or unfit. (A complete list of the research can be found in the *American College of Sports Medicine's Guidelines for Exercise Testing and Prescription,* 2006). In their 6-year study of 302 adults between the ages of 70 and 82, Manini and colleagues (2006), for instance, found that exercise helped the elderly extend their lives. Their study revealed that those who expended more energy had a longer mortality. The National Institutes of Health (2007b) explains:

> For 2 weeks, researchers used advanced methods to measure the subjects' free-living energy expenditures, or how many calories they burned doing their daily activities. Participants were followed up an average of 6 years later, when researchers collected mortality data. Results showed that death rates decreased as daily energy expenditure went up. Those who were in the highest third energy expenditure had a 69% lower risk of death than those who were in the lowest third. It was estimated that for every 287 calories burned per day, the risk of mortality is reduced by 30%. (p. 3)

That regular physical activity has considerable benefits should come of no surprise. The consensus in the medical community is that regular exercise is the best medicine, because it is associated with fewer hospitalizations, physician visits, and medications (Williams, 2007). But what exactly is regular physical activity and how much do we really need?

CONTRAST BETWEEN PHYSICAL ACTIVITY, EXERCISE, AND PHYSICAL FITNESS

Different terms are associated with physical activity, namely *exercise* and *fitness*. While *physical activity* and *exercise* have been used interchangeably thus far, there is a difference between the two. *Physical activity* is a broad term that defines any bodily movement that expends energy (i.e., burns calories). It can include physical tasks associated with domestic chores like vacuuming, washing the car (by hand), cleaning the gutters, or raking the leaves. It also encompasses activities performed throughout the day like walking to and from the car or climbing the stairs at work. Physical activity consists of unstructured, leisure activities like walking, hiking, dancing, and gardening. Think of moderate physical activity as an activity that expends about 150 calories a day (Hoeger & Hoeger, 2007). Exercise, on the other hand, is planned and structured physical activity that compels the body in repetitive movement. With exercise, a person seeks to become fit or maintain fitness. Some examples of exercise are performing a series of stomach curls, using a Stairmaster for 30 minutes, and cycling for an hour.

Physical fitness suggests the ability—by way of an array of attributes or skills—to effectively perform physical activity. The many dimensions of fitness can be categorized into two components: skill-related fitness and health-related fitness. Skill-related—sometimes called sports-related—fitness is about agility, balance, coordination, speed, power, and reaction time, elements generally associated with competitive athletes (American College of Sports Medicine, 2006). Health-related fitness deals with muscular and cardiovascular endurance, strength, flexibility, and body composition—the physiological aspects that affect how efficiently and effectively the body functions (Bounds et al., 2006).

To balance energy "in" (calorie consumption) with energy "out" (energy expenditure by way of physical activity), the American Heart Association (2001) suggests this formula:

- To maintain your body weight: multiply the number of pounds you weigh now by 15. This represents the average number of calories used in one day if you're moderately active.

- To maintain your body weight if you get very little exercise: multiply your weight by 13 instead of 15. Less active people burn fewer calories. (p. 90)

However, a convenient way to remember how much regular physical activity is required to maintain a healthy lifestyle is to remember 30-60-90, which represents increments of time in minutes. In the 1996 surgeon general report *Physical Activity and Health*, the federal government recommended that adults be physically active (of moderate to vigorous intensity) for at least 30 minutes on most, though preferably all, days of the week. This 30-minute recommendation is well publicized in nearly all federal health publications, including *Dietary Guidelines*, *Healthy People 2010*, and MyPyramid.

Adults who want greater health benefits are encouraged to engage in at least 60 minutes of physical activity on most days of the week. This will also help them manage their weight or prevent weight gain so long as they do not exceed their caloric requirements. Incidentally, this can be fulfilled at one period of time or in intervals throughout the day. The 60-minute recommendation applies to children and adolescents as well. They too are encouraged to engage in moderate physical activity each day. Medical researchers have noted that a 90-pound child can prevent gaining a pound of fat a year by walking 10 extra minutes a day (Tartamella et al., 2004). Children and adolescents should pursue physical activities they find interesting and fun so that they will be motivated to pursue physical activity or exercise throughout their lives.

Last, for people who want to lose weight or maintain weight loss, health experts strongly encourage 90 minutes of moderately intense activity. Whatever a person's goal may be, the more exercise that is added in a given day, and the more vigorous the activity, the more energy will burned, generating greater results.

FULFILLING THE PHYSICAL ACTIVITY RECOMMENDATIONS

There are many ways to be physically active for 30, 60, or 90 minutes on most days of the week. Consider:

Domestic Chores

Children and adults alike often overlook housework, but chores can burn calories too. In 30 minutes of house or window cleaning, a 130-pound person burns about 123 calories and 105 calories, respectively (Bauer,

2005). Do not lose sight of the fact that washing the car by hand, raking leaves, vacuuming, shoveling snow, mowing the lawn, and weeding contribute to being physically active.

Leisure Activities

Archery, bicycling, canoeing, dancing, fishing, gardening, golfing, hiking, jogging, judo, karate, rollerblading, skating, swimming, and walking are all fine examples of physical activities that can be pursued leisurely (and in competition). Walking is worth mentioning because it seems a modest means of physical activity, but the benefits are noteworthy. Walking is easy, inexpensive, and relatively safe, and walking a mile can burn 100 calories, which corresponds to 10 pound of weight loss in a year (Fenton, 2008). For children, free play, which includes traditional games like hide-and-seek, tag, and so forth, counts as physical activity too. Ginsgburg (2007) explains, "Encouraging unstructured play may be an exceptional way to increase physical activity levels in children, which is one important strategy in the resolution of the obesity epidemic" (p. 183). Positive associations have been found between free play and the cognitive, physical, social, and emotional development and well-being of children (Stanford University School of Medicine, 2007). One 2010 report noted that children's academic achievement, social development, and well-being improve with regular periods of recess (Robert Wood Johnson Foundation, 2010).

Sports and Competitive Games

Sports-oriented activities keep players moving and vigorously engaged. Badminton, baseball, basketball, bowling, football, kickball, soccer, tennis, and volleyball are physical activities that are not only fun and inexpensive but also can lead to improved fitness and feeling good.

Structured Exercise

Doing aerobics; lifting weights; cycling; jumping rope; and using a treadmill, Stairmaster, or other kind of gym equipment are excellent ways to whip the body into shape.

Fenton (2008) and Dunn, Marcus, Carpenter, Jaret, and Blair (2001) suggest that physical activity should substitute inactivity as often as possible to optimize the amount of calories burned in the day. Fenton offers these easy ways to be more active throughout the day:

1. Use a bathroom on another floor at work or school.
2. Get a post office box and walk to pick up the mail.
3. Choose to go to a more distant cafeteria or restaurant for lunch; if you make your own lunch, walk to a park or mall to eat.
4. Walk to a corner store for the newspaper, milk, or bread.
5. Carpool with a friend and walk to his or her house for the ride.
6. Occasionally skip e-mail and hand-deliver messages to people.
7. Walk the kids to school, a friend's house, or soccer practice rather than driving them (they'll end up healthier, too)!
8. Take a quick stroll rather than sit down for midmorning snack. (p. 35)

To give consumers ideas of activities that are of "moderate to vigorous intensity" as recommended by the surgeon general, the Centers for Disease Control (2009) published a scale of activities and the amount of time required of each to get the maximum benefit. See the recommendations found in Figure 5.1. The range of activities at the top require more time because they are less intense than those at the bottom of the scale. Conversely, the activities closer to the bottom of the scale require less time because they are more vigorous than those at the top. Not everyone can perform the activities at the bottom, nor should people if they are too young or too old and the general condition of their body cannot handle the intensity or they have medical problems (Reisser, 2006).

To encourage children to pursue physical activity and fulfill the daily recommendations, the federal government (U.S. Department of Agriculture, 2000b) launched a campaign with a visual in the shape of a pyramid of whimsical cartoons depicting different activities. Figure 5.2 presents the poster "Move it! Choose your FUN!" The campaign endorses the notion that children need at least 60 minutes a day of moderate activity on most days of the week. At the base of the pyramid are illustrations of activities that should be pursued with more frequency than the activities found at the top. Alleman (1999), the author of *Save Your Child from the Fat Epidemic*, created a pyramid to include specific physical activities with a frequency that children can aim for. The four levels of her pyramid divide the kinds of activities that children should be encouraged to pursue: (1) everyday (e.g., playing outdoors, walking, biking, and volleyball), (2) three to four times a week (swimming, shooting hoops, helping in the yard and garden), (3) two to three times a week (e.g., gymnastics, in-line skating, racquetball, rapid walking), and (4) one to two times a week (jumping rope, stair walking, running, and basketball). The less vigorous activities, which should be pursued more regularly, are found at the base of the pyramid (i.e., Every Day); the more vigorous activities are found at the top.

FIGURE 5.1. Scale of Activities

Less vigorous, more time

> Washing and waxing a car for 45–60 minutes
> Washing windows or floors for 45–60 minutes
> Playing volleyball for 45 minutes
> Playing touch football for 30–45 minutes
> Gardening for 30–45 minutes
> Wheeling self in wheelchair for 30–40 minutes
> Walking 1 3/4 miles in 35 minutes (20 min./mile)
> Basketball (shooting baskets) for 30 minutes
> Bicycling 5 miles in 30 minutes
> Dancing fast (social) for 30 minutes
> Pushing a stroller 1 1/2 miles in 30 minutes
> Raking leaves for 30 minutes
> Walking 2 miles in 30 minutes (15 min./mile)
> Water aerobics for 30 minutes
> Swimming laps for 20 minutes
> Wheelchair basketball for 20 minutes
> Basketball (playing a game) for 15–20 minutes
> Bicycling 4 miles in 15 minutes
> Jumping rope for 15 minutes
> Running 1 1/2 miles in 15 minutes (10 min./mile)
> Shoveling snow for 15 minutes
> Stairwalking for 15 minutes

More vigorous, less time

Source: Centers for Disease Control. (2009). *What is a moderate amount of physical activity?* Retrieved December 1, 2010, from http://www.cdc.gov/NCCDPHP/sgr/ataglan.htm.

PHYSICAL ACTIVITY AND EXERCISE AT SCHOOL

Youth can potentially get much of their physical activity at school in recess, PE, or organized sports, which make schools ideal for promoting physical activity. At school, youth can be exposed to exercise science information that can influence their behavior and benefit their health, and they can use the knowledge to lay a foundation that can serve their health well into adulthood. School personnel, however, must institute health and physical education programs that promote physical activity, exercise, and physical fitness in varied ways (not just in an isolated PE program) and actively engage youth through an array of experiences.

A number of organizations (among them the National Association for Sport and Physical Education and the American Association of Physical Ac-

FIGURE 5.2. Move it! Choose your FUN!

Source. U.S. Department of Education (2000). *Move it! Choose your FUN!* Retrieved May 18, 2010, from http://www.fns.usda.gov/tn/Resource/Nibbles/moveit_poster.pdf

tivity and Recreation) offer guidelines that schools can consult in planning for an optimal PE program. Some, as they relate to physical activity and PE, are presented in Figure 5.3. Here are some essential elements, modified from a position paper on preventing child obesity (Iowa Child and Adolescent Obesity Task Force, 2001), that should be found in PE programs:

Essential Element 1: Full Student Participation in PE

The program should contain meaningful lessons and activities that engage all youth from prekindergarten to high school seniors, including those with physical or mental disabilities and English language learners. All youth should be able to successfully fulfill the PE goals and objectives to the best of their ability. For more information on including students with disabilities in, and adapting, PE, the American Association for Active Lifestyles and Fitness (2004) offers *A Position Statement on Including Students with Disabilities*

FIGURE 5.3. Guidelines to Promote Physical Education

Promoting PE. Requiring all students to participate in PE programs and developing curricula that take into account the limitations of students with physical and mental disabilities will enhance the health of all students. The following recommendations should be considered:

A. Plan a PE program that is inclusive, promotes lifelong physical activity, and is rewarding for all children.
    •   Offer a variety of experiences including both team sports and individual activities.
    •   Expose children to lifetime recreational activities such as walking, biking, rollerblading, swimming, fishing, and canoeing.
    •   Adapt PE instruction for students with special needs, include special needs students in regular classes wherever feasible
    •   Provide both indoor and outdoor facilities.
    •   Maintain facilities and equipment to meet safety standards.
    •   Provide quality equipment and supplies in sufficient quantity to allow all student to participate.

B. Allow adequate time for PE
    •   Provide at least 30 minutes daily in Grades K–3 with 20 minutes spent in actual PA.
    •   Provide a minimum of 45 minutes daily for Grades 4–8
    •   Require a minimum of 2 years in daily PE for grades 9–12, with the option of taking an additional two years of PE on an elective basis.
    •   Keep class size similar to other subjects in the school curriculum, preferably not more than 30 students.
    •   Establish minimum standards for PE at state or local district levels to ensure equal benefits for all children.

C. Recognize PE as an important part of the total school curriculum
    •   Mandate the PE instructors are certified for the grade level taught
    •   Include PE grades in the overall GPA
    •   Disallow exemptions for students for participating in any curriculum or extra curricular activities

D. Emphasize physical fitness, including concepts that will encourage the achievement of personal physical fitness, as a vital component of the curriculum at all levels.
    •   Conduct an annual fitness evaluation of all students and report results to their parents. Utilize the following criteria to ensure that the program provides opportunity for aerobic and/or skill building:
        three 10 minutes bouts of moderate to vigorous PA daily (5 school days each week);
        three or more 30 minute bouts of moderate to vigorous PA at least;
        three or more 30 minute sessions of motor skill practice and or development each week.

Recess and before and after school programs are important to a school's total PA program. Schools are encouraged to offer both structured and free time for PA.

Source: Iowa Child and Adolescent Obesity Task Force. (2001). Preventing child obesity in Iowa. *Healthy Weight Journal*, 15(4), 55–57. Reprinted with permission.

in Physical Education through the American Alliance for Health, Physical Education, Recreation, and Dance. As an additional resource, the Public Schools of North Carolina (n.d.) offers PE teaching strategies for English language learners in a brochure titled *Limited English Proficient (LEP) Students in Physical Education*. See the References for website addresses.

Essential Element 2: Fun, Varied, and Developmentally Appropriate Activities

The students should look forward to PE because they know they will have a good time participating in the activities while fulfilling the instructional objectives and demonstrating competencies. PE instructors should plan to teach youth indoor and outdoor activities, ranging from moderate to vigorous, that involve them in collaborating with others (e.g., team activities or sports) or participating individually (e.g., jumping rope, jogging). As often as possible, the activities should vary, sometimes focused on building endurance and other times working toward improved flexibility and strength. PE teachers should be enthusiastic and motivating and avoid using physical activity as punishment or degrading youth whose performance is below standard. In all, PE should aim to directly or indirectly teach youth a lifelong lesson that physical activity is worthy of pursuit because it can be rewarding, beneficial, and easily integrated in life.

Essential Element 3: Adequate Time for Physical Activity

As noted earlier, youth should have about 60 minutes or more of physical activity on most days of the week, which can include PE coupled with recess. Several national organizations such as the American Heart Association, the American Cancer Society, the American Diabetes Association, and the Centers for Disease Control recommend that children in the elementary grades get 150 minutes of PE each week and that middle and high school youth get about 225, with at least half the time spent in moderate to vigorous activity (Statement from the American Cancer Society, the American Diabetes Association, and the American Heart Association on Physical Education, n.d.). So that youth fulfill the recommended time, school personnel should consider developing after-school programs that engage youth in team sports or offer recreational kinds of activities (like walking, biking, swimming, and rollerblading) that are not offered through the formal PE program. Above all, youth should spend as much time actively participating in these endeavors as possible. PE, recess, or other structured physical activity benefits no child when he or she is waiting passively for the time to pass.

On that note, PE teachers should assign every student a part in the activities as well as provide enough quality equipment and supplies for everyone.

Essential Element 4: Physical Activity That Is Described in the School Wellness Policy

The School Wellness Policy, and the state's and district's standards, guide the delivery of physical activity and nutrition services on campus. So that children and their parents, teachers, and administrators fully understand the school's commitment to PE and physical activity, it is important that it is well advertised. The policy can include how PE will be structured (e.g., the frequency that it is offered and its duration), rules about PE and recess (e.g., that physical activity will not be used as punishment), and commitments to additional physical activity opportunities (e.g., physical activity clubs, how school administrators will work to establish a safe walking or biking route to school, partnerships with organizations that offer physical activity programs). A well-published policy holds the learning community accountable to the expectations, which can be modified to reflect its changing needs and interests.

Essential Element 5: Emphasis on Sportsmanship and Teamwork

Motor skill development and movement performance are the very nature of PE; however, students should also learn about sportsmanship and teamwork and the value of being a responsible and respectful team member. As positive, contributing team members, students begin to appreciate that collaborating with dignity maximizes effectiveness and efficiency (U.S. Department of Health and Human Services, 2008b).

Essential Element 6: Promotion of Physical Fitness

Work with students to forge developmentally appropriate physical fitness, emphasizing that fitness is indispensible in life. As Hoeger and Hoeger (2007) point out, "Physically fit people of all ages have the freedom to enjoy most of life's daily and recreational activities to their fullest potential. . . . Sound physical fitness gives the individual a degree of independence throughout life that many people in the United States no longer enjoy" (p. 17). To shape students' fitness, allocate time in PE for students to practice agility, balance, coordination, speed, power, and reaction time, as well as engage in exercises that build cardiovascular endurance, strength, and flexibility.

CONCLUSION

That being physically active is good for the body and mind is not a new notion. Hippocrates and Plato alluded to the idea that physical activity is beneficial in life and the message still has value today as it is among the top 10 leading health goals for the nation. But modern conveniences make it difficult to engage in physical activity regularly, and the excessive—and attractive—availability of TV and other technologies fascinates the young-est of children, pulling them away from routine exercise. Because physical activity is essential to the balance of what is consumed, it can, if consistent over time, help reduce the risk of dying prematurely, or acquiring cancer, heart disease, high blood pressure, and osteoporosis. Thus, it is crucial that children learn early on that physical activity improves health and fitness and how to incorporate it in life as daily routine. The next chapter presents just that: the Ideas on how to influence children to pursue physical activity on a regular basis.

CHAPTER 6

Ideas to Increase Physical Activity

The Youth Risk Behavior Surveillance is a national survey that monitors health-risk behaviors that high school youth in this country exhibit. The behaviors on the survey include those associated with morbidity and mortality, covering matters such as alcohol and drug use; violence; sexuality; and the topic at hand, obesity and physical inactivity. The most recent report (2007) had an expected, and lamentable, finding: Youth are physically inactive. Nearly 65% did not meet the recommended levels of physical activity; 70% did not attend physical education classes daily; 35% watched television for 3 or more hours a day on the average school day; and 25% engaged in 3 or more hours a day of playing video games or time spent on the computer (on an average school day), which was not for schoolwork (Centers for Disease Control, 2008c). These findings are germane to high school students; however, research strongly supports that children become more sedentary as they grow older (Berg, 2004). It stands to reason, then, that children need to develop the habits that lead them to regular physical activity before they become set in sedentary ways.

With the Ideas that are presented in this chapter, students learn that physical activity can be enjoyable, and with commitment, support, and encouragement they can develop healthy habits to practice throughout their lives. The Ideas and the framework from which they come are discussed in three sections:

- Assumptions Guiding the Ideas
- Background on the Ideas
- The 13 Ideas

ASSUMPTIONS GUIDING THE IDEAS

A number of assumptions guide these ideas, which are designed to promote physical activity in the lives of children. They include

1. Routinely engaging in physical activity contributes positively to health. Indeed, it helps reduce the risk of developing chronic diseases such as heart diseases and type 2 diabetes; improve blood and oxygen circulation; build and maintain bones and muscles; improve fitness, leading to increased energy and endurance; and increase self-confidence and self-esteem. Physical activity is also associated with enhanced mental well-being, which reduces anxiety, stress, and depression, and has been known to support a good night's sleep. If all this holds true, so does the converse: A lack of it contributes to a wide range of health problems. Because physical activity is a fundamental component of the energy balance equation, energy/calories "in" (by way of consumption) should be duly expended by energy/calories "out" (through daily bodily sustenance and physical activity). Unmistakably, too much "in" and not enough "out" causes weight gain, over time leading to overweight and obesity. Children who adopt a routine that includes physical activity will enjoy a healthier life.

2. Children do not get enough physical activity and the lack impinges their quality of life. The spotlight cannot be cast on children alone, since most Americans are physically inactive. Only a quarter of all people in this country get 30 minutes of physical activity a day (Fenton, 2008). The conveniences of modern life and captivating technology discourage the best of people from devoting time and energy to physical activity. Especially now, most children fall short of accumulating the 60 minutes of physical activity a day (on nearly all days) that the National Association for Sport and Physical Education recommends. Only a third of children take physical education daily (Centers for Disease Control, 2008c), and there is no assurance that all children have recess every day. That said, children have to be taught and encouraged to pursue physical activity because they do not, and, some would argue, cannot, get enough of it during the school day.

3. Children need to know why physical activity is important in their daily lives. That they do not get enough of it at school or home, or witness people they esteem being physically active sends a powerful indirect message: physical activity is not that important. Dalton (2004) believes that youth are underwhelmed with positive messages about being physically active. But myriad media exchanges (i.e., ads and commercials) influence them about food and eating, and as a result of modern-day social conventions and persuasions, they inevitably adopt the habits of their peer groups:

watching TV, playing video games, surfing the Internet, writing and responding to e-mail, talking on the phone, and listening to music. Reportedly, 62% of youth between 9 and 13 years old do not participate in organized physical activity, and nearly a quarter do not pursue physical activity during their free time (Centers for Disease Control, 2003b). It is a sure bet that they are pursuing those alluring, though sedentary, pastimes. It is simply appalling that most youth spend extended periods being physically inactive. Children need to realize that physical activity is important to their health and begin to devote their attention, time, and energy to developing the very habits that amount to a better quality of life.

4. Starting a habit focused on physical activity is easier to accomplish early in life than later when a person is set in sedentary ways. Health experts agree that younger children are more physically active than their older counterparts and become more sedentary as they grow. There are two complementary reasons why it is important to address physical activity at the early stages of life. For one, children are more active by nature and tend to seek out activities that are fun. Other than athletes, children are the most physically fit and active of any age group in this nation (Berg, 2003). Second, they gravitate toward physical activities as part of their natural development to obtain, practice, refine, and master their motor skills (Zembar & Blume, 2009). In effect, the early stage in life offers the best opportunity to confirm that the very physical activity they are attracted to is essential to their health. Failing to do so smoothes the pathway that many youth already take, developing sedentary tendencies throughout their lives.

5. Children can be taught that they control their physical activity habits. Because children have been dependent on their caregivers for all their young lives, they often believe that others fully determine circumstances and events and make decisions on their behalf. True, others are accountable for their sustenance, but children are just beginning to take responsibility for what they do (e.g., doing chores, completing their homework, behaving at school). Childhood is an opportune time to teach them that they can create and pursue practices that positively affect their health. When they learn that they have control over their health and that the decisions they make avoid the dreadful effects associated with sedentary practices (84% of the leading causes of death are preventable, Hoeger & Hoeger, 2007), they will be inclined to adopt lifestyle habits that include physical activity.

6. Physical activity should be fun. When it is not, and it makes children feel awkward, embarrassed, or inept; or they experience

discomfort, soreness or pain; or perceive it a dreaded chore with few redeeming benefits, they will lose interest in it and avoid it altogether. So that they avert such incidents, children should be encouraged to pursue physical activities that appeal to them the most. When activities are fun, children are more likely to pursue them with increasing intensity and frequency. They should be advised to try assorted activities, cast away those they disfavor and seek out those they find appealing. No one has to be athletic or especially skilled in a sport or game to have fun.

7. Aiming for physical activity (during childhood) is not about losing weight or having a slender body. Instead, it is about making it a daily routine because it is enjoyable and it benefits health.

BACKGROUND ON THE IDEAS

These Ideas are designed to help children fully conceive that physical activity is critical in and to life. As a matter of course, the Ideas stress that physical activity improves health and helps children overcome some of the challenges to making it a part of their daily routine. While the principles associated with motor skills, movement concepts, and exercise are certainly essential to physical education and valuable to children, the Ideas do not cover these matters because they are discoursed extensively in their respective disciplines. The comprehensive work of Graham, Holt/Hale, and Parker (2009) in *Children Moving*, Gallahue and Donnelly (2003) in *Developmental Physical Education for All Children*, and Pangrazi and Beighle (2010) in *Dynamic Physical Education for Elementary School Children* can be consulted, which are specific to the science of teaching a quality contemporary PE program. These sorts of books also impart the dynamics of sports and games and how to play them effectively.

The Ideas were created with the National Standards for Physical Education (NASPE, 2004) and the 2008 Physical Activity Guidelines for Americans (U.S. Department of Health and Human Services, 2008a) in mind. PE programs, by design, help students fulfill the NASPE standards, but the Ideas here serve to help children acquire fundamental competencies associated with physical activity, which lend themselves to meeting the national standards. Figure 6.1 illustrates how each Idea helps meet the NASPE standards. Consult with the PE teacher, school coach, or PE district administrator to determine how to best use the Ideas in the classroom. And on that note, seek their advice for clarity on physical activity issues, supplementary exercises or games, and safety measures.

These Ideas are tools teachers can use to enrich what PE teachers are accomplishing in their programs. That these Ideas are imparted in additional

FIGURE 6.1. National Standards for Physical Education Addressed by Each Idea

Physical activity is critical to the development and maintenance of good health. The goal of physical education is to develop physically educated individuals who have the knowledge, skills, and confidence to enjoy a lifetime of healthful physical activity.

A physically educated person:

Standard 1: Demonstrates competency in motor skills and movement patterns needed to perform a variety of physical activities.

Standard 2: Demonstrates understanding of movement concepts, principles, strategies, and tactics as they apply to the learning and performance of physical activities.

Standard 3: Participates regularly in physical activity.

Standard 4: Achieves and maintains a health-enhancing level of physical fitness.

Standard 5: Exhibits responsible personal and social behavior that respects self and others in physical activity settings.

Standard 6: Values physical activity for health, enjoyment, challenge, self-expression, and/or social interaction.

Jump Start Health! Ideas	National Standards for Physical Education					
	1	2	3	4	5	6
Idea 16 Physical Activity Is Important			✓			✓
Idea 17 Levels of the Physical Activity Pyramid		✓	✓			✓
Idea 18 FITT		✓	✓	✓		
Idea 19 Health-Related Fitness		✓	✓	✓		
Idea 20 Warm-up and Cool-down	✓	✓				
Idea 21 Flexibility Exercises	✓	✓	✓	✓		
Idea 22 Overcoming Excuses			✓		✓	✓
Idea 23 Make It Fun			✓			✓
Idea 24 Find a Buddy			✓		✓	✓
Idea 25 Responsible Behavior					✓	✓
Idea 26 Hydrate with Water				✓	✓	
Idea 27 Limit Television Time			✓			✓
Idea 28 Making and Tracking Goals			✓	✓		✓

Source: National Association for Sport and Physical Education. (2004). *Moving into the future: National standards for physical education* (2nd ed.). New York: McGraw-Hill.

settings other than PE or the gym and by an adult other than the coach contributes to two outcomes. One, the students begin to realize that physical activity is important enough to be covered in two separate settings, and two, they see that physical activity is not just about one domain in their life. In addition, the Ideas benefit children who attend schools that offer PE infrequently. By no means are the Ideas an exercise program designed for children to lose weight. In fact, the Ideas never address the issue of weight loss or body size. Such programs do exist and should be considered only under the recommendation of a pediatrician who specializes in overweight and obesity.

In terms of the design and delivery of the Ideas, there are essential instructional practices to keep in mind, which are addressed in Chapter 4. But rather than replicate the discussion, refer instead to that background section. As a point of reemphasis though, because the Ideas are intended for a wide range of children, always consider children's age-related characteristics and their respective developmental factors (i.e., physical, social, and cognitive) when administering the Ideas (Gallahue & Donnelly, 2003). One aspect represented in these Ideas that sets them apart from those in Chapter 5 is the notion that children have to be continually encouraged to be physically active. After all, whether to be physically active on one's personal time is completely voluntary these days. To create this constant wave of motivation where children feel supported to take risks and stimulated to invest their interests, see the helpful hints outlined in Figure 6.2. Indeed, children need a positive environment and a teacher who shows that the pursuit of physical activity is worthwhile.

A unique feature of the guided activity section in these Ideas is that nearly all of them engage the students in a participatory practice, a welcome opportunity to reinforce the lesson at hand. The guided activities last about 30 minutes, but should be adjusted according to unique circumstances. Some teachers may be apprehensive about allowing students to become physically active out of fear that they will become loud, disruptive, and unruly. Indeed, most children can get out of hand when they are excited, but they need to be active to fully recognize and appreciate the value of physical activity. So that the students are disciplined throughout the physical activity, good behavior management strategies should be practiced. To that end

- Review the classroom rules before starting the physical activity;
- Review the behavior management plan in use, drawing students' attention to the hierarchy of punishments (e.g., "If I have to warn you three times, you will be sent to time out");
- Set the behavioral expectations, which should be explicit and apparent (e.g., "I expect everyone in their own space," "I expect

FIGURE 6.2. Creating a Physically Active Classroom Environment

Below are some helpful hints for classroom teachers to use to create a physically active environment.

1. Create a positive atmosphere that enhances the self-esteem for all students. Each student should feel respected and valued. We do not all move alike or at the same speed. Value each child based on individual abilities. Modify activities when needed.
2. Have a signal or sign that can refocus students quickly so that they can "freeze" and listen to you when you need to speak or end the activity.
3. Share appropriate personal information with your students. Students respond favorably to the instructor who shares personal anecdotes or participates with them actively.
4. Be fair. Make certain each student understands the teacher's expectations prior to the state of the activity.
5. Expect success! Assume all students can, and want, to be active— including those with special needs.
6. Model enthusiasm for physical activity. Be aware that students (at first) may seem apathetic or silly. These are common expressions of being self-conscious about trying something new in front of their peers. With practice, this discomfort can be minimized and students will be more relaxed and willing to participate.
7. Give instructions before and after arranging the room to get ready for participation. Remind students of the rules for the activity and the "freeze" signals.
8. Take time to make sure that objects are out of the way for safe movement.
9. Set a time limit for the activity before beginning movement. Be sure to share with students.
10. Compliment groups or individuals so that all groups or individuals feel as though their participation was valued.

Source: Mahar, M.T., Kenny, R.K., Scales, D.P., Shields, A.T., & Miller, T.Y. (2006). *Science middle-school energizers: Classroom-based physical activities.* Raleigh, NC: North Carolina Department of Public Instruction. Reprinted with permission.

everyone to keep their hands and feet to themselves," "I expect everyone to use their quiet voice");

- Stress safety at all times;
- Immediately praise children for good behaviors;
- Immediately warn or reprimand students for bad behaviors;
- Be consistent in enforcing the behavior management plan; and
- Use time limits (e.g., "You will have seven minutes to stretch, at that time switch with your partner").

Upon completion of the guided activity, the students return to the classroom for the independent activity, where they reflect on the matter at hand. Just as in the Ideas to promote healthy eating, consider asking the students to keep a journal and record their thoughts about the lessons. Specifically, they could respond to

- What physical activity did I do?
- For how long?
- How did I feel afterwards?
- Was it fun?
- Why would I do it again?
- What I'm learning about myself . . .
- Questions I have . . .
- Connections I have made . . .

A reproducible with these introspective-like stems is found in Idea 16, but can be used for each Idea.

THE 13 IDEAS

The 13 Ideas that follow are titled Physical Activity Is Important; Levels of the Physical Activity Pyramid; FITT; Health-Related Fitness; Warm-up and Cool-Down; Flexibility Exercises; Overcoming Excuses; Make It Fun; Find a Buddy; Responsible Behavior; Hydrate with Water; Limit Television Time; and Making and Tracking Goals.

IDEA 16: PHYSICAL ACTIVITY IS IMPORTANT

Rationale

In her book *Underage and Overweight,* Berg (2004) identifies an ironic occurrence in our society: Despite our bodies being uniquely equipped for movement and exercise, youth and adults alike are underwhelmed by physical activity advice. Indeed, efforts have been made by the federal government and private organizations to stress to the public the importance of regular physical activity, yet research continues to find that Americans, as a whole, do not engage in the recommended amounts of physical activity. Because engaging in physical activity is voluntary, and there are so many attractive sedentary options, children have to be taught to pursue physical activity (U.S. Department of Health and Human Services, 2000b). There is not enough time in the school day for children to fit in the recommended

60 minutes of daily physical activity. Hence, they have to be motivated with messages that physical activity is important (as a healthy diet) so that they learn to integrate it in their personal time.

Objectives

After learning about the importance of physical activity, the students will

- Evaluate whether a behavior is physically active
- Create a time capsule and include five reasons why physical activity is important in daily life

Download and use Reproducibles 1.1, 1.4, and 16.1–16.5 for this Idea.

To Motivate the Students

Invite the students to describe some of the things they did over the weekend. Write their responses on the board, using a Venn diagram as a graphic organizer. Write "physically active" on one side, "sedentary" on the other, and "similar qualities" in the center; their responses can be organized accordingly (the center can include activities such as "walked to the movies" or "biked to a friend's house to play video games"). Describe some of the activities you did over the weekend. Underscore how you are pleased with the amount of physical activity you had, or express disappointment that you did not have more. Turn the students' attention to the MyPyramid for Kids illustration, which can be easily retrieved online and displayed on a computer projection system. Briefly review some of the concepts they have learned thus far (e.g., the food groups, energy balance). Call on some students to describe what the children on the poster are doing. Emphasize that nearly all of them are engaged in some activity. Mention that based on the activities they did over the weekend, many of them, like the children on the poster, endeavor to engage in physical activity. Ask the students to share how they are physically active every day.

Frame the Instruction

Explain that the federal government and health experts alike want children (and adults) to engage in physical activity every day. This explains why there are children in motion depicted on MyPyramid for Kids (Reproducible 1.4) along with the food groups and other important health messages. The symbolism is simple: Being physically active is just as important as eating healthy foods. Emphasize that part of the energy balance is to be physical active every day so that some of the "in" energy is expended. Explain that in this lesson, the students will learn about the importance of physical activity.

Step by Step

1. Redirect the students' attention to the MyPyramid for Kids illustration and read, "Eat Right. Exercise. Have Fun." and, "Find your balance between food and fun." Ask the students to contemplate what the statements suggest. Reinforce that the message is a reminder to include exercise and physical activity in daily routines along with healthy eating. Show the students the adult version, MyPyramid, so that they see a similar image of a person climbing the stairs alongside the pyramid. Mention that the steps are symbolic in that any person can take steps at their own pace toward physical activity. Read the MyPyramid message, "Find your balance between food and physical activity." (See Figure 2.2 or Reproducible 1.4.) Underscore that regular physical activity is important for physical and mental health. Share the many ways that you are physically active. Explain that the activities you do are enjoyable, and that they too should seek out physical activities that are fun.

2. Use Reproducible 1.1 to review the concept of balance. Review how food consumption is one side of the scale and physical activity is the other. Emphasize that there can be dreadful results when people do not practice balance in their daily life, especially when they do not balance their food intake with physical activity. Review: "Energy in" is what is consumed by way of food, foods are composed of energy-producing values known as calories, some foods have more calories than others, and the body needs energy (calories) to function. Explain that the calories add up whenever a person eats or drinks and they are burned off by way of physical activity and continual support of the body. Mention that in a later lesson they will learn how some activities burn more energy than others. Younger children may better understand the energy balance concept by suggesting that food is fuel the body needs to function and grow, and too much of it without sufficient physical activity results in the body's storing it as fat. Stress that when they balance the foods they eat with physical activity, they burn fuel/energy.

3. Explain that there are many benefits associated with being physically active every day. Ask the students to speculate on what some of the benefits may be. As they ponder, ask them to consider how they feel physically and mentally when they engage in physical activity and how they feel afterward. Compare their answers with some of the benefits found on Reproducible 16.1. Summarize how being physically active is important because it improves and maintains mental health throughout life and also enhances the body's strength, balance, flexibility, and ability to move, which they will learn about in the

subsequent Idea. Mention that the more physically active they are, the better, and that any amount or form of physical activity counts toward meeting the federal recommendations. Stress that they should contemplate how they can be active at home, school, and places they often frequent such as a relative's or neighbor's home or even when they are running errands with their parents (e.g., they can ask their parents to park farther away).

4. Take them outside to walk around the school grounds, and to perform assorted exercises that they may be familiar with such as jumping jacks, running in place, and so forth. When they are finished, return to the classroom and ask them to think about all the activities they have done since waking up. Based on their responses, have them create a definition for physical activity, which should approximate "bodily movement." Stress that there are many ways to be physically active, most of which do not require formal rules, special training, or skills. Indicate that daily and recreational tasks as well as organized sports count as physical activity. Have them think about all the physical activities they can do indoors and outdoors as well as those they can do by themselves, with a friend, a group, or family. Remind them that the MyPyramid campaign emphasizes that they enjoy their physical activities, so they should pursue those they find appealing.

5. Contrast physical activity with sedentary behaviors, which include watching TV, playing video games, playing on the computer/Internet, and lying down and talking on the phone. Ask them to reflect on the times they have engaged in these kinds of activities for prolonged periods. Add that it is easy to engage in them because they can be relaxing and pleasant, but too often and too long can produce harmful effects. Underscore that sedentary activities do not require much energy and consequently burn few calories, and more important, continual sedentary behaviors can lead to a diminished quality of life. Stress that they have the power to choose physical activity over sedentary behaviors, and they should strive to combine the right food choices with the right amounts of daily physical activities. Indicate that if they develop good physical activities habits now, they are likely to incorporate them throughout their lives.

Activities

Guided. Distribute double-sided copies of the cards (Reproducible 16.2) to a pair of students. Instruct the students to cut out the cards and spread them face down on their desks. Each child selects a card and determines whether the scenario is worthy of the distinction "physically active." If it is, the student gives a reason for why it is important. If it is not, the student can offer a physical activity alternative. The game continues until all of the cards have been played.

Independent. Pass out Reproducible 16.3 to each student. On the handout the students describe why being physically active is important and follow with a picture of what they do to keep physically active. After the students are finished, assemble their products into one book using Reproducible 16.4, A Class Book for a Time Capsule, as the cover.

Conclusion

Read the book to the class and mention that future lessons will focus on how to incorporate physical activity in their lives.

Tips

- Pass out copies of Reproducible 16.5 and have the students fill in the blank cards with new scenarios.
- Show the students pictures of sedentary behaviors (type in *couch potatoes* or *sedentary lifestyles* on the Google image search) and invite them to offer suggestions for physical activity.

IDEA 17: LEVELS OF THE PHYSICAL ACTIVITY PYRAMID

Rationale

Here students learn about the Physical Activity Pyramid (U.S. Department of Agriculture, 2000b) and the notion that physical activity can be divided into varying levels of intensity. It may seem absurd that children know about these levels; however, they need to begin to understand that different amounts of energy (i.e., calories) are expended according to the intensity and duration of the physical activity. In short, they need to know that not all physical activity is the same and each has unique benefits. With this knowledge, students can increasingly work their way from activities that require minimum levels of energy toward those that are more intense and require more energy, and consequently produce preferred results. They learn to engage in exercises that hone specific muscles and bones, which maximizes their ability to move, reach, lift, and so forth (Reisser, 2006), because not all physical activity builds and strengthens every muscle (Willett & Skerrett, 2005). If these arguments do not suffice, children need to at least know the vocabulary associated with levels of physical activity because they are used throughout the *Dietary Guidelines* (U.S. Department of Health and Human Services, 2005b). The key recommendations associated with physical activity use the terms *moderate-intensity* and *moderate- to vigorous-intensity activity* to guide Americans to develop a better ability to perform more intense activities.

Objectives

After learning about the importance of physical activity, the students will

- Perform a series of physical activities and guess at the level of intensity (inactive, light, moderate, vigorous, or stretching)
- Create their own personal plan for physical activity that incorporates at least three types of activity per "plenty" (moderate) and "more" (vigorous) levels, and one for "enough" (stretches) and "less" (inactivity) levels

Download and use Reproducibles 17.1–17.3 for this Idea.

To Motivate the Students

Take the students outdoors and divide them into small teams. Inform them that they will pantomime physical activity while their respective team members attempt to identify it. Ask the students to pantomime their favorite physical activity, the physical activity they like the least, a physical activity that can be played indoors, a sport they want to learn more about, a recreational physical activity, a daily task that requires physical activity, a physical activity that can be accomplished by themselves, a physical activity that requires at least two people, and a physical activity they have never tried.

Frame the Instruction

Return to the classroom after the outdoor activity. Invite the students to pantomime some of these for the class, especially those that were difficult to figure out, those they were surprised to learn that their teammates did not like, and those that their teammates wanted to learn. Inform them that the purpose of the activity was to show them the varied kinds of activities that are available to them. Tell them that they are going to learn how these physical activities can be categorized and about principles they need to keep in mind when they engage in physical activity.

Step by Step

1. Review how the body uses energy for its daily essence and to fuel physical activity. Call the students' attention to the pantomime activity and ask them to contemplate how some of these physical activities were the same and how they were different. Mention that the physical activities are unique, not just in their appearance, the movement of the

body, or the degree of skills needed to execute them fittingly, but also because each expends different amounts of energy. Relay in simple terms that the number of calories burned differs according to the intensity of the physical activity and the duration engaged in it. Explain that minimum levels of energy are needed to complete basic tasks like household chores and leisure activities (e.g., walking for few minutes, dancing to a song), so fewer calories are burned. Alternatively, more energy is burned the longer or more intense the physical activity (Baird, Branta, Mark, & Seremba, 2006). Give the students some examples: Light physical activity that burns little energy might be sweeping a front porch, picking up clothes, playing a board game, walking from the bedroom to the kitchen, or working on a puzzle; more intense physical activity that burns more energy might include jogging for 30 minutes, swimming for an hour, or actively playing a game of soccer. Call on some students to explain how some of the physical activities that were pantomimed are more intense than others. Stress that all physical activity is worthwhile because each develops and strengthens the heart, lungs, muscles, and bones in a unique way.

2. Explain that there is an activity pyramid that can be used to guide them toward varying levels of physical activity. Show them the pyramid, which is part of a USDA campaign and can be easily located by way of an Internet search with its title, Move It! Choose Your Fun! (See Figure 5.2). Read the title and the additional messages that append the illustration: "Your body counts on you to be active to help strengthen your bones and heart, and build muscles," and "How much physical activity do kids need? Get at least 60 minutes a day of moderate activity, most days of the week." Ask how these messages resonate with the initial lesson on how physical activity is important in daily life. Transition to the four levels of the pyramid. Ask the students to identify what the drawings at the base depict the children doing. Mention that these illustrations are associated with the pyramid advice "Do plenty: walk, wiggle, dance, climb stairs. Just keep moving whenever you can." Explain that the next level encourages, "Do more: Do more intense activities that warm you up and make you glow!" At this point, have the students contrast the activities in the base with those found at the next level, which are more intense. Read the recommendation tagged with next level, which relates to stretches, "Do enough: Do enough strengthening activities to keep your muscles firm." Have the students contrast the pictures in this level with those of the former. Point out that stretching is a critical endeavor that increases the body's range of motion (American Heart Association, 2006b). Finally, identify what the child at the tip of the pyramid is

doing, and ask them to contemplate why the recommendation for this level is considered inactivity. Read, "Do less. Spend less time sitting around watching TV or using the computer." Assert that there are times when they will be inactive (e.g., playing a board game with friends, painting/drawing), but they should balance inactive times with physical activity.

3. Based on the pantomimes and the physical activity pyramid, have the students define light, moderate, and vigorous physical activity, as well as stretches. You may have to frame their contributions with your own definition of intensity. Tell them that the purpose of learning about these terms and their respective definitions is that our federal government recommends that adults—which they will become—engage in moderate to vigorous intensity physical activity for longer periods of time.

4. Pass out a card cut from Reproducible 17.1 for each child. Draw your own physical activity pyramid on the board or display Reproducible 17.2 on the overhead. Call on students to read their card and subsequently tape it to the appropriate level on the pyramid. The cards range from Less (watch TV, play video games, talk on the phone, watch a DVD), Enough (reach for the stars stretches, touch your toes stretches), More (vigorous physical activity such as run, jog, jump rope, rollerblade), and Plenty (moderate physical activity such as walk, play catch, work on the yard). Underscore that these are simple, hypothetical examples that can vary where they are placed on the pyramid because the activity depends largely on the intensity and the duration. Use the example of walking. At a fast pace for an hour, it would be considered vigorous, while walking from one room to the next would be considered light. The same holds true for rollerblading; for instance, a 3-minute trial would be light, but a 5-mile trek would be vigorous.

5. Tell the students that they can move from regular bouts of light activity to routine moderate to vigorous physical activity tailored in each day. Ask the students how they might include light, moderate, and vigorous physical activity (and stretches) in a 60-minute period.

Activities

Guided. Take students on a physical activity adventure. Each time they perform an activity, you will call on them to verbally respond whether the activity was inactive, light, moderate, vigorous, or stretching. Assemble the students and instruct them to touch their toes (stretch). Then have them do a round of 25 jumping jacks (moderate) and 50 jumping jacks at a faster speed (vigorous), walk four times around the parameter (moderate), and then jog four times (vigorous). Give them a few minutes of rest to compose themselves (inactive). Have them lie on their backs and do 10 sit-ups (stretches). Have them stand and walk heel to toe (stretch). Consider playing a round of kick ball, and ask the students to estimate the amount of time they spent inactive, or in light, moderate, or vigorous physical activity.

Independent. Distribute copies of Reproducible 17.3 and instruct the students to identify at least three types of activity per "plenty" (moderate) and "more" (vigorous) levels, and one for "enough" (stretches) and "less" (inactivity) levels they would like to accomplish in a 2-day period.

Conclusion

Invite the students to share their personal physical activity plan. Reinforce that the purpose of learning about the levels and types of physical activity is for them to incorporate a variety of physical activities in their daily lives. They will likely develop and strengthen their bones, muscles, and their cardiovascular system so that they are able to perform vigorous activities without physical challenge.

Tips

- Show the students images of physical activity (and inactivity) and have them identify the respective level and how it could be adapted so that it could be considered a different degree of physical activity
- Show the students the range of physical activity in your own life
- Have the students take a poll of the physical activity a sample (of children, adults, or family members) like the most and determine whether most of it is inactive, light, moderate, vigorous, or stretching

---

IDEA 18: FITT

Rationale

The acronym FITT stands for the principles associated with physical activity (and exercise), which are frequency, intensity, type, and time. Until now, the students have learned to use the Physical Activity Pyramid to pursue varying levels of physical activities on all or most days of the week. Because the general spirit of the Physical Activity Pyramid serves to encourage and motivate youngsters, it does not publicize or make the distinction of the FITT principles. Yet students need the knowledge of these principles for different reasons. With this knowledge comes the understanding of the correct amounts of specific physical activity to pursue on most days, and as they learn that some types of physical activity yield specific results, they begin to seek them out and build them into their routine. Moreover, they can pace themselves and gradually work toward fulfilling the respective physical activity recommendations when they know their initial limitations. More important, by practicing these principles, they build stronger muscles, joints, and bones and become fit, which gives them the boost of energy to be physically active for longer periods of time. Students must also be familiar with the FITT principles because some states, such as Texas (Texas Education Agency, 2009), assess students' fitness beginning in third grade. Quite often the battery of tests is associated with the FITT principles.

Objectives

After learning about the principles of physical activity, the students will

- Identify the respective FITT principles assigned to a physical activity
- Identify their own physical activities that satisfy the FITT principles for 60 minutes a day, for a full week

Download and use Reproducibles 17.3, 18.1, and 18.2 for this Idea.

To Motivate the Students

Invite the students to share how successful they have been in fulfilling their Physical Activity Pyramid (Reproducible 17.3). Ask them to explain the challenges they faced in participating in "plenty," "more," and "enough" physical activity. Next, tell them that a friend has asked for their advice about pursing 60 minutes of daily physical activity. In particular, the friend has asked, "How often should I do stretching exercises? How much time should I spend doing vigorous activity? What types of physical activity should I do?" Call on students to provide him the best advice they can. Then mention that they will learn about some principles that will help them refine their own physical activity routine, and with this knowledge they will be better able to advise others.

Frame the Instruction

Explain that they will learn about the four principles associated with physical activity that can be easily remembered by way of the acronym FITT (U.S. Department of Health and Human Services, n.d.): Frequency, Intensity, Type, and Time. These principles are often associated with the term *exercise* because the activities imply planned, structured, and repetitive movement. Some health professionals use the FIT formula without the use of the extra "T" (Corbin et al., 2008).

Step by Step

1. To teach "frequency," invite the students to identify a place they visit regularly, foods they eat often, and places they shop at frequently. Use their examples to convey the notion of frequency and define the term. Explain that the term is comparable to terms such as *regular*, *constant,* and *occurring* often. Use the term to convey the importance of making time for it every day. Encourage them to keep a daily schedule of physical activity or at least attempt it on most days of the week. Explain that it is easier to be physically active if they consider it part of their day (e.g., playing outside for an hour after school or right after doing homework, walking the dog after dinner). Tell them that frequency in this context has an additional meaning that is closely tied to the prior lesson: They should engage in different levels of physical activity in frequent bouts (e.g., stretching activities for at least 2 to 4 days a week). Explain that they will learn the established names associated with the different levels.

2. To teach "intensity," review how the term *intense* was used in the prior Idea. Ask the students to define it, and then reinforce their understanding by suggesting that it is the degree to which a person exerts him- or herself in physical activity (i.e., how easy or hard a person is exercising (American Council on Exercise, n.d.). Explain that more intense physical activity increases their heart rate, they breathe heavier, and they sweat. Discuss how some physical activities are more intense than others, using examples they are familiar with, such as running is more intense than shooting baskets, pushing a stroller for 30 minutes is less intense than shoveling snow for 15 minutes. (See Figure 5.1, the scale of physical activities, for additional examples). Explain that they should engage in physical activities that range in intensity, from light to moderate to vigorous. In other words, in the span of a week students should have engaged in physical activities that required them to exert minimum and maximum levels of energy. To further illustrate the point, explain that the physical activity they participate in should include light levels (i.e., they can talk and do the activity with ease, they are not sweating, their heart rate is normal), moderate levels (i.e., their heart rate is increased, but they are not breathing or sweating heavily), and vigorous levels (i.e., their heart is significantly increased, they are sweating, and they are breathing faster and heavier) of intensity. Warn them that if they are out of breath (or to the point of collapse) during their physical activity, they are exerting themselves too hard, which can cause them injury. Underscore that they should be able to talk during physical activity (with the exception

of swimming laps) and recover composure within few minutes (American Heart Association, 2006b).

3. For "type," explain that this refers to the type of physical activity that is being done. There are three types of physical activity (exercise): flexibility, aerobic, and strength. Write these terms on the board, and define each (students in the upper grades may be familiar with these terms and can define of each with your guidance). *Flexibility* refers to stretching, where they extend their body to reach and bend. Review that stretching is beneficial because it increases the body's range of motion and improves their muscle and joint pliability (American Heart Association, 2006b; U.S. Department of Health and Human Services, 2005a). *Aerobic* is about moving muscles in the arms and legs in a repetitive fashion for extended periods of time. Explain that aerobic activities are sometimes referred to as cardiovascular activities because they make the heart work hard to pump blood throughout the body. These kinds of activities improve their heart and lung efficiency (Bounds et al., 2006). Last, *strength* activities are those that build muscle and strength, such as weight lifting. These help to increase their ability to move, reach, lift, and so forth (Reisser, 2006). (For the youngsters in the primary grades mention that because of their age group, it is important to know the concepts of aerobic and strength so that they can seek out these exercises when they are older. For now, though, have them focus their attention and efforts on pursing physical activities that they have come to know as moderate and vigorous. Note that the American Academy of Pediatrics (1990) states, "Children and adolescents should avoid the practice of weight lifting, power lifting, and body building, as well as the repetitive use of maximal amounts of weight in strength training programs" (p. 802).

4. For "time," indicate that this represents the length of time they participate in physical activity. Health experts recommend that children get at least 60 minutes of physical activity on most, and preferably all, days of the week. This amount of physical activity (and more) will help them maintain or improve their health. Emphasize that they should plan for this time in addition to whatever physical activity they get at school by way of recess or PE. If the physical activity cannot be carried out in one period, encourage them to participate in short bouts of activity that amount to 60 minutes (e.g., 20 minutes here, 30 minutes there). Remind them that their physical activity does not have to be the same, recurring activity; on the contrary, it should vary. "Time" also refers to the amount of time they spend in the different types of physical activity.

5. Distribute photocopies of Reproducible 18.1 to the students. Point out how the pyramid resembles the federal one, but specifies FITT at the

different levels. Review each level, calling on students to identify the frequency, intensity, type, and time and the range of activities located for each.

Activities

Guided. Take the students outside and divide them into teams. Each team should have at least one Reproducible (18.1) to participate in the activity. Inform them that you are going to instruct them to do a physical activity and they have to respond with the accurate F, I, T, or T. Have them perform light stretching, run in place, walk their pretend dog around the parameter of a square, jump rope, dance, and so forth. As a culminating activity, allow them to play on the playscape for a few minutes or arrange for a relay race.

Independent. When the students return from outside, distribute Reproducible 18.2 and have them write in their own physical activities that could fulfill the FITT principles for 60 minutes a day, for a full week.

Conclusion

Invite the students to share their pyramids with the class. Reinforce that if they do what they plan to commit to the FITT principles they will stay fit and they will witness significant health benefits.

Tips

- Assign the students a physical activity and have them identify its place on the pyramid according to the frequency, intensity, type, or time.
- Have the students create and recite a pledge to fulfill their pyramid

---

IDEA 19: HEALTH-RELATED FITNESS

Rationale

A great outcome of engaging in regular physical activity is fitness. By definition, fitness is having an enhanced body with the ability—by way of a stronger heart, lungs, and muscles—and the energy to perform many kinds of activities. Now that the students know the FITT principles, they can apply them in their physical activity routines to develop their fitness. As they do, they increase their capacity to meet the physical demands of daily life, to exercise, and to participate in vigorous sports for longer periods of time without difficulty or premature fatigue. As fitness contributes to well-being, it increases a person's ability to cope with stressful events (President's Council on Physical Fitness, n.d.). Further, physically fit youth perform better in school and on achievement tests (Texas Education Agency, 2009), a fact that has motivated some states to measure their students' fitness as early as third grade. In brief, fitness and better health are closely associated (Sharkey & Gaskill, 2007). Youth need to know the components of fitness so as to keep them in mind as they seek to improve their body's vitality.

Objectives

After learning about the importance of health-related fitness, the students will

- Engage in physical activity to enhance their cardiovascular endurance, muscular strength, and muscular endurance
- Create a logo that represents three health-related fitness components

Download and use Reproducible 19.1 for this Idea.

To Motivate the Students

Invite the students to share what they remember from the *Dietary Guidelines*. Write their responses on the board. Then introduce the "ABC" of the *Dietary Guidelines*: "Aim for fitness," "Build a healthy base," and "Choose sensibly" (U.S. Department of Agriculture, 2000c). Inform them that "B" and "C" are associated with healthy eating. "Choosing sensibly" refers to consciously consuming the right foods and exercising moderate intakes of sugary, salty, high calorie, high fat foods. Tell them that "building a healthy base" represents using the MyPyramid food groups to guide their choice of foods. Ask the students to share what they believe "aim for fitness" is about and to define fitness to the best of their ability (up to now, the terms *fit* or *fitness* have not been used). After they have had the opportunity to do so, follow that *fit* refers to the state of being in good physical condition and that fitness is the body's ability to completely sustain itself during physical activity performance.

Frame the Instruction

Explain that there are two aspects of fitness. On the board, write the two terms associated with fitness: *health-related* and *skill-related*. Ask the students to contrast the two terms and to contemplate how the terms would generate two different sets of components. Validate that the term *health-related* refers to the organic functions of the body, whereas *skill-related* refers to how the body moves and performs during physical activity. Mention they will learn about health-related fitness because skill-related fitness is closely associated with performance (e.g., speed, power, reaction time), which is not critical to children, as it is among adolescent athletes seeking to improve their motor skills in their pursuit of competitive sports.

Step by Step

1. There are five health-related components of fitness. They include cardiovascular (sometimes known as cardiorespiratory or aerobic) endurance, body composition, muscular strength, muscular endurance, and flexibility. For the component cardiovascular endurance, ask the students to recall the definition of *cardiovascular* (from Idea 18) or define it for them by dividing the term in two: *cardio* and *vascular*. Explain that *cardio* means "heart," and *vascular* refers to vessels or ducts (i.e., the circulatory system) that carry bodily fluids such as blood throughout the body. Tell them that *cardiovascular* refers to the heart's ability to efficiently work with the lungs to deliver blood, composed of oxygen and essential nutrients, to the muscles, joints, bones, and tissues. Define the term *endurance*, which is the ability to sustain or hold up before surrendering to fatigue, and indicate that cardiovascular endurance is the heart and lung capacity to support a person to persist through an activity. Physical activities like jogging, swimming, walking, and cycling build endurance.

2. Another component is *body composition*, which refers to the degree of fat found throughout the body. Underscore that fit people tend to have leaner bodies than those who do not exercise often. The leaner the body, the easier it is for it to perform physical activity; excess fat tends to encumber it. To develop leaner bodies, encourage the students to pursue physical activity as often—and under the right conditions—as possible.

3. Muscular strength is another component, which is the amount of force that muscles exert against the resistance of body weight (e.g., push-ups or curl-ups) or free weights (e.g., barbells). Muscular endurance, a fourth component, is the ability to exert that force repeatedly over a period of time or as long as the body is able. Tell the students that muscular strength is the degree to which people can use muscles to lift free weights or resist/control their own body weight (Corbin et al., 2008) and that muscular endurance is about the body's ability to exert that force repeatedly without premature fatigue or stress. Fit persons, that is, persons with sound muscular endurance, can engage in vigorous physical activity for longer periods of time than unfit persons who are likely tire easily. Exercise strengthens muscles and bones as well as enhances posture (President's Council on Physical Fitness, n.d.). There are a range of activities that in repeated motion build muscular strength and endurance: curl-ups, push-ups, rope climbing, and so forth.

4. The fifth component is flexibility, which is characterized by how limber the body is. Inform the students that flexibility is about the combined ability of the muscles and joints to move within respective inherent ranges (i.e., bend and stretch). People who are fit can move their muscles and joints more easily than people who are not. The benefits of and exercises that work toward flexibility are covered in Idea 21.

Activities

Guided. Inform the students that they will engage in physical activity to enhance their cardiovascular endurance, muscular strength, and muscular endurance. Flexibility is addressed in Idea 21, and body composition is determined by recording their body fat by a trained technician using methods that would prove implausible in the classroom (e.g., testing by way of water immersion, a caliper, a pressure chamber, and bioelectric conducting). Take the students outside and for cardiovascular endurance, have them run, jog, or briskly walk for a quarter mile (6- and 7-year-olds) or half mile (8- and 9-year-olds). For muscular strength and endurance have them do rounds (as many as they can do in a minute or 2, repeating after their partner has had his or her turn) of push-ups, pull-ups, curl-ups, crunches, or leg lifts. Use the *Get Fit and Be Active* (President's Council on Physical Fitness and Sports, n.d.) handbook, which can be found at http://www.presidentschallenge.org/pdf/getfit.pdf, to show the students how the exercises are performed.

Independent. Hand students their own copies of Reproducible 19.1, which lists three of the health-related fitness components with respective examples. Define the term *logo*, and show them some brand, organization, company, and trademark logos. Explain that logos are easily recognized symbols that represent unique products or missions. Their task is to design a logo that captures the spirit of the three components. Encourage them to use different shapes, colors, and easy-to-read text. If the activity proves a too much of challenge for your students, ask them to create a print advertisement instead.

Conclusion

Review the health-related fitness components and ask students to explain the importance of knowing about them. Invite the students to share their logos with the class.

Tips

*   Have the students create a logo for each component

- Have the students identify specific physical activities they plan to do that evening, week, or weekend that builds their cardiovascular endurance, muscular strength, and muscular endurance

IDEA 20: WARM-UP & COOL-DOWN

Rationale

Warming up is a well accepted practice (Bishop, 2003). Essentially, a warm-up increases breathing, blood flow, and temperature, preparing the body for vigorous physical activity (Corbin et al., 2008; American Heart Association, 2006b). Reisser (2006) explains that a warm-up is important to do before any physical activity or exercise because the heart requires lead time to increase its rate. The vascular system also benefits from a warm-up because it has to provide increasing amounts of blood to the muscles, which depend on added oxygen as they are called upon to work harder than usual. A warm-up makes the muscles limber, which reduces the risk that they, and tendons, will be torn if they are suddenly exerted to their limits. Cooling down is also a critical practice that allows the cardiovascular system to gradually slow down to normal breathing and heart rate (President's Council on Physical Fitness, n.d.). Youth need to know the elements of warming up and cooling down so that they begin to make them part of their physical activity routine. Failing to do so overtaxes the cardiovascular system that is likely to fatigue early and overburden the muscles, which places them at risk for injury.

Objectives

After learning about the importance of warming up and cooling down, the students will

- Practice four warm-ups and a cool-down
- Complete Reproducible 18.2 by writing warm-ups and cool-downs for their respective routines

Download and use Reproducible 18.2 for this Idea.

To Motivate the Students

Invite the students to imagine the times they have accompanied their caregivers on a drive. Call on a student or two to report on what the drivers did to prepare for it. Expect answers such as buckling of seat belts, checking the mirrors, inserting the key, and turning on their car. Ask if most of the drivers took off immediately or if they let the car idle before driving and ask students to consider why some drivers allow the car to warm up. Mention that machinery and mechanical equipment often need to be warmed up prior to usage so that they function efficiently. Emphasize that the body also has to be warmed up before engaging in vigorous physical activity.

Frame the Instruction

Inform the students that they will be learning about the importance of including a warm-up and cool-down as part of their physical activity routine.

Step by Step

1. Underscore that it is good practice to warm up before engaging in physical activity. Add that warming up is a safety measure that prepares the cardiovascular system, the muscles, the joints, and the tendons for work. During a warm-up, the muscles become stretched, which makes them pliant and capable of bending readily, making them less susceptible to injury. Moreover, a workout without a warm-up leaves the cardiovascular system exerted because it must supply added oxygen to the muscles as they are called upon to work harder. A warm-up increases the blood flow to the muscles.
2. Explain that warming up before a physical activity or exercise should take 5 to 10 minutes. Warming up can encompass simple measures such as slow walking before running, marching in place, biking on level ground before trekking up steep hills, or simplifying the vigorous activity (U.S. Department of Health and Human Services, 2006a).
3. Visit the National Institute of Health website (http://win.niddk. nih.gov/publications/walking.htm#warmup) and download the e-brochure to show the students four types of warm-up stretches they can do: side reaches, wall push, knee pull, and leg curl. A sketch appears with each stretch with an explanation for how to posture the body and how long to hold each pose prior to repeating the inverse. Advise the students to perform the stretches slowly and to gauge the range of motion their muscles, joints, and tendons will give. The warm-up stretches should be comfortable, smooth, and without bounces.
4. Tell the students that a cool-down is the process of slowing down from a physical activity and that it is just as critical as warming up. Explain that through a cool-down the body gently slows down to allow the cardiovascular system, blood circulation, and breathing to recover and return to normal levels. An abrupt end to a workout can lead to cramping of the muscles, dizziness, and blood pooling (i.e., blood accumulations) in the legs (Bounds et al., 2006). In short, cooling down—like warming up—protects the body from injury. To cool

down, the exertion level is reduced from vigorous to light intensity in the way of slowing down from a run to a walk, slowing down from high-speed biking, stretching for a few minutes after an aerobic dance workout, or phasing the exercise to a gradual stop by way of reversing the events that occurred in the warm-up (Reisser, 2006).

Activities

Guided. Direct the students to open spaces in the classroom. Model the first stretch: side reach. Use the National Institutes of Health link above or conduct an Internet image search to retrieve additional pictures to show them how to position the body. Have the students try the stretch. Remind them to perform the stretch slowly, to the extent that they can, and not to bounce. Model the knee pull, wall push, and leg curl in the same fashion, each for 10 seconds before trying the inverse. (Walls are needed for the wall push). Then take the students outside for vigorous physical activity such as running, jogging, jumping rope, and brisk walking. Allow time for them to cool down.

Independent. Have the students take out Reproducible 18.2. Instruct them to write how they intend to include a warm-up and cool-down as part of their routine.

Conclusion

Invite the students to share the importance of beginning their physical activity routine with a warm-up and concluding with a cool-down.

Tips

- Conduct an Internet search for additional warm-ups and cool-downs for children and share them with the students
- Share images of professional athletes warming-up and cooling-down

IDEA 21: FLEXIBILITY EXERCISES

Rationale

Although children are quite flexible, health experts recommend that they learn exercises to maintain or increase their flexibility (Branner, 1993). Children benefit from such exercises for three primary reasons. First, as they age, their muscles and tendons tighten and become less flexible and their physical range of motion diminishes without the aforementioned exercises (Reisser, 2006). Second, without the knowledge of flexibility, children may learn to perform exercises incorrectly that can cause acute injuries that can lead to chronic maladies, such as cervical, thoracic, lumbar, and vertebral disk injuries (Branner, 1993). Third, because flexibility exercises enhance specific muscles and joints, children begin to understand that relationships exist between specific exercise and their effects on individual parts of the body (Graham, Parker, & Holt/Hale, 2007). As Sears and colleagues (2003) point out, flexibility exercises "improve muscle flexibility, strengthen tendons and ligaments, increase joint mobility, improve body posture and body symmetry, decrease lower back pain, delay muscle fatigue, minimize muscular soreness after activity, decrease stress, and increase blood circulation" (p. 126). In all, learning about flexibility is worthwhile insofar as children can begin to develop this component of fitness, which holds a respective position on the Physical Activity Pyramid.

Objectives

After learning about flexibility exercises, the students will

- Perform some stretches carefully adhering to the associated rules
- Identify flexibility exercises to perform in a week

Download and use Reproducibles 18.1, 18.2, and 21.1 for this Idea.

To Motivate the Students

Prior to the lesson ask the students to bring comfortable, loose clothing to wear for the activity. After they have had time to change into their workout clothes and have convened for the lesson, have them contemplate the purpose of wearing loose clothing. Invite the students to share their thoughts. Show them the FITT Pyramid (Reproducible 18.1) and ask what *flexibility* means and how they currently perform exercises to enhance their flexibility. Remind them that health experts recommend they perform flexibility exercises at the frequency of 2 to 3 times a week. Doing so will keep their muscles elastic, which improves their ability to complete their physical activity routine more effectively and decreases the likelihood of suffering an injury.

Frame the Instruction

Explain that the students will learn how to fulfill the flexibility component of fitness.

Step by Step

1. Indicate that *flexibility* refers to the ability to use joints and their connective tissues (i.e., muscles, tendons, and ligaments) to their potential range of motion. Elaborate that flexibility exercises are similar to stretching exercises that are performed as warms-ups and

cool-downs, but rather than *leading* to physical activity, they *are* the physical activity. Explain that muscles and tendons tend to tighten as they age unless they are regularly stretched (Reisser, 2006). Flexibility exercises, done regularly, lengthen the muscles and over time afford them a greater ability to efficiently maneuver through strenuous situations (Roizen & Oz, 2007). Stress that flexibility is a fitness component, and hence to become fit they have to do exercises that enhance flexibility.

2. Point to the area of the FITT Pyramid that concerns flexibility. Emphasize that it is important to commit to flexibility exercises because they enhance the joints and muscles, tendons, and ligaments, which improves the body's general mobility. Such exercises, which are stretches per se, help maintain or increase the body's range of movement (Branner, 1993). Stress that a limited range of movement may not be an issue for them now because as children they are quite flexible, but as they age the body loses elasticity and limits their mobility. Flexibility exercises also help prevent injuries, such as torn muscles and tendons, and improve body posture, reduce stress, decrease lower back pain, keep the muscles from premature fatigue, and minimize muscle soreness after physical activity (Sears et al., 2003).

3. Tell them that they will learn a type of flexibility exercise known as static stretching. Define *static* by way of comparable concepts such as fixed and stationary, and convey that static stretching is about arranging the body into a specific pose, stretching in that position until tension is felt, and holding it without movement for prescribed time (Branner, 1993). Flexibility is joint specific, which implies that the connective tissues supporting each joint require their own unique stretches to be enhanced. It is feasible that the connective tissues supporting some joints may be more flexible than others. Underscore, however, that there are a few hundred joints throughout the body, and the exercises they learn will increase the flexibility of essential joints and their connective tissues, such as the legs, lower and upper back, and shoulders (Graham et al., 2007).

4. Explain the common rules associated with static stretching: Make static stretches part of the physical activity routine; perform static stretches 2 to 3 times a week; perform slow, relaxed, and focused stretches (Sears et al., 2003); warm up with light exercise before starting the stretch; slowly stretch in a position until tension is felt; hold the stretch for 10 to 30 seconds; breathe slowly, calmly, and comfortably (Reisser, 2006); gradually release stretches; repeat the stretch 2 times; and learn new stretches to add to the collection. (These

rules are found in Reproducible 21.1, which can be displayed as the students engage in the guided activity). Alternate with the caveats never stretch without a warm-up, resist bouncing or jerking while holding the stretch, never rush through the stretches (Reisser, 2006), and avoid stretching to the point of pain.

5. Teach the students specific flexibility exercises. The federal government, through the President's Challenge Physical Activity and Fitness Awards Program, promotes such exercises for children. To download the exercises, visit http://www.presidentschallenge.org/pdf/getfit.pdf and display these for the children to see: neck stretch, reach to the sky, reach back, arm circles, toe touch, twister, knee to chest, butterfly, hurdler's stretch, thigh stretch, calf stretch, child's pose, and cat and camel. Choose as many to teach as time allows, and introduce the remaining in subsequent lessons.

Activities

Guided. Divide the students into pairs and space them around the room. Have them warm up with some light exercises. Teach the stretches one at a time. In pairs, one student performs the stretch while the other ensures that the rules (found on Reproducible 21.1) are carefully followed. The students then alternate so that each has a chance to stretch and monitor. Have the students complete as many stretches as time allows.

Independent. Have the students complete Reproducible 18.2 by identifying the flexibility exercises they would like to perform in a week.

Conclusion

Have the students share their reflections as well as summarize why flexibility exercises are important for their health.

Tips

-   Use a rubber band to simulate how tight, inflexible muscles are more likely to become injured
-   Have the students come up with appropriate times throughout the school day when they could perform stretching exercises

IDEA 22: OVERCOMING EXCUSES

Rationale

As established in earlier chapters, children in the United States lack physical activity in their lives. Many are currently cultivating hard-to-break sedentary habits that will likely transform them into inactive and over-weight adults (Berg, 2004). Data clearly suggest that as youth grow older they become more sedentary. With only a third of children attending PE classes daily, they need support and encouragement to be regularly active outside school (Centers for Disease Control, n.d.a). Youth need 60 minutes of daily physical activity to achieve and maintain physical health, yet, many of them are following short of this recommendation. There are myriad reasons—typically excuses—that stand in the way of their physical activity. To ensure that youth pursue physical activity as recommended, they have to learn to recognize excuses and be able to counter them with productive activities. When they can devote their attention and time to physical activity and recognize it as a way of life, they are in control of their habits and can gracefully keep physical activity destroyers at bay.

Objectives

After learning some of the common excuses associated with physical activity avoidance, the students will

- Advise others how to initiate regular physical activity
- Complete contracts to engage in at least 60 minutes of physical activity per day

Download and use Reproducibles 22.1 and 22.2 for this Idea.

To Motivate the Students

Explain that a recurring message throughout the Ideas has been that it is important for youth to participate regularly in physical activity. Add that sometimes it is difficult to fulfill this recommendation. Hand each student a slip of paper, and instruct all the students to write what keeps them from engaging in daily physical activity, or what had made it challenging to fulfill their pyramid goals (Reproducibles 17.3 and 18.1). As they do, write, "I lack . . ." on the board with these broad categories: *time, energy, ability, knowledge,* and *other* (Discovery Education, 2006). When the students are finished, write their responses under each respective category. Then add your own reasons for not engaging in physical activity.

Frame the Instruction

Tell the students that they will learn how to counter the common reasons (i.e., excuses) that keep persons from engaging in physical activity. Mention that the purpose for learning about excuses is so they can avoid them altogether or learn to deal with them effectively.

Step by Step

1. Reference how some students wrote, "I don't have time." Mention that this is a common reason that people give for not participating in physical activity. Explain how difficult it can be to engage in daily physical activity when they are busy. However, the best approach to counter this excuse is to remember that the 60 minutes does not have to occur at one setting. Hence, they can be active in bouts of physical activity before and after school. They can use their chores as time for physical activity, since cleaning house, walking the dog, raking leaves, and so forth burn calories as well. Stress how it does not take much to become physically active. They just have to think creatively about how to fit it in. Emphasize that 15 minutes of physical activity here and there add up, and this may be a more effective alternative. Another approach to counter this excuse is to plan for physical activity and stick to it faithfully. Some of them will have to negotiate this with their parents and accomodate chores, homework, and errands around planned physical activity.

2. Tell them that some people often believe that they will be made fun of by others for being physically active. Explain that they think they look amusing when they are jumping rope, walking, or skating and they fear that they will be laughed at. In developmentally appropriate language, define the notion of being self-conscious and give examples about how self-consciousness manifests. One approach to counter students' embarrassment is to initiate physical activity indoors, in the backyard, or when no one is around. Also, they can get creative and make opportunities to be active so that it is not readily apparent that their intent is to be physically active. This might include seeking out opportunities to clean house, play music and dance, walk the neighbors' dog or wash their car or rake their yard, walk around the store several times while shopping with their parents, or ask their parents to park farther away from stores' entrance. The students can opt to enlist their friends to participate in group activities. Point out that when two or more students are engaged in physical activity, attention—if there is any—is generally given to the group rather than attention focused on an individual.

3. A strand of similar excuses includes "I just don't like to be physically active," "It's not fun," "I'm not motivated," "I don't know how." Often many persons have these excuses because they regard physical activity as militant, inflexible, hard-core exercises, which is enough to scare any novice away. However, physical activity is not just about push-ups, running, or playing a competitive sport; it is about a wide

range of activities from the moderate to the vigorous. Emphasize that people have many to choose from. They should choose those they enjoy that include lifetime activities (such as golfing, bowling, and fishing) and recreational ones (e.g., tennis, basketball, racquetball). Because there are so many choices, they can vary their physical activity from day to day to keep from getting bored. Alternatively, they can stick to physical activities they like. The important thing is that they get up and move to benefit from physical activity.

4. Another vein of excuses is "It's hard to do physical activity," "It's such a chore," and "I don't have the energy for physical activity." People with these excuses need to realize that physical activity does not have to be difficult. Explain that physical activity is not as hard as some think because they can choose what they want to do, and they can start off in small increments with moderate sorts of activities and progress to more vigorous ones. (Remind them that the 60 minutes does not have to happen at one setting). They should start with activities that leave them feeling good, which should encourage them. After all, as they commit to regular physical activity they will have more energy and find other physical activity easier to pursue. They should also keep in mind the time of day they are engaged in physical activity. They may become quickly disenchanted with physical activity if they have to get up too early or stay up too late, or more important they are exercising when it is too hot or cold outside.

5. Excuses are also masked as procrastination: "I'll do some physical activity tomorrow," "I'll start next week," or "I'll do twice as much on the weekend." Define *procrastinate* with synonyms such as *postpone*, *suspend*, *delay*, and *put off*. Invite the students to share examples of times when they were in procrastinating moods and to explain why. Mention that people often procrastinate participating in physical activity because they think that a later time is the best time. But instead, they keep putting it off. Before long it never happens and the bad habit of inactivity is created. To counter this excuse, the students should ask themselves, "Why wait?" and affirm that the current time is the best time. Having a regular schedule for physical activity helps avoid procrastinating behaviors.

6. Finally, explain how some persons believe that they are exempt from the physical activity recommendation: "I don't have to" or "Why do I have to?" Emphasize that many people do not recognize the importance of physical activity. While some may believe that eating right or being thin is enough for a healthy lifestyle, others may see no wrong with sedentary behaviors. Reinforce that sedentary habits increase the risk of developing a range of diseases. Underscore that it is

a fundamental principle that everyone benefits from physical activity. (Review the material in Idea 16, Physical Activity Is Important, if warranted).

Activities

Guided. Display a copy of Reproducible 22.1. Inform the students that these are excuses that children their age commonly mention. Read each excuse and call on the students to counter with some advice.

Independent. Distribute photocopies of Reproducible 22.2 to each student. Have them read the contract and determine their unique schedules that could fulfill the terms of the contract, at least 60 minutes of physical activity a day. Ask that they review their contracts with their parents to finalize a feasible commitment and to enlist their support. Then, if it is convenient, take the students outside for physical activity of their choice. When they return to the classroom, instruct them to note how they participated in physical activity that day.

Conclusion

Call on students to summarize in their own words the importance of knowing the common excuses that people have for not engaging in physical activity. Invite others to share their contracts with the whole class.

Tips

- Create a class contract for fulfilling as much physical activity as possible during the school day
- Create affirmative reminders that students can place around their homes

---

IDEA 23: MAKE IT FUN

Rationale

It is crucial to teach children to perceive physical activity as fun. Indeed, it is an element of the MyPyramid for Kids campaign "Eat right. Exercise. Have fun" for good reason: If children do not find physical activity fun, they will seek out other options. They will embrace technology without equivocation, yet the ever fascinating TV, video games, computers, and so forth engender sedentary behaviors. The pursuit of physical activity is voluntary. So while most children find physical activity enjoyable, those who do not can easily avoid it. Certainly, children who find it a chore are sensitive about their physical competence, are conscientious about how they look when they are physically active, and have been unsuccessful at organized physical activity view physical activity unfavorably. To counter the skepticism some may have about it and inspire all children to aim for it wholeheartedly, they must learn to explore all kinds of physical activity and choose those that appeal to them most. When they do, they will discover that physical activity can be fun, and they can begin pursuing it.

Objectives

After learning why physical activity should be fun, the students will

- Choose and participate in two physical activities they enjoy most
- Identify six physical activities they find most enjoyable

Download and use Reproducibles 1.4, 23.1, and 23.2 for this Idea.

To Motivate the Students

Share the general activities that you find fun. Explain that you like to pursue your personal interests because they are fun and balance with the stressors in your life. Invite some of the students to share what they find fun. Display MyPyramid for Kids (Reproducible 1.4) and read its maxim, "Eat right. Exercise. Have fun." Underscore that everyone should find physical activities fun. Explain that when people find enjoyment in moving their bodies they will want to partake in physical activity. And when physical activity seems a chore or a bore, they are likely to avoid it.

Frame the Instruction

Explain that in this lesson they will learn the importance of recognizing physical activity as fun and the circumstances that can lead to avoiding it.

Step by Step

1. Underscore that physical activity should be fun. When students think it is boring, is a matter of routine, or leads to exhaustion, or when they do not feel good playing a competitive sport, they lose their enthusiasm for physical activity and begin to avoid it altogether. For this reason, they should seek out physical activities they enjoy and that make them feel good (President's Council on Physical Fitness, n.d.). When they do, they will find it easier to adhere to a routine; they are likelier to increase the frequency and duration of physical activities they love.
2. Explain that they should seek out physical activity that fits their needs. Variety is the key. Encourage them to engage in as many activities as possible and make note of those that interest them most. Ask them to think about physical activities they like to do: in teams

(as in sports), individually, that are moderately intense, in leisure. Display Reproducible 23.1 and review the various types of physical activity there are. Call on students to name their favorite activities. Tell them to vary their physical activities so that they do not tire of repeating them. Point out that they should vary the physical activity by season and companion (e.g., the associate can be a friend, sibling, dog, or parent) (Reisser, 2006; Anspaugh et al., 2006). They can also diverge from these activities by creating alternative ways of playing sports or games to include new rules, roles, and responsibilities for the players.

3. Advise students that other factors can influence the degree to which they like an activity. The time of day (too early or in the blazing sun of midday, for instance), the location (walking at the mall may not be as fun as walking through the park), the temperature (some may not find it fun to play when it is too hot or too cold), the intensity of the activity, and whether they experienced an injury can affect their desire to pursue physical activity again. So that they do not become discouraged with physical activity, recommend that they choose comfortable times and locations that inspire them.

Activities

Guided. Have the students identify two activities from Reproducible 23.1 they like the most. Take them outside for a warm-up. Have them find a partner who, or group that, shares an affinity for the first physical activity they like most. Allow the students 10 minutes to engage in that physical activity. Repeat the process for the second physical activity. Ensure that the students have some time for a cool-down before retreating to the classroom.

Independent. Pass out copies of Reproducible 23.2 to the students. Instruct them to identify the top six activities they like to do most and write each one on the side of the die. After assembling the die accordingly, they can roll it and agree to commit 15 minutes to the activity it lands on. They can roll the die a few more times to plan for 60 minutes of physical activity. If extra dice are warranted (i.e., the students can identify more than six activities), additional copies of the die should be provided. Underscore that they should use the dice to vary their physical activities.

Conclusion

Call on different students to cast their die to determine the physical activities they plan to engage in, and ask them why they chose these activities. Then invite a student or two to summarize why physical activity should be fun.

Tips

- Review Reproducible 23.1 and build consensus over the activities they do not know how to play. Subsequently, find an expert to teach the class how to play or perform the physical activity.
- Use Reproducible 23.2 as a die to vary location, the amount of time spent on each activity, and companion.

IDEA 24: FIND A BUDDY

Rationale

Most children are naturally social and tend to seek out playmates. In this lesson they learn that having a companion while they engage in physical activity can be positive and rewarding. Indeed, there are many reasons why children should have a buddy while they are being physically active. A friend, sibling, parent, or cherished adult can encourage them to stay focused and keep being active physically. Plus, children are likelier to fulfill the recommended amounts of physical activity when they know they are accountable to someone else. Having a companion also makes for a bonding opportunity to talk about facets of life and school, which can make the activity fun and safe. Coupled with the idea that having a social network of friends and family members can reduce the negative health effects of stress (Roizen & Oz, 2007), having a companion during physical activity enhances children's social skills as well as refines their motor skills.

Objectives

After learning about the importance of having a physical activity buddy, the students will

- Identify classmates to serve as their physical activity buddy at school
- Create "wanted" posters that detail the characteristics of a physical activity buddy they seek

Download and use Reproducibles 24.1 and 24.2 for this Idea.

To Motivate the Students

Ask the students to imagine a good friend or trusted adult they like to spend time with. Have them reflect on these questions:

- Who is your friend?
- Why is your friend important to you?

- Why do you like to spend time with your friend?
- What do you like to do with your friend?
- How does your friend support you?

Invite some students to share their answers to these questions.

Frame the Instruction

Mention that they will learn about the importance of having a friend to associate with while they engage in physical activity.

Step by Step

1. Explain that when physical activity is social, it can be more fun. For that reason, they should invite a friend, sibling, parent, guardian, or relative (or group) that will support their physical activity routine. Ask the students to contemplate why it can be beneficial to have a physical activity buddy. Confirm that as companions they can motivate one another. Add that with a buddy's encouragement, they can keep each other focused on fulfilling the daily physical activity requirements. It is seemingly easier to be physically active when they have someone cheering them on. Mention that when they have physical activity buddies, they are accountable to them. That is, it is easier to keep to a routine when they know that someone is relying on them.
2. Emphasize that having a physical activity buddy makes for great opportunity to touch base with each other. Through conversation, they can release some of the stress they have associated with school or home. State that talking out a problem with a buddy can help them see a different point of view and come to a solution all while they are engaged in physical activity. Having a buddy is also beneficial for safety reasons. If one of them becomes seriously injured, the other can get help. And should they confront stranger or bully danger they have someone to confirm their intuitions and advise them to seek a trusting adult.
3. Tell them that they should negotiate with their buddy over the physical activities to do, the length of time to do each, and where to do them. Stress that to be fair, each should have their way sometimes. Advise them to carry on with their physical activity when their buddy is not available for physical activity.

Activities

Guided. Distribute photocopies of Reproducible 24.1 to each student. Have them identify a classroom buddy to write on each hour of the "clock." Take the students outside for a warm-up and physical activity and ask that they bring their "clocks" with them. Select a "time" from the clock and instruct the students to find their corresponding classroom buddy for physical activity. Ask that the two compromise on an activity and reasonable location. After 10 minutes repeat the process. Allow for a cool-down before returning to the classroom.

Independent. Distribute photocopies of Reproducible 24.2 to each student. Have them create a "Wanted" poster that details the characteristics of a buddy they seek to accompany them during their physical activities periods.

Conclusion

Have the students share their posters with the class and identify the friend, sibling, parent, or cherished adult they hope to have as their physical activity buddy.

Tips

- Discuss the buddies in your own life who encourage you to engage in regular physical activity
- Have the students create rules for their physical activity time with their buddy (e.g., take turns cheering each other's efforts)

IDEA 25: RESPONSIBLE BEHAVIOR

Rationale

Many of the physical activities that children seek out include playing with others. Of course, there will be times when they are physically active on their own and other times when they have a companion, but more often than not they will find themselves in situations where they are forced to play with groups of children. So that they get the most out of physical activity and stay encouraged, they should learn personal and social behaviors that enhance cooperative play. Here, children learn to be accountable and responsible for their own behavior and well-being, as well be socially responsible, which implies that they are sensitive to the rights, feelings, well-being, and needs of others (Gallahue & Donnelly, 2003; Graham, Holt/Hale, & Parker, 2009). In fact, there is a National Association for Sport and Physical Education (NASPE) standard assigned to responsible behaviors and the concepts they represent (i.e., respect for others and perspective taking) because they are deemed so critical to the development and maintenance of good health. Children cannot be expected to develop responsible behaviors on their own or merely by playing with others (Rink, 2002). Learning such behaviors has to be planned for, taught, and reinforced and, like any skill, takes time and practice to establish (Pangrazi & Beighle, 2010).

Objectives

After learning about the importance of being personally and social responsible during physical activity, the students will

- Create ground rules for when they are engaged in physical activity with others
- Create a poster that illustrates appropriate and inappropriate behavior during physical activity

To Motivate the Students

Make a t-chart on the board. Ask the students to identify the feelings they experience when they are engaged in physical activity with others who are nice, fair, supportive, and encouraging. Write them on one side of the chart. Invite students to tell what they feel when others are abusive, intimidating, or interruptive, and write their responses on the other side of the chart. After calling on a few students to share their experiences, have them contemplate the repercussions of being in physical activity where one or more children are undisciplined and uncooperative. Confirm that such instances make physical activity seem dreadful, and hence lead many children to avoid it altogether.

Frame the Instruction

Explain that they will learn about the importance of personal and social responsibility when they play with others.

Step by Step

1. Share the four levels of personal and social responsibility that are directly from Don Hellison's (1995) model and well cited through much of the elementary physical education literature: respect, participation, self-direction, and caring. Write these concepts on the board, and explain that learning these values will help them make wise decisions that can lead to a satisfying life (Rink, 2002). Have them create a definition for the term *value*. Confirm that everyone looks forward to playing with others who are courteous, follow rules, treat each other with respect, help out, play fairly, are good sports, and are sensitive to the team's and team member's needs (Graham, Holt/Hale, & Parker, 2004).
2. For Level I, respect, explain that when they are in a physical activity with others they should show respect for the rights and feelings of others (Gallahue & Donnelly, 2003). Ask the students to share how respect is manifested when they are playing with others in structured and unstructured physical activities. Confirm that respecting others is about cooperating, taking turns, helping others participate

successfully, regulating behavior (e.g., no outbursts, no abusive language, no intimidating), contributing positively to the activity and allowing others to do the same, and taking the lead or following when appropriate. Emphasize that teachers, adults, or peers should not have to remind individual students to respect one another. Indicate that respect is also about resolving conflicts in a peaceful, constructive way. To do so, they will have to negotiate their differences through conflict resolution (a process that should be taught separately).

3. For Level II, participation, mention this is about the effort they exert to explore physical activities that are foreign to them. This means learning new games and exercises, working constructively with unfamiliar play and sports equipment, and creating alternative ways of playing traditional games. Stress that often they receive encouragement from adults and peers, but they should endeavor to fashion internal encouragement to explore a wide range of physical activities. Emphasize that they should contemplate what success and defeat means to them. Ask them to identify ways they can graciously handle the two without offending others. Write their responses on the board and remind them not to become preoccupied with winning or losing, but to focus their efforts on playing cooperatively.

4. For Level III, self-direction, explain that this is the ability to behave independently without being reminded to do the right things (e.g., pay attention, carry out the expectations of others, contribute to the greater good of the team, put away play equipment). Introduce the term *self-reliant*, and use age-appropriate examples to expand on the concept. Add that self-direction is also about being assertive and expressing their ideas clearly so that they are successful in fulfilling their needs and accomplishing their goals (Gallahue & Donnelly, 2003). Illustrate that all the behaviors can build their confidence so that they stand up against peer pressure and resist succumbing to behaviors that clash with the spirit of physical activity (e.g., not participating in physical activity because some peers do not like it). To further illustrate self-direction, write these two rules on the board and have the students think about what they mean: "I am responsible for myself, my actions, and my behavior," and "There are always choices to be made; each choice presents either positive or negative consequences" (Graham, Holt/Hale, & Parker, 2004, p. 57).

5. For Level IV, caring, ask the students how this concept manifests in physical activity. Confirm that caring is about helping and supporting others, being empathetic to the feelings and needs of others, and showing sincere concern when others are injured or unhappy. Gallahue and Donnelly (2003) add that caring students "possess interpersonal listening skills, are nonjudgmental, and consistently demonstrate a

wholesome absence of arrogance. They are truly empathetic toward others and strive to make positive contributions to the group or class" (p. 676).

Activities

Guided. Instruct the students to create ground rules (for each of Hellison's levels) for when they are engaged in physical activity with others. Have them write these onto a poster board and sign it as a symbol of contractual commitment. Display the board in a prominent place in the classroom. Take them outside for a warm-up and structured physical activity, and have the children role play responsible personal and social behaviors. Allow for a cool-down before returning to the classroom.

Independent. Have the students choose one of Hellison's levels and make a "Do and Don't" poster illustrating appropriate and inappropriate behavior during physical activity. Hang these on a bulletin board and review them each time before going out for physical activity.

Conclusion

Invite the students to share their posters with the class, and select an ideal place to hang them for others to see.

Tips

- Role play scenarios at each level of Don Hellison's model
- Ask the students to reflect on a time when they did not embody respect, participation, self-direction, and caring, and have them discuss how they could have changed their behavior

---

IDEA 26: HYDRATE WITH WATER

Rationale

Most children understand that they cannot live without water. But these days, children have tempting alternatives to water—typically sodas—which they often choose to quench their thirst. Children need to learn that drinking water regularly, especially since they are becoming increasingly physically active, is essential to a healthy body. Staying hydrated with water is advantageous for many reasons. For starters, drinking adequate amounts of water maintains bodily fluid balance, organ function, and blood viscosity, which allows for the effective transport of nutrients. And because the body loses water by way of sweating, breathing, and waste discharge, drinking water prevents dehydration. A dehydrated body can make a person feel sick and perform poorly. The body needs several glasses of water a day, and more when it is physically active. Some health experts claim that 8 glasses of water a day is sufficient and others claim that 15 cups is better, but there is no magic number as the "right" amount varies by activity level, gender, and size (Roizen & Oz, 2007). Children should be encouraged to drink water prior to, during, and at the end of their physical activity (Kidshealth.org, 2009). Learning to drink water regularly helps children establish an excellent lifetime habit (Dalton, 2004).

Objectives

After learning about the importance of drinking water to keep hydrated, the students will

- Identify the need for drinking before, during, and after physical activity
- Create a company logo and label design for a water bottle using at least one health benefit as the promo

To Motivate the Students

Ask the students to identify times throughout the day when they are most thirsty. Call on others to speculate why people have an inherent thirst periodically and why is it important to drink when we are thirsty. Ask what they reach for when they are thirsty. Have them reflect from the lesson on snacks and beverages (Idea 8) and recall what the ideal thirst quencher is and what they know about water thus far.

Frame the Instruction

Inform the students that they will be learning why it is important to keep hydrated, especially while they are engaged in physical activity. It is expected that the reasons will compel them to make water the beverage of choice.

Step by Step

1. Explain that water is vital to life and that no living organism can survive without it (Alpert, 2005). Without water, humans can live only for a few days. Note that water is essential in the body, as nearly 60% of it is water (Bounds et al., 2006). Some estimate that the body loses about 2.5 quarts of water a day from sweat, breathing, urinating, and bowel movements; hence it is important to replace fluid loss by drinking water throughout the day (Baird et al., 2006).
2. Underscore that there are many benefits to drinking water. Have the students contemplate what these might be and write their answers on the board. Inform them that water keeps the body healthy by

keeping a fluid balance in the body, which helps with digestion, dissolving and transporting nutrients throughout the body by way of blood, flushing out toxins and waste, maintaining regularity and relieving constipation, regulating body temperature, preventing kidney stones, lubricating and cushioning joints, boosting concentration, and maintaining muscle tone. Remind students that water is also an appetite suppressant.

3. Tell the students that drinking water is particularly critical because it prevents dehydration. Ask the students to define *dehydration* and confirm that it means that the amount of fluids (i.e., water) in the body is low, which occurs when water loss is not replaced. While mild degrees of dehydration are rarely detected, significant dehydration could leave a person tiring easily and not performing well; having poor concentration (the brain relies on water); and feeling sick (i.e., becoming constipated, experiencing headaches). All organs and parts of the body rely heavily on water to function accordingly. Hydration should be a continuous process (Bounds et al., 2006), especially whenever children are engaged in physical activity.

4. Most health experts, among them staff at the Mayo Clinic, recommend that adults consume eight 8-ounce glasses of water on a daily basis (MayoClinic.com, 2010). However, there is no recommended amount of water for children to drink daily. The rule of thumb is that they should drink water whenever they are thirsty and before, during and after physical activity, especially in warm and humid climates (Kidshealth.org, 2009). Tell them that relying on their thirst when they are physically active is not always a good idea because in those times thirst is poor gauge of dehydration (American College of Sports Medicine, n.d.). Remind students that many vegetables and fruits contain a significant amount of water (see Idea 4) and that they can reach for water alternatives, but plain water is the better choice. Water is considered the foremost thirst quencher and hydrates the body the best (Thompson & Shanley, 2004).

Activities

Guided. Take the students outside for a warm-up, two 10 minute physical activities (of their choice), and a cool-down. Ask that they bring a water bottle with them. Stop at the water fountain and ensure that everyone has a drink. Instruct them to drink from their water bottles between the two activities and at the end of cool-down. Call on a student or two throughout this whole process to identify the need for drinking before, during, and after physical activity.

Independent. Prior to the lesson, have the students bring a water bottle to class. Instruct them to create a company logo and design for their water bottle, using at least one health benefit as their promo. Provide each student with a self-adhesive label and ask them to attach it to their water bottle.

Conclusion

Invite the students to share their water bottle designs and logo, and call on some students to summarize critical aspects associated with drinking water.

Tips

- Display the nutrition facts labels for beverages and compare these to water
- Have the students research flavored water and sports drinks and evaluate their benefits

IDEA 27: LIMIT TELEVISION TIME

Rationale

In this country, watching television is a favorite pastime, especially among children. And children today spend a lot of time in front of the screen (e.g., playing on the computer, watching DVDs, and playing video games). Youth spend more time watching television each year than they spend in school, and more combined time in front of a screen than anything else besides sleeping (Gelbard, 2006). Statistics reveal that one out of three children watch 3 or more hours of TV a day (Centers for Disease Control, 2010b; Dalton, 2004). The amount of time spent in front of a screen increases to 4 hours (and 15 minutes) when videos and DVDs are introduced and up to 6 hours when computers and video games are factored in (Hersey & Jordan, 2007). Such news makes for a simple axiom: The more time that children spend in front of the screen, the less time they have for physical activity. Indeed, this is a concern because research further suggests that the more TV a child watches, the likelier it is that he or she will be overweight. In fact, Anspaugh and colleagues (2006) have noted that "the risk for obesity increases 23% for each 2-hour increment in daily TV watching" (p. 252). It is no surprise that limiting the amount of television children watch to 2 hours or less (American Academy of Pediatrics, 2001a) and replacing sedentary activities (such as video game playing) with physical activities (U.S. Department of Health and Human Services, 2005b) are two leading enterprises that seek to improve children's health. Here, the students learn to cut down on television viewing and opt for physical activity.

Objectives

After learning about the importance of limiting their television watching, the students will

- Brainstorm ways to limit the amount of television they watch
- Create a list of the independent and group physical activities they will do instead of watching television

Download and use Reproducible 27.1 for this Idea.

To Motivate the Students

To spark a discussion about their television viewing habits, ask the students to contemplate the amount of time they spent watching TV (in minutes and hours) the day before the lesson. Instruct them to then calculate the amount of time they spent on the computer (using software or surfing the Internet) and playing video games. After an appropriate response time, invite a few students to share their amounts. Express that health experts agree that television viewing should be limited to 2 hours a day and that physical activity be pursued instead. Ask the students to contemplate why.

Frame the Instruction

Explain that they are going to learn about the importance of limiting the amount of time they spend watching television.

Step by Step

1. Emphasize that most children across the nation watch excessive amounts of television. While the average child spends about 3 hours watching television, some watch even more. Mention that some children spend more time watching television in 1 year than they spend at school (Cheung et al., 2007) and more time in front of a screen than they spend on anything else except sleeping (Gelbard, 2006). This is particularly harmful to their health because they move very little during this time. Explain that health experts report that almost any other activity expends more energy (i.e., burns calories) than watching television, and that no other activity burns fewer calories than watching television (Kaiser Family Foundation, 2004). This time watching television is time they could spend in physical activity. Define the term *sedentary* (getting little exercise) and affirm that too much time engaged in sedentary activities can be harmful to their health. In fact, the more television they watch, the more likely it is they will gain weight (Cheung et al., 2007; Dalton, 2004; National Institutes of Health, 2007a).

2. Assert that there are three concerning matters that occur when they watch too much television. First, as mentioned above, the more time they are in front of a screen is less time they are being physically active and burning calories. Second, not only do they burn few calories watching television, they may consume more because there is a tendency to snack excessively on nutrient-inferior foods while watching television (Kaiser Family Foundation, 2004). Explain that some studies have found that the average child eats 600 calories while munching in front of the television (Rimm, 2004). Third, they are exposed to about 40,000 television ads a year, most of which are for food products (Dalton, 2004). The commercials that dominate the airwaves are for tasty—albeit nutritionally poor—foods, such as fast and junk foods (Anspaugh et al., 2006). Mention that television viewing is associated with making unhealthy food choices, which could be attributed to the commercials that seek to stimulate their appetite for them.

3. Discourage the children from watching too much television. Ask that they work toward watching 1 to 2 hours a day at most, and if they do not have favorite programs, not watch any television at all. Encourage them to choose physical activities instead. Emphasize that when the television is off, they increase the likelihood that they will become physically active. To that end, they should have in mind some physical activity alternatives. Mention that limiting the amount of television they watch will have a positive effect on their health. Some studies have found that children who managed their television-viewing habits had less body fat than children who watched more television (Dalton, 2004). For the students who have a difficult time accepting these 2-hour limits, have them consider ways to slowly reduce the amount of television they watch and set initial limits they find acceptable.

Activities

Guided. Divide the students into groups and instruct them to brainstorm ways they can avoid the television (e.g., have a parent hide the remote, choose a physical activity before turning on the television, plan for a physical activity with a friend immediately after school). Record their answers on the board.

Independent. Distribute Reproducible 27.1 and have the students create a list of the independent and group physical activities they can pursue instead of watching television.

Conclusion

Invite the students to share what they plan to do instead of watching television. Call on one or two students to summarize what they learned.

Tips

- Divide them into pairs and have them negotiate the shows they could stop watching
- Have them create and sign a classroom pledge to limit the amount of television they watch to 1 to 2 hours

---

IDEA 28: MAKING AND TRACKING GOALS

Rationale

Having children change their sedentary ways can be difficult, especially when they have no goals or self-monitoring tools in effect to guide them. Making and tracking physical activity goals is one way to help them think about and plan to work toward specific habits. In fact, most health experts agree that doing so is an important step in starting a fitness program (President's Council on Physical Fitness, n.d.). Teaching children to make and track physical activity goals helps them make realistic goals that meet federal recommendations, anticipate and circumvent their challenges in accomplishing their goals, monitor their progress and adjust accordingly if warranted, and become accountable to self-initiated goals. It also helps their caregivers strategize on how to support their efforts. Here, the students learn to make and track physical activity goals according to the SMART principles (described in Idea 15), and to call to mind that being physical active is an enjoyable process toward healthy living.

Objectives

After learning about the importance of making and tracking physical activity goals, the students will

- Choose a self-monitoring tool to keep track of meeting their goals
- Write two goals (according to the SMART principles) they would like to achieve and track their progress

Download and use Reproducibles 28.1–28.3 for this Idea.

To Motivate the Students

Underscore that all the lessons they have completed thus far have invited them to commit to physical activity. Now, they will begin using what they have learned to set goals that can generate behavioral changes, which could last a lifetime and lead to healthy living. Ask the students to volunteer some of the information on physical activity that they have learned thus far. Record their answers on the board. If they do not mention these aspects, remind them to be active every day, not to force themselves to the point of discouragement, to choose activities they enjoy and vary them according to the FITT principles, to aim for 60 minutes of physical activity a day, and to find a friend to be accompany them during their physically activity. Explain that if they have not yet achieved some of these behaviors, having a physical activity goal or two can help.

Frame the Instruction

Tell the students that they are going to learn about making physical activity goals and self-monitoring practices.

Step by Step

1. Emphasize that sedentary behaviors are bad habits, which can be difficult to change. Explain that making and tracking physical activity goals can help alter specific sedentary habits. To that end, physical activity goals (i.e., goals that are aimed at increasing and maintaining physical activity behaviors), especially those that are written, obligate persons to regularly reexamine them, which engenders behavioral change. The goals hold people accountable to their intentions. Tell them that written physical activity goals will help them consider and work toward meeting recommended levels of physical activity, anticipate and plan to overcome obstacles and challenges associated with having a physical activity routine, and adjust their goals when they are too lofty or effortless to achieve.

2. Express that selecting the right goal is a critical first step (U.S. Department of Health and Human Services, 2005a). Indeed, it is easier to make and plan for a physical activity goal when they have carefully considered habits they would like to alter or adopt. Second, they should focus on two or three specific behaviors they would like to target; these will evolve into goals. Convey that too many goals can be overwhelming, seem insurmountable, and influence the likelihood that they will not be achieved. Many people, unfortunately, assume the attitude, "With too many goals to accomplish, why bother trying?" Remind them that their goal is self-initiated, which implies that they will construct their goals based on their unique situations and circumstances, and control—by way of their decisive actions—whether their goal is fulfilled. Encourage the students to make a genuine audit of their lives to determine how to make their lives healthier as only they know how.

3. The next step is to construct the goals and write them down. Effective goals are those that follow the SMART goals principle, which is discussed in Idea 15. The acronym SMART represents goals that are specific, measurable, attainable, realistic, and timely. These five tenets, which can be recorded on the board, ensure that the goals are reasonable and reachable. Review each of them with physical activity as the foreground. *S*, which stands for *specific*, indicates that the goal is not vague or general. "I will not watch as much TV," "I will be more physically active," are not specific; "I will only watch an hour a TV per weekday," "I will be physically active for 30 minutes when I get home from school," are goals that are. *M* represents *measurable*. The students should construct goals that can be easily determined whether they were reached (e.g., "Yes, I walked for 30 minutes today," or "No, I watched more TV than I said I would"). A checkmark or similar mark in a daily journal, for instance, could be used to discern that the goal was fulfilled, *A* stands for *attainable*, for example. The goals should not be too grandiose: "I will exercise for 4 hours every day," "I will never watch TV again," and "I will join every sport this school offers," are nearly impossible to achieve. A youth is more likely to fulfill goals such as "I will be physically active for an hour and half on the weekends," "I will limit my screen time to 2 hours a day," and "I will explore organized sports that offered at school." The goals should also be *realistic*, which is represented by way of the letter *R*. They should not be too easy or insignificant (e.g., "I will walk faster") or too difficult (e.g., "Every day I will run for a continuous hour"). Finally, *T* stands for *timely*. The goal should be meaningful at the present time and take into account their current needs within the context of all the recommendations that have been presented thus far.

4. After constructing their goals and writing them down, motivate the students to wholeheartedly commit to fulfilling them to realize healthy changes. In fact, they should regard these goals as the path to fitness. At this point, they should consider the possible challenges to achieving their goals and approaches to effectively dealing with them. Ask the students to reflect on some of the goals they are considering and have them name their roadblocks. Record some of these on the board and brainstorm strategies to overcome them. Affirm that quite often unexpected circumstances will thwart their efforts, but they should not be discouraged (American Heart Association, 2010). Instead, they should acknowledge these as minor setbacks and decide on how to deal with them or adapt their goals so they take reasonable effect within their confines.

5. Inform them that tracking their physical activity goals (i.e., recording how they are meeting their goals) is another important step. Explain that this is called self-monitoring, which is observing and recording specific behaviors (U.S. Department of Health and Human Services, 2005a). Self-monitoring affords the students the opportunity to reflect on their progress and appraise how well the goal is achieved. Self-monitoring also serves as an indirect motivator because seeing a goal being fulfilled can encourage people to forge ahead, especially when the benefits are readily apparent (i.e., feeling good, becoming fit). Point out that it can be rewarding to see progress, and once goals are fulfilled they are considered habits and new goals can be made. Mention that they can keep track of meeting their physical activity goals by recording their behaviors each day (or week) in a journal, where they write a narrative of what they accomplished (Reproducible 28.1); an activity log, where they check off how they fulfilled their goals and write brief statements about what they did, the length of time, and how they felt (Reproducible 28.2); or calendar, where they check off on corresponding days when they fulfilled their goals (Reproducible 28.3). Show the students the three reproducibles and indicate that they should choose the one of their liking.

Activities

Guided. Divide the students into small groups. Have them contemplate some of their sedentary habits and discuss two physical activity goals they would like to consider. Distribute a copy of each reproducible to each group. Have the students examine the three, evaluate the benefits and disadvantages of each, and choose one they would like to try to keep track of meeting their goals.

Independent. Distribute a copy of a reproducible to the students. Have them write two goals (according to the SMART principles) they would like to achieve and track their progress toward making the goal a behavior.

Conclusion

Invite the students to share their goals. As a class, brainstorm ways they can be encouraged to fulfill them. Request that they show the goals to their parents, family, and friends so that they can be supported in their efforts. After a few days or so, have them comment on their progress. Ask questions focused on their self-monitoring practice, such as "How well are you meeting your goals?" "What seems to be working?" "What effect is this having on you?" "What changes will you make to ensure that you meet your goals?" For the students who have not been successful in fulfilling their goals, ask the class for suggestions to help them overcome their challenges. Allow opportunities for the students to rewrite their goals.

Tips

- Visit and encourage the students to use online interactive tracking tools such as
  http://aom3.americaonthemove.org/get-active/activity-tools.aspx
  http://www.presidentschallenge.org/activity_log/index.aspx
  http://www.mypyramidtracker.gov/
- Construct two physical activities goals for the class (according to the SMART principle) and strategize how to best track their progress

Part IV

BEYOND THE CLASSROOM: THE SCHOOL AND COMMUNITY AS CHANNELS FOR PROMOTING HEALTH

CHAPTER 7

School and Community Collaboration

By now, it is apparent that the two sets of Ideas (found in Chapters 4 and 6) were designed to be delivered in a classroom setting and the respective knowledge and skills reinforced in forums such as the cafeteria, gym, home, or recreation areas. Lacking is the additional support youth could receive by way of school and community initiatives that also espouse the message that health is a worthy lifelong pursuit. Presented in this chapter are a number of ideas designed to further encourage children to pursue healthy dietary and physical activity practices. These ideas can be accomplished on a broader scale outside the classroom: the school level, and with its support, the local community. After all, it can be difficult to convince children to alter their habits when they only have one source—the teacher—relaying the message that these practices are significant to their health and well-being. When the message is resounding and children witness their whole learning community embracing a genuine pursuit of health, they will be more inclined to change.

This chapter is about ideas for involving the whole community. The discussion is presented in two sections:

- Preparation for Action
- Ideas for School and Community Collaboration

PREPARATION FOR ACTION

While the Ideas presented in Chapters 4 and 6 were designed to be delivered in the classroom and comparable settings, school- and community-wide activities should also be considered to help children develop habits that positively contribute to health. When health is promoted often through a variety of means, settings, and people, children begin to consider it an important—and rewarding—pursuit. Prior to exploring how schools and local communities can encourage children's strides toward better health, however, oblige this discussion to shift to some general matters that can help actualize the very activities that support the Ideas. These matters are not arranged in particular order of importance or implementation, but they should be a prelude to the activities that follow in the next section.

Build Support

Spearheading any initiative, without a support network, can be arduous. To mitigate serving as the lone driving force, it is important to attract and convene a team of colleagues as allies to help convince the leadership staff, faculty, and PTA that routinely promoting health at the school level is a good idea. A team of professionals (including parents and community members) offers diverse skills and backgrounds and can set forth a clear agenda and see it through the multiple steps of what can be an extensive process. The advantage herein is that each member can assume specific assignments that capitalize on their strengths and can spread the message—that the initiative is paramount—to a wider audience. If the team becomes larger than expected, subcommittees can be organized to work toward more specific kinds of tasks.

The team's primary responsibility is to assure the leadership staff, faculty, and PTA that children's development of healthy dietary and routine physical activity practices can be enhanced when they receive increased exposure to the benefits of health. This can be accomplished any number of ways, such as

- Meeting with them directly and providing an outline of the latest statistics and figures associated with childhood health and obesity (many of these can be taken from Chapters 1 and 2 and can also be retrieved by way of an Internet search);
- Providing them with journal and news articles or brochures to read about childhood health or obesity;
- Sharing what other schools and PTAs are doing to promote health apart from classroom instruction;
- Sharing the federal recommendations for school-level initiatives (see the websites of the Department of Health and Human Services, the Centers for Diseases Control, and the Department of Agriculture).

Each team member can also earn support and commitment for this initiative by influencing their mutual acquaintances.

Keep in mind that the leadership staff and faculty are likely to be wary of supporting another initiative because they have the heavy burden of increasing or maintaining the school's standardized test scores. Indeed, many teachers already feel overwhelmed with their daily responsibilities. Most understand, however, that if children's health is on the line and that guiding them to engage in good health practices leads to a finer quality of life, they will recognize that the initiative needs their support. What will help the team build support is that this is a local school personnel-driven initiative, and because it is not a district directive, it will be easier to attract the support and commitment of the leadership staff and faculty. In short, the school personnel (and PTA) will have ownership of this health initiative and can come to decide how to carry out activities to meet the unique needs of their learning community. The disadvantage is that without the district authority there are destined to be personnel who will avoid the initiative altogether. In such cases, convey that millions of Americans aspire for health throughout life (Reisser, 2006). In this country, most parents nurture the health of the fetus and maintain comparable care to protect their children's health through their development into young adulthood. Thereafter, most adults aim for it until the time of death. A school-level initiative is just one way to ensure that future generations have the knowledge and skills to improve and maintain their health through life.

Involve Parents

Because the PTA can be immensely resourceful, it should be involved with any initiative that the school personnel seek to materialize. The PTA holds a pool of potential volunteers, fund-raisers, skilled professionals, and members who can campaign a health agenda. Some PTAs are so commanding they may want to launch their own health-focused projects. Keep in mind, though, that not all parents are members of the PTA, but most have an interest in participating in endeavors that promote children's health. Some parents may want to be involved directly (e.g., volunteering their time) or indirectly (e.g., speaking to their children about healthy dietary practices) with the school's health initiative.

For that reason, all parents should receive regular notice of what is happening on campus (related to the initiative), what activities their children can expect in and outside the classroom, and a calendar of important events. Consider sending home weekly newsletters that inform parents how to promote healthy eating and physical activity at home. It can include information about why childhood health is essential with specific ideas they can enforce when children are in their care. A simple one-page note or pamphlet, such as the play pledge found in Figure 7.1, reminds parents that their children's health deserves their persistent attention. Such missives can have far-reaching effects because parents can see to it that their children eat healthier and spend some of their free time engaged in physical activity, and they may inspire other parents with the advances in health their children are making.

FIGURE 7.1. The Voice of Play, Play Pledge

Source. Voice of Play (2010). *Play pledge.* Retrieved May 14, 2010, from http://www. voiceofplay.org/public/uploads/playpledge.pdf. Reprinted with permission.

Collaborate with Community Businesses and Organizations

Teaming up with others outside of school can advance efforts to help youth and adults understand that health is a valuable asset. Children begin to see that even community individuals—through their own campaigns—are champions of health. Consider these sorts of community establishments that can create alliances of people who can further the cause:

- National health organizations that have local affiliates, such as the American Heart Association, the American Diabetes Association, and the American Stroke Association often offer free brochures or discounted books that promote a healthy lifestyle, as well as representatives who can talk about matters closely associated with their affairs;
- Local clubs whose mission is focused on health, like a running club, or a biking club;

- National, state and local parks representatives who could talk about innovative uses of their grounds;
- Businesses, such as grocers or other types of stores, that can sponsor (e.g., financially or in-kind contributions such as space) school events;
- Schools (middle and high, community college and university) that can recruit potential student volunteers and could co-sponsor an event;
- Public libraries that can create a display of their resources on healthy eating or exercise, sponsor a viewing of a documentary on health, or allow use of their bulletin board to post health information or children's work; and
- Civic organizations, such as the Junior League, the Chamber of Commerce, food banks, Women's Club, and Lion's Club that aim to improve communities through their volunteer efforts.

Remember that professionals whose career is promoting health, such as physicians, nurses, and dieticians; teachers and college professors who teach and write about the subject; university extension program agents; and gym owners or physical trainers are also a pool of potential collaborators.

Create Health Goals and Objectives for the School

At some point, assemble the team of collaborators to compose an overarching mission for the school that provides the knowledge and skills associated with healthy dietary and physical activity practices to children. The mission statement should be broad enough so that the team and advocates can articulate it with ease (e.g., "We believe our children need perpetual affirming information on diet and physical activity that is developmentally appropriate"). Then, follow with goals and subsequent objectives, which can guide the team to fulfill the mission statement (e.g., Goal 1: Children will learn about the food groups represented in MyPyramid; Objective A: Children will learn about the benefits of eating varied fruits; Objective B: Children will learn the recommended amounts of food to consume; and so forth).

School districts already have wellness policies (as mandated by the Child Nutrition and WIC Reauthorization Act of 2004) in effect that explain how they are committed to promoting and protecting children's health, but often they are expansive—as they should be—and cover matters such as the qualifications of the food service staff and food marketing in schools. But the mission statement, goals, and objectives, which should reflect the district's wellness policy, are more aligned with the unique needs of the school and are the very base of the eventual schoolwide activities that promote change in the way children eat and exercise. Consider posting the mission statement or goals in high-traffic areas, especially in areas such as the cafeteria and the gym, where they can readily be seen by children and adults alike.

In all, the environment should be one that promotes health, not detracts from it. So that this is a consistent mantra and provided that there are no contractual or regulatory restraints, make sure that the vending machines are stocked with healthy options, not nutrient-inferior ones; remove fast food and soft drink logos from campus advertising, unless they promote healthy products; teachers do not take away recess or make children sit out from PE as a form of punishment for improper behavior; and children do not receive nutritionally inferior snacks at classroom parties or as rewards for good behaviors. Children should not have to reconcile these sorts of mixed messages.

Focus on Children

Be sure that the health initiative is child centered and that all the activities are intended to improve their health in meaningful and challenging ways. Whatever activities are planned should be developmentally appropriate. That is, they are not so simple that the students become bored, or so complex and demanding that students are left discouraged. The goal is that they have fun with the activities (so that they recognize that health is affirming) as they gain knowledge and skills they can practice in settings apart from the school and the classroom. Do not allow the students to act as passive participants and expect them to subtly learn the information. Instead, make certain that they are actively processing it (e.g., making snacks, exercising).

To ensure that the activities are fun and stimulate active participation, consider sampling children to determine how they want to learn about dietary practices and physical activity. With adult guidance, they, too, should be involved in the design of the initiative that seeks to serve them. Children who enjoy the activities are likely to become avid supporters of the initiative and enthusiastically spread the message that health is worthy of pursuit. Finally, think of ways to celebrate children's successes. Collaborate with others to create a forum that rewards children who embrace health and promotes the strides they are making.

Assess What the School Can Offer

A useful starting point is to assess what the school can offer the students. In other words, take a careful inventory of the school's environment, financial resources, and personnel and how these combined can be used to actualize the activities. The physical sites that can be used to carry out some of the activities include the cafeteria, gym, open and sport-specific fields (such as baseball or football), playgrounds, and other flat, open areas (paved or otherwise) where group exercises, games, and sports can be performed.

In the cafeteria, determine whether posters or other promotional literature can be displayed to reinforce messages of healthy dietary practices. Also, evaluate the feasibility of the cafeteria service, including the preparation and selling of healthy snacks (in addition to government-supplied meals) instead of offering ice cream, cookies, or pastries, which have become standard in many school cafeterias. Explore whether a salad bar or deli can be created so that children who can and want to choose healthy à la carte items can do so. The logistics associated with their operation would have to be considered as well, including whether there is sufficient physical space; personnel to supervise the entire process (including a staff to create the items, stock the supplies, and generate guidelines for the children and their parents); and funding to sustain their indefinite enterprise without compromising taste and food items, charging outrageous prices, or digging in to the school budget.

This is a good time to think about the actual times that lunch is served to children. Aim to avoid feeding children too early (because they will be hungry when they get home and may oversnack if a meal is not ready for them), or too late (because they may be very hungry by lunchtime and hence eat rapidly and as much as they can), or rushing them through the dining experience (they may develop the habit of eating fast).

In terms of the gym and the flat, open spaces, survey whether there is ample space for the children to run and play safely. Although this kind of assessment has likely been performed by the PE teachers and district administrators in the past, it is a good idea to gauge how to configure teams of students simultaneously playing games or exercising and to decide on how many adults are needed to appropriately supervise the children. Make note of how well groups of students can safely play inside and outside concurrently, as well as indicate how groups of children could play while gym classes are being held. An inspection of the fields should follow. There should be no unstable ground or hazardous trash on the open field, and the sports fields should be functional and attractive so that children are encouraged to use them. Also, contemplate how the gym, the fields, and the playground could be used after school or on the weekends without draining the school's finances. Then, with permission of the PE teachers, take inventory of the equipment they would allow the children to use for playing games and sports. In the event that a school has no outdoor space, find the nearest parks and playgrounds, and determine if they are feasible for use by the schoolchildren. A city's department of parks and recreation website can help locate these outdoor spaces. In some instances, another school may have outdoor space that can be shared. If these spaces are convenient for regular visits, consider partnering with the school (or department of parks and recreation) and use the space often. If such a collaboration is not possible, inform parents of the location of the nearest public parks and playgrounds and remind them that outdoor spaces are excellent settings for children to be physically active.

The next piece worth appraising is the school's human resource capital, which is about exploring the strengths and talents of the teachers, the administrative staff, and the PTA. Here, seek to determine who can, and more important, wants to

- Teach children, their parents, or both how to prepare healthy snacks or cook healthy meals;
- Create professional-looking posters for the cafeteria and hallways and literature for schoolwide distribution;
- Teach children how to play specific sports and games or how to swim;
- Teach children martial arts or yoga;
- Teach an age-appropriate dance class;
- Start and manage an after-school or weekend Little League;
- Find sponsors for the Little League;
- Lend their personal sports equipment when there is short supply;
- Volunteer their after-school time or Saturday mornings to open up the gym and playground and supervise the children; and
- Enlist the help of local high school or colleges students or organizations like the Junior League, the American Heart Association, and university extension programs.

The third piece in this informal audit deals with the financial resources that may be available to support the proposed activities. More often than not, expect limited funding because a school's budget is generally fixed, with most funds allocated for the expenses associated with curriculum and instruction. However, this does not suggest that there are no funds whatsoever. So consider a thorough check of the school budget, which may reveal line items to tap or available funding at the district level. Private organizations and community donors might also prove worth a probe. Foundations like the Robert Wood Johnson Foundation, and insurance companies like Blue Cross Blue Shield, often award grants (through a call for proposals) for schools to fund special projects that promote health. Fund-raising is also an option; just avoid having the children sell candy, baked goods, and so forth unless they are healthy alternatives. Inform the children how the funds will be used and the equipment that will be purchased so that they know what they are working for. This, too, is an opportunity to promote the message that health is important—so important, in fact, that they are raising money to ensure its fixed position in their learning community. Last, consider asking the site-based management committee and the PTA to allocate funds for healthy eating and physical activity sorts of enterprises.

Explore What Others Are Doing

Take the opportunity to check out what other schools are doing to promote health. There are creative school programs across the country that seek to motivate children to develop good dietary and physical activity practices, but they may not be readily promoted. A little research could unveil an efficient program or two. For example, one private school in South Texas inspired its students to be physically active while at home. In the "Mi Vida Challenge," the students were asked to document the amount of physical activity they had each month. Prizes were then awarded to the students or their classrooms with the most amount of participation (St. Anthony Catholic School, n.d.). Such a program could be easily adapted so that it is suitable for your population of students. In like manner, conduct an Internet search of schools, including community colleges and universities, to identify how their sponsored projects or annual health fairs operate and how they collaborate with others to stimulate their community's quest for health and wellness. The results of the search may prove incompatible with the conditions of your own school; therefore, some consideration will have to given to how the ideas could be modified to best meet your school's needs. Remember to explore the kinds of health expos local grocers, pharmacies, medical clinics, and so forth have and take note of what can be learned from them. Also, look into how organization-sponsored annual marathons—such as Hoop It Up, walkathons, bike marathons (or bike rodeos), and dance marathons— could be adapted for children. Collect as much information as possible, including digital photos and videotapes (of visited sites), so that it can be shared with the team, leadership staff, and faculty.

Encourage the Leadership Staff and Faculty to Become Fit

Find ways to spark teachers' interest in improving their personal health. Because one out of three adults in this country carries excess weight, there are likely to be adults in the learning community who could benefit from adopting healthier dietary practices and a routine that includes physical activity. The adults can also enjoy the benefits of improved health when they intentionally alter the way they eat and exercise. Of course, some adults will trivialize this health initiative, but some will gladly receive it.

Consider sponsoring activities to attract those like-minded adults, such as convening a Weight Watchers group that meets regularly on campus, creating a club that either walks on the track and field or meets for a daily aerobic or dance class, having a party or luncheon where all of the potluck dishes are healthy alternatives, drafting volunteers to prepare a healthy dish or snack that can be sampled at faculty meetings or throughout the day in the lounge, exploring whether a commercial gym would offer discounted rates for groups of teachers or if the nearest high school would avail their exercise equipment and gym for use, and creating a bulletin board that celebrates the success stories of teachers becoming fit. When the adults become health conscious and fit, they become exemplars who can inspire children and adults alike.

Promote Healthy Eating and Physical Activity Often

The pursuit of healthy eating and regular physical activity habits should be a crusade at school. Think about promoting this message through visuals such as posters in the cafeteria, gym, hallways, and where children and their parents congregate, or through bulletin boards that display children's work on health and physical activity matters (the final products in many of the Ideas can be used). Also, consider the morning announcements (perhaps have the children create a commercial to broadcast) or school/class newsletters to include a health tip for the day or week, praise of children who are improving their health through deliberate change of habits, and encouraging invitations to health fairs (focused on diet or physical activity) in the community. At some point, a team of teachers should convene to explore how diet and exercise could be addressed to meet content area standards for each grade level.

Insist That Children Have Recess and Opportunities for Free Play at School

There are few better ways to promote physical activity than to include it in children's school routine. These days, because such importance is placed on improving students' standardized test scores, recess and other time allotted for free play are often cut to make time for added instruction. It also seems that some teachers (and administrators) mistakenly believe that is good classroom management to take away recess from children who misbehave. Research, however, supports otherwise: Play is crucial for social, emotional, and cognitive development (Wenner, 2009). It is so important, in fact, that the United Nations High Commission for Human Rights recognizes play as a right of children (Ginsburg, 2007). Ginsburg noted, "Encouraging unstructured play may be an exceptional way to increase physical activity levels in children, which is one important strategy in the resolution of the obesity epidemic" (p. 183). Indeed, children expend calories when they play; as Mayo Clinic (2008) childhood obesity experts point out, "Free play activities, such as playing hide-and-seek, tag, or jump-rope, can be great for burning calories and improving fitness" (cited in Alliance for Childhood, 2010, p. 2). Voice of Play (n.d.) further underscores, "Research has shown that the physical benefits of play include learning reflexes and movement control, developing fine and gross motor skills, increasing flexibility and balancing skills; learning to walk, run, jump, throw, climb, slide and swing. These activities all lead to improved physical health and fitness." As an added bonus to children's development, research strongly suggests that play

- enhances self-regulation, empathy, and group-management skills;
- reduces the severity of symptoms associated with attention disorders; and
- reduces anxiety and depression. (Alliance for Childhood, 2009)

These kinds of findings should be promoted often to parents, teachers, and school district officials so that the message is resounding: Taking children to the playground, offering recess daily, and allowing children to play freely can be one of the most fun and healthy things adults can do to enhance children's wellness (Voice of Play, n.d.). Look to the organizations listed in Figure 7.2 for ways to generate play opportunities for children.

IDEAS FOR SCHOOL AND COMMUNITY COLLABORATION

Now that an alliance between the school and community is established and the assembled team of professionals and parents has attended to important matters, the time has come to start thinking about the activities to put into action. At this time, the team and fellow advocates can visit the decided goals and objectives and plan for activities that will fulfill the corresponding mission. The tasks at hand are to deliberate over the activities to offer and how often they are executed, given the community's resources and restraints. On that occasion, consider some of these ideas:

Plant and Maintain a Garden

Invite children from all the grade levels to plan for, grow, and maintain a garden to be cultivated on school or community grounds. The children could arrange to plant specific vegetables and fruit that when harvested

FIGURE 7.2. Play Advocacy Organizations that Offer Tips and Resources for Creating Play Opportunities

Alliance for Childhood: http://www.allianceforchildhood.org/

The Alliance for Childhood, which is composed of leading childhood experts, advocates on behalf of children's healthy development. The alliance sponsors national projects that lead to policies and practices that support childhood and work to protect (and restore) play from the influences of media, commercialization, and obesity. Alliance reports, articles, briefs, booklets and fact sheets are available by way of a link on their respective website.

KaBOOM!: http://kaboom.org/

KaBOOM!, a national nonprofit, believes that play has a purpose in children's lives and seeks to help communities build playgrounds across the country. website links show how to find and build playscapes in local communities.

International Play Association: http://ipaworld.org/

IPA groups throughout the world endeavor in projects that promote play, which include seminars and conferences. Their publications link will access their *Playright* magazine and assorted concept papers, book reviews, and other IPA brochures.

Playborhood: http://playborhood.com/

The organization offers a wide range of ideas to foster play opportunities, highlights how some communities mobilize to foster play, and offers a bibliography of books, articles, and other web resources associated with children's play.

Playworks: http://www.playworksusa.org/

The Playworks mission reads, "To improve the health and well-being of children by increasing opportunities for physical activity and safe, meaningful play." In addition to posting recent research that supports the benefits of play, the Playworks website offers links to news, videos, and events focused on play specific to cities nationwide.

US Play Coalition: http://usplaycoalition.clemson.edu/

The coalition is composed of individuals and organizations committed to play. Through their yearly conference (The Conference on the Value of Play) and the projects of various action committees, members seek to publicize how play is a valuable and necessary part of a healthy and productive life. Online resources include current news postings, videos, and links to research to the purpose of play.

Wild Zones: http://www.wild-zone.net/www.wild-zone.net/Home.html

Wild Zones is committed to helping children, adolescents, and adults alike create public spaces that engender unstructured free play. The website clarifies, "Wild Zones differ from parks and nature reserves because they offer opportunities to interact with the environment rather than leaving it untouched." The tool kit link will retrieve a PDF of various ways to structure Wild Zones.

Source: Alliance for Childhood. (2010). *Free play is the missing link in anti-obesity campaign, says children's health group*. Retrieved May 15, 2010, from http://www.allianceforchildhood. org/sites/allianceforchildhood.org/files/file/Anti-Obesity_Campaign.pdf.

could be ingredients of a healthy dish that they (and others) could consume; sold in a venue such as a farmer's market; or exhibited at a fairlike event where others can see the results of their labor and toil. The instructional benefit of planning for and managing a garden is that teachers can teach lessons about this topic across varied disciplines. For instance, in science, children could learn about organic matter; in social studies, they could learn about the economics associated with selling organic products; in reading, they could read about plants that are climate appropriate; and in writing, they could journal their experiences. And, more important, the garden could be used as the centerpiece for teaching about matters associated with the two food groups found on MyPyramid, vegetables and fruit. A garden also lends itself to teaching children about the responsibilities of caring for living organisms. Each classroom could be assigned to research what it takes to effectively grow plants in the respective climates, and teams of volunteers could keep a schedule to ensure that the crops will be bountiful.

Have a Healthy Eating and Physical Activity Day

Many schools already have an annual field day, which is generally offered near the end of the school year, where students spend an entire day engaged in sorts of physical activity outside and in the gym. The spirit of that day is a fun one with the ambiance of a well-organized festival as the students rotate between planned outdoor and sports games, physical contests, play with recreation equipment, or free play where they decide what to play (hide-and-go-seek, tag). Consider having such an event more than once a year or offering supplementary condensed versions on a half day or Saturday morning. Use World Health Day, which is generally held in April, to motivate youngsters to think about health far beyond their communities. World Health Day themes in the past have included urbanization and health (2010), protecting health from climate change (2008), and working together for health (2006). Teachers could use such an event to instruct children to research an aspect of health (including dietary practices) and teach others about it. Such a health and wellness fair would give community members, especially medical practitioners, the opportunity to conduct health screenings and inform others how to effectively maintain their health. An international food fair could also be held that afforded the children the opportunity to prepare and sample a variety of healthy meals and dishes that effectively integrated the food groups represented on MyPyramid (see Figure 2.2).

Sponsor an Adapted Version of a Marathon

An adapted marathon can motivate children to become physically active as well as raise awareness about a particular cause. Of course, children are not developmentally able to run in a bona fide marathon, but they can take part in a friendly race of sorts modified for their age-appropriate abilities. The school and community could sponsor their own version of a walk-, jog-, dance-, or bike-a-thon for children and their families. A variant of Hoop It Up (www.hoopitup.com) could also be organized where the children could use their basketball skills to make as many baskets as possible. Another idea worth considering is Jump Rope for Heart (www.americanheart.org) where children jump rope to raise money for the American Heart Association. (Each year schools nationwide raise hundreds of thousands of dollars to support children with heart disorders that require costly treatments. One school alone raised nearly $67,000). Alternatively, a mini marathon could be offered where the children could walk, jog, dance, jump rope and so forth during a 20-minute time period other than recess (children should have recess for play that they initiate and direct) (Alliance for Childhood, 2009). To arouse their interest, the principal or local celebrity (e.g., a news anchor) could be asked to lead the way, or their caregivers, friends, or neighbors could be invited to join. Last, if weather is a persistent issue and it is too cold or hot outside for these sorts of activities, a local indoor mall could be used.

Encourage Healthy Parties

Major holidays are regularly celebrated in this country with a party. Schools enlighten children about national holidays, with many teachers electing to close out their lessons with a ceremonial classroom party replete with sweet treats. Traditionally, the party feasts included markedly sugary sorts of pastries and candies. In light of the childhood obesity crisis, however, school districts more recently have imposed policies that curb the amount of confections in the classrooms, which is a noteworthy practice. Be that as it may, teachers should be encouraged to plan for classroom parties that are healthier for children but still convey that spirit of festivity. For instance, the children could be invited to bring fruit, vegetables, or healthy dishes, or the party itself could be about taste tests (the teacher could even teach a lesson on graphs, supply and demand, or comparisons) or learning how to prepare a meal. Physical activity could serve as a corresponding theme that challenges the students to move for the duration of the party. Or they could learn and play a series of fun games.

FIGURE 7.3. Goals of International Walk to School Month, October

"iwalk" is the official website of International Walk to School. The organization's goals are described below:

The goal of the walk varies from community to community. Some walks rally for safer and improved streets, some to promote healthier habits and some to conserve the environment. Whatever the reason, International Walk to School events encourage a more walkable world—one community at a time.

International Walk to School is more than just getting together with children and going for a walk to school as a special event. This is certainly important, but the event's greater aim is to bring forth permanent change in communities across the globe. Below are just a few of its goals:

Encourage physical activity by teaching children the skills to walk safely, how to identify safe routes to school, and the benefits of walking

Raise awareness of how walkable a community is and where improvements can be made

Raise concern for the environment

Reduce crime and take back neighborhoods for people on foot

Reduce traffic congestion, pollution, and speed near schools

Share valuable time with local community leaders, parents, and children

Source: iwalk. (2010). *About the walk*. Retreived April 4, 2010, from http://www. iwalktoschool.org/about.htm. Reprinted with permission.

Revise School Routines

It may seem easier to get Congress to pass an act than it is to get district personnel to change a school routine. Administrators, faculty, staff, and parents are often resistant to change because there is comfort in familiar procedures and it can take lead time to work though the complications associated with a new routine. However, school routines should be examined to determine if changes could occur before, during, and after school to enhance children's health. For that reason, consider the feasibility of making changes such as having parents drop off and pick up their children farther away from the building (so they walk more) on nice days; having an extra 10- or 15-minute period of physical activity (including stretching) before class starts; offering PE on a daily basis; increasing the amount of time children have at recess or adding an extra short period of time where they play freely; organizing a walk- or bike-to-school event (see KidsWalk-to-School at www.cdc.gov for additional information on this community-based program and Figure 7.3 for goals associated with International Walk-to-School Month, October); providing healthy snacks, fruit, and vegetables throughout the day at no to low cost for children; and inviting children to bring water bottles from which they can drink throughout the day. These kinds of changes may seem lofty, but they are achievable with an army of volunteers who could lift some of the burden that teachers would assume to monitor and safeguard the children.

Offer Attractive Before- and After-School Programs

Another approach to encourage children to pursue health is to offer them before- and after-school programs focused entirely on healthy eating or physical activity. Many schools already offer care for children apart from school hours where they are tutored, helped with homework, or provided fun sorts of activities. Consider, however, creating a series of classes, a club, or a team where groups of students gather to learn a skill that leads to a practice that contributes positively toward health. Think about creating a jogging, walking, biking, or stretching club; offering classes on yoga, dance, or the martial arts; opening the playground, gym, and fields to allow children to play freely (with supervision); and teaching children how to play a specific sport, giving them the opportunity to practice and try out for a team and then compete with others. To attract as many participants as possible, offer a variety of programs that accommodate a wide range of interests and developmental abilities. Also consider sponsoring a cooking class where the children learn to prepare healthy meals and snacks for themselves and their family members. Schools often fund after-school tutoring to help children pass their state's standardized test. Why not offer tutoring on how to become a healthier person?

Spotlight a Food Item or Game for the Day

Each morning the principal at a south Texas elementary school announces a science word of the day. (All the words are in some way integrated into the state's standardized test). She defines it, discusses it with some detail, and encourages teachers to teach about in the day. The word is then posted on a bulletin board at the entrance of the cafeteria alongside visuals of properties associated with it. Quite often as the children wait to enter the lunch line, teachers use the board as a tool to elaborate on the science term. This instructional strategy could be used similarly to introduce a product from one of the food groups found on MyPyramid. In effect, a food item could substitute a science word. Someone from the leadership staff could present the word, describe its nutritional qualities, and recommended portion sizes. Teachers could then address it in class and review it as they and their students pass the bulletin board, which could be located in a high-traffic area. As an alternative, the corresponding process could be used to teach students how to play a game each day or week (see books such as *The Incredible Indoor Games Book* (Gregson, 1982), *The New Games Book* (The New Games Foundation, 1976), and *The Outrageous Outdoor Games Book* (Gregson, 1984) for examples of games).

Create a Food Lab

An authentic experience that allows children to manipulate tangible items can make a lesson meaningful. For that reason, consider establishing a lab akin to a simulated grocery store stocked with real food products and packages that affords children the opportunity to explore their nutritional benefits, as well as their potential for harm when they are consistently over-consumed. In terms of how it could operate, teachers would first present the matter in this text by way of the Ideas and follow with a visit to the lab to plan for a healthy meal, compare and contrast serving and recommended sizes, and propose how to stretch a limited budget to encompass healthy dishes. The students could also prepare and sample real snacks and meals. In this fashion, classrooms could adopt a food group or food product to re-search and share their findings and recipes with others. If creation of a lab is not feasible, reserve a bulletin board that publicizes their work or celebrates the success of students who are pursing health.

Hold Health Competitions

To encourage children's reading habits, many schools across the coun-try often hold a friendly competition that draws attention to classes with the most number of minutes the students have read for the week. Winning classes are awarded a prize that further promotes reading (e.g., a class set of books, an extra visit to the school library, a local celebrity that reads to them). This approach could work similarly with a health initiative, but in-stead of reading per se, healthy eating or physical activity practices could be tracked by some means and the class that demonstrates the healthiest gains wins. For instance, classrooms could compete on who ate the recommended amounts of vegetables and fruit most often, spent the most time engaged in physical activity, and so forth. Moreover, a competition could be held for the most inspiring ad campaign or the most imaginative physical activity game created by a class.

Have "Healthy" Field Trips

Consider planning for field excursions that focus on students' health. Sure, many teachers already take children on field trips, but the task here is to show children how the surrounding community can be used to benefit their health. To that end, children could take a walking tour of the city; learn about and visit national, state, and local parks; and travel through farms and ranches to learn how foods originate. In these instances, teachers could emphasize the primary objective—to develop the habit of looking for opportunities in the community to improve their health—as well as address secondary objectives that are more content area specific, such as to learn about the native plants of the state or to recognize community interdependence. In any case, make sure that the children have plenty of free time to walk, run, and play on these excursions, and take an active role in planning and preparing healthy meals, snacks, and drinks that will be consumed on their journey.

Sponsor a Night Off from the Screen

According to the Kaiser Family Foundation (2010), youth from 8- to 18 years old today spend nearly 8 hours engaged in a medium with a screen (over 10 hours, including music/audio and print). As one way to show children exactly how these types of activities engender sedentary behaviors, consider sponsoring a night where they are encouraged to spend their evening completely away from the screen. The students could first learn how use of electronic media deprives them of time that could be spent being physically active, and then promise to honor that evening screen free. They could learn sorts of activities to substitute the time spent in front of the screen, or the school could remain open late that the day so that the students could participate in a series of special enterprises, which could range from the academics to the health related.

Conduct a Fitness Assessment

Some school districts already mandate that their students undergo a series of tests that assess their overall fitness. If your district is not one of them, consider doing so at the beginning of the school year when the students are examined for vision and hearing disparities (some districts now check for acanthosis because of the increasing incidence of type 2 diabetes). The most prominent commercial test available is FITNESSGRAM (created by the Cooper Institute of Dallas, www.cooperinstitute.org), which assesses children as early as third grade in the areas of body composition, aerobic capacity, strength, endurance, and flexibility. Some of the activities involve the children running a mile and performing curl-ups, push-ups, trunk lifts, and shoulder stretches (Texas Education Agency, 2009). If such a test is not accessible, consider collaborating with your district's physical education division and the PE teachers in your school to determine how to best assess the children's fitness. With the added help of a school nurse and medical volunteers, the children's height and weight could be measured, Body Mass Indexes (BMIs) calculated (using the BMI for growth charts), and body fat assessed using a caliper test. Report the general findings to the faculty and individual results to the children and their parents. Use that information as a baseline from which to improve the children's overall health.

Finally, after sponsoring these sorts of events, remember to inform others about what was accomplished so that they have an idea for how to improve their own community's health. Invite the local media to cover the event, and send letters to parents and influential community members who could lend their support to future events.

CONCLUSION

The Ideas presented in Chapters 4 and 6 demonstrated how individual teachers could help children acquire a knowledge base and a body of skills to improve and maintain their health. However, if the national expectation is to stifle the childhood obesity epidemic, it is going to take the collaborative effort of the school and community to regularly expose children to healthy practices beyond their classroom walls. The Centers for Disease Control and Prevention (2008a) assert, "Reversing the obesity epidemic requires a long-term, well-coordinated approach to reach young people where they live, learn, and play. Schools have a big part to play. Working with other public, voluntary, and private sector organizations, schools can play a critical role in reshaping social and physical environments and providing information, tools, and practical strategies to help students adopt healthy lifestyles." Hillary Clinton's often quoted mantra of our time, "It takes a village to raise a child," holds profound relevance when it comes to the topic of children's health. Indeed, it takes the whole community to raise a health-conscious child.

References

Action for Healthy Kids. (2003). *Building the argument: The need for physical education and physical activity in our schools*. Retrieved September 29, 2007, from http://www.actionforhealthykids.org/filelib/facts_and_findings/Need%20for%20PE-PA.pdf.

Action for Healthy Kids. (2005a). *Better nutrition and more physical activity can boost achievement and schools' bottom line*. Retrieved October 23, 2007, from http://www.nutritionexplorations.org/pdf/educators/SpecialReportFactSheet.pdf.

Action for Healthy Kids. (2005b). *Childhood obesity: The preventable threat to America's youth*. Retrieved December 27, 2009, from http://www.nationaldairycouncil.org/SiteCollectionDocuments/child_nutrition/nutrition_in_schools/ChildhoodObesityFactSheet.pdf.

Advertising Age. (2009). *Marketer trees 2009*. Retrieved June 25, 2009, from http://adage.com/marketertrees09/index.php?marketer=69#69.

Alleman, G. P. (1999). *Save your child from the fat epidemic: 7 steps every parents can take to ensure healthy, fit children for life*. Rocklin, CA: Prima.

Alliance for Childhood. (2009, November). The loss of children's play: A public health issue. *Policy Brief, 1*, 1–2.

Alliance for Childhood. (2010). *Free play is the missing link in anti-obesity campaign, says children's health group*. Retrieved May 15, 2010, from http://www.allianceforchildhood.org/sites/allianceforchildhood.org/files/file/Anti-Obesity_Campaign.pdf

Alpert, P. (2005). Sharing the secrets of life without water. *Integrative and comparative biology, 45*(5), 683–684.

America on the Move Foundation. (2010). *Balance first: Balance what you choose with how you move*. Retrieved January 2, 2010, from http://school.discoveryeducation.com/balancefirst/pdf/teachersGuide.pdf.

American Academy of Family Physicians. (2008). *Will the habits I have now really make a difference when I'm older?* Retrieved April 23, 2008, from http://familydoctor.org/online/famdocen/home/children/teens/prevention

American Academy of Pediatrics. (1990). Strength training, weight and power lifting, and body building by children and adolescents. *Pediatrics, 86*(5), 801–802.

American Academy of Pediatrics. (1999). Calcium requirements of infants, children, and adolescents. *Pediatrics, 104*(5), 1152–1157.

American Academy of Pediatrics. (2001a). Children, adolescents, and television. *Pediatrics, 107*(2), 423–426.

American Academy of Pediatrics. (2001b). Media violence. *Pediatrics, 108*(5), 1222–1226.

American Association for Active Lifestyles and Fitness. (2004). *A position statement on including students with disabilities in physical education*. Retrieved March 11, 2009, from http://www.aahperd.org/aapar/pdf_files/pos_papers/inclusion_position.pdf

American College of Sports Medicine. (n.d.). *Dehydration and aging*. Retrieved

January 2, 2010, from http://www.acsm.org/AM/Template.cfm?Section=Current_Comments1&Template=/CM/ContentDisplay.cfm&ContentID=8614

American College of Sports Medicine. (2006). *ACSM's guidelines for exercise testing and prescription.* Philadelphia: Lippincott Williams & Wilkins.

American Council on Exercise. (n.d.). *Operation fit kids.* Retrieved October 13, 2009, from http://www.acefitness.org/ofk/youthfitness/default.aspx

American Dietetic Association. (2004). Position paper update for 2004. *Journal of the American Dietetic Association, 104*(2), 276–278.

American Heart Association. (1997). *365 ways to get out the fat: A tip a day to trim the fat away.* New York: Clarkson Potter.

American Heart Association. (2001). *To your heart: A guide to heart-smart living.* New York: Clarkson Potter Publishers.

American Heart Association. (2006a). *Nutrition.* Retrieved August 8, 2008, from http://www.americanheart.org/downloadable/heart/1156966377994SYH_Nutrition_Repros.pdf

American Heart Association. (2006b). *Physical activity.* Retrieved October 5, 2009, from http://www.americanheart.org/downloadable/heart/1156966821600SYH_Phy Activity_Repros.pdf

American Heart Association. (2010). *Why should I be physically active?* Retrieved September 19, 2010, from http://www.americanheart.org/downloadable/heart/119618454295630%20WhyShldIBePhyllyActve%209_07.pdf

American Heritage Stedman's Medical Dictionary. (2008). *Health.* Retrieved May 23, 2008, from http://dictionary.reference.com/browse/health

Anspaugh, D. J., Hamrick, M. H., & Rosato, F. D. (2006). *Wellness: Concepts and applications* (6th ed.). Boston: McGraw-Hill.

Baird, K., Branta, C., Mark, C. B., & Seremba, D. (2006). *Jump into foods and fitness.* East Lansing, MI: Michigan State University Extension.

Bauer, J. (2005). *The complete idiot's guide to total nutrition* (4th ed.). New York: Alpha.

Beckman, S. (2001). Emergency procedures and exercise safety. In J. L. Pointman (Ed.), *ACSM's resource manual.* Philadelphia: Lippincott Williams & Wilkins.

Begley, S. (2009, September 21). Born to be big: Early exposure to common chemicals may be programming kids to be fat. *Newsweek,* 56–62.

Berg, F. M. (2004). *Underage and overweight: America's childhood obesity crisis—what every family needs to know.* Long Island City, NY: Hatherleigh Press.

Berkey, C. S., Rockett, H. R., Gillman, M.W., & Colditz, G. A. (2003). One-year changes in activity and in inactivity among 10- to 15-year-old boys and girls: Relationship to change in body mass index. *Pediatrics, 111*(4), 836–843.

Birdwell, A. F. (2006). *Bullying keeps overweight kids off the field.* Retrieved October 12, 2007, from http://news.ufl.edu/2006/04/19/bullies/

Bishop, D. (2003). Warm up I: Potential mechanisms and the effects of passive warm up on exercise performance. *Sports Medicine, 33*(6), 439–454.

Bogden, J. (2000). *Fit, healthy, and ready to learn: A school health policy guide.* Alexandria, VA: National Association of State Boards of Education.

Booth, F. (2001). *Sedentary death syndrome is what researchers now call America's second largest threat to public health.* Retrieved December 16, 2008, from http://hac.missouri.edu/RID/PressRelease.pdf

Bounds, L., Shea, K. B., Agnor, D., & Darnell, G. (2006). *Health and fitness: A guide to a healthy lifestyle* (3rd ed.). Dubuque, IA: Kendall/Hunt.

Branner, T. T. (1993). *The safe exercise handbook: Everyone's guide to lifetime, injury-free fitness* (2nd ed.). Dubuque, IA: Kendall/Hunt.

Burgeson, C. R., Wechsler, H., Brener, N. D., Young, J. C., & Spain, C. G. (2001). Physical education and activity: Results from the school health policies and programs study, 2000. *Journal of School Health, 71*(7), 279–293.

California Department of Health. (n.d.). *California 5 a day campaign: Key health messages.* Sacramento, CA: Author.

California Pan-Ethnic Health Network. (2005). *Out of balance: Marketing of soda, candy, snacks, and fast foods drowns out healthful messages.* Oakland, CA: Author.

Center for Science in the Public Interest. (2003a). *Anyone's guess: The need for nutrition labeling at fast-food and other chain restaurants.* Washington, DC: Author.

Center for Science in the Public Interest. (2003b). *Pestering parents: How food companies market obesity to children.* Washington, DC: Author.

Center for Science in the Public Interest. (2005a). *Healthy snacks for children.* Washington, DC: Author.

Center for Science in the Public Interest. (2005b). *Salt assault: Brand-name comparisons of processed foods.* Washington, DC: Author.

Center for Science in the Public Interest. (2008). *Don't say cheese.* Retrieved July 29, 2008, from http://www.cspinet.org/smartmouth/articles/cheese.html

Centers for Disease Control. (n.d.a). *60: Play every day. Any way.* Retrieved October 17, 2009, from http://www.cdc.gov/youthcampaign/marketing/adult/tip.htm

Centers for Disease Control. (n.d.b). *KidsWalk-to-school: A guide to promote walking to school.* Retrieved September 30, 2007, from http://www.cdc.gov/nccdphp/dnpa/kidswalk/pdf/kidswalk_brochure.pdf

Centers for Disease Control. (2002). Youth risk behavior surveillance—United States 2001. *MMWR, 51*(SS04), 1–64.

Centers for Disease Control. (2003a). *Physical activity and good nutrition: Essential elements to prevent chronic diseases and obesity.* Retrieved September 20, 2007, from http://www.cdc.gov/nccdphp/aag/pdf/aag_dnpa2005.pdf

Centers for Disease Control. (2003b). Physical activity levels among children aged 9–13 years—United States, 2002. *Morbidity and Mortality Weekly Report, 52*(33), 785–788.

Centers for Disease Control. (2004). Youth risk behavior surveillance—United States, 2003. *Morbidity and Mortality Weekly Report, 53*(SS-2), 1–95.

Centers for Disease Control. (2006). Youth risk behavior surveillance—United States. *Morbidity and Mortality, 55*(5), 1–108.

Centers for Disease Control. (2008a). *Make a difference at your school!* Retrieved December 28, 2009, from http://www.cdc.gov/HealthyYouth/KeyStrategies/pdf/make-a-difference.pdf

Centers for Disease Control. (2008b). *Physical activity for everyone.* Retrieved December 16, 2008, from http://www.cdc.gov/nccdphp/dnpa/physical/everyone/index.htm

Centers for Disease Control. (2008c). Youth risk behavior surveillance—United States, 2007. *Morbidity and Mortality Weekly Report, 57*(SS4), 1–136.

Centers for Disease Control. (2009). *Physical activity and health: At a glance 1996.* Retrieved March 8, 2009, from http://www.cdc.gov/NCCDPHP/sgr/pdf/sgraag.pdf

Centers for Disease Control. (2010a). State-specific trends in fruit and vegetable consumption among adults—United States, 2000–2009. *Morbidity and Mortality Weekly, 59*(35), 1125–1130.

Centers for Disease Control. (2010b). Youth risk behavior surveillance–2009. *Morbidity and Mortality Weekly Report, 53*(SS-2), 1–95.

Cheung, L. W. Y., Dart, H., Kalin, S., & Gortmaker, S. (2007). *Eat well and keep moving.* Champaign, IL: Human Kinetics.

Corbin, C. B., Welk, G. J., Corbin, W. R., & Welk, K. A. (2008). *Concepts of fitness and wellness: A comprehensive lifestyle approach* (7th ed.). Boston: McGraw-Hill.

Dalton, S. (2004). *Our overweight children: What parents, schools, and communities can do to control the fatness epidemic.* Berkeley, CA: University of California Press.

Datar, A., & Sturm, R., (2004). Physical education in elementary school and body mass index: Evidence from the early childhood longitudinal study. *American Journal of Public Health, 94*(9), 1501–1505.

Discovery Education. (2006). *Balance first: Balance what you choose with how you move.* Retrieved September 19, 2010, from http://school.discoveryeducation.com/balancefirst/pdf/teachersGuide.pdf

Dunn, A. L., Marcus, B. H., Carpenter, R. A., Jaret, P., & Blair, S. N. (2001). *Active living every day: 20 weeks to lifelong vitality.* Champaign, IL: Human Kinetic.

Dwyer, T., Coonan, W. E., Leitch, D. R., Hetzel, B., & Baghurst, R. A. (1983). An investigation of the effects of daily physical activity on the health of primary school students in South Australia. *International Journal of Epidemiology, 12*(3), 308–313.

Fenton, M. (2008). *The complete guide to walking for health, weight loss, and fitness.* Guildford, CT: Lyons Press.

Fouts, G., & Burggraf, K. (2000). Television situation comedies: Female weight, male negative references, and audience reactions. *Sex Roles: A Journal of Research, 42*(9/10), 925–932.

Fox, K. (1997). *A summary of research findings on body image.* Retrieved June 12, 2008, from http://www.sirc.org/publik/mirror.html

Gallahue, D. L., & Donnelly, F. C. (2003). *Developmental physical education for all children* (4th ed.). Champaign, IL: Human Kinetics.

Gardner, H. (1993). *Multiple intelligences. The theory into practice.* New York: Basic Books.

Gassenheimer, L. (2007). *The portion plan: How to eat the foods you love and still lose weight.* New York: DK.

Gelbard, N. (2006). *Do more, watch less.* Sacramento, CA: California Obesity Prevention Initiative.

Gerrior, S., Putnam, J., & Bente, L. (1999). Milk and milk products: Their importance in the American diet. *Food Review, 21*(2), 29–37.

Ginsburg, K. R. (2007). The importance of play in promoting healthy child development and maintaining strong parent-child bonds. *Pediatrics, 119*(1), 182–191.

Gleason, P., & Suitor, C. (2000). *Changes in children's diets: 1989–91 to 1994–96.* Washington, DC: U.S. Department of Agriculture, Food and Nutrition Service.

Good Housekeeping. (2008, August). Sweep the blues away. *Good Housekeeping, 247*(2), 37.

Graham, G., Holt/Hale, S. A., & Parker, M. (2007). *Children moving: A reflective approach to teaching physical education* (8th ed). Boston: McGraw-Hill.

Greenfield, S. A. (1995). *Journey to the centers of the mind.* New York: W.H. Freeman.

Gregson, B. (1982). *The incredible indoor games book.* Fearon Teacher Aids: Carthage, IL.

Gregson, B. (1984). *The outrageous outdoor games book.* Fearon Teacher Aids: Carthage, IL.

Hargreaves, D., & Tiggeman, M. (2002). Idealized women in TV ads make girls feel bad. *Journal of Social and Clinical Psychology, 21*(3), 287–308.

Harrison, K., & Cantor, J. (1997). The relationship between media consumption and eating disorders. *Journal of Communication, 47*(1), 40–67.

Healthgrain Project. (2008). *Healthgrain.* Retrieved July 4, 2008, from http://www.healthgrain.org/pub/chapter-three.php

Hellison, D. (1995) *Teaching responsibility through physical activity.* Champaign, IL: Human Kinetics.

Hersey, J. C., & Jordan, A. (2007). *Reducing children's TV time to reduce the risk of child-hood overweight: The children's media use study.* Washington, DC: Centers for Disease Control and Prevention Nutrition and Physical Activity Communication Team.

Hill, J. C., Wyatt, H. R., Reed, G. W., & Peters, J. C. (2003). Obesity and the environment: Where do we go from here? *Science, 299*(5608), 853–855.

Hoeger, W. K., & Hoeger, S. A. (2007). *Lifetime physical fitness and wellness: A personal program* (9th ed.). Belmont, CA: Thomson Higher Education.

Institute of Medicine. (2004). *Industry can play a role in preventing childhood obesity.* Retrieved April 7, 2006, from http://www.iom.edu/Object.File/Master/22/613/fact%20Sheet%20-%20industry%20finalBitticks.pdf

Institute of Medicine. (2010). *Strategies to reduce sodium intake in the United States.* Retrieved September 23, 2010, from http://www.iom.edu/~/media/Files/Report%20Files/2010/Strategies-to-Reduce-Sodium-Intake-in-the-United-States/Strategies%20to%20Reduce%20Sodium%20Intake%202010%20%20Report%20Brief.ashx

Iowa Child and Adolescent Obesity Task Force. (2001). Preventing child obesity in Iowa. *Healthy Weight Journal, 15*(4), 55–57.

Jacobson, M. F. (2005). *Liquid candy: How soft drinks are harming Americans' health.* Washington, DC: Center for Science in the Public Interest.

Jahns, L., Siega-Riz, A., & Popkin, B. (2001). The increasing prevalence of snacking among US children from 1977 to 1996. *Journal of Pediatrics, 138*(4), 493–498.

The Joint Committee on National Health Education Standards. (2007). *National health education standards: Achieving excellence* (2nd ed.). Atlanta: American Cancer Society.

Kaiser Family Foundation. (2004). *The role of media on childhood obesity.* Retrieved December 6, 2009, from http://www.kff.org/entmedia/upload/The-Role-Of-Media-in-Childhood-Obesity.pdf

Kaiser Family Foundation. (2010). *Generation M2: Media in the lives of 8- to 18-year-olds, 2009.* Retrieved September 19, 2010, from http://www.kff.org/entmedia/upload/8010.pdf/

Katan, M. B., & Ludwig, D. S. (2010). Extra calories cause weight gain—but how much? *JAMA, 303*(1), 65–66.

Kidshealth.org. (2009). *Why drinking water is the way to go.* Retrieved December 1, 2009, from http://kidshealth.org/stay_healthy/food/water.html

Kirschmann, J. D. (2007). *Nutrition almanac: Fight disease, boost immunity, and slow the effects of aging* (6th ed). New York: McGraw-Hill.

Let's Move. (n.d.). *Healthier schools.* Retrieved May 16, 2010, from http://www.lets-move.gov/schools/index.html

Manini, T. M., Everhart, J. E., Patel, K. V., Schoeller, D. A., Colbert, L. H., Visser, M., Tylavsky, F., Bauer, D. C., Goodpaster, B. H., & Harris, T. B. (2006). Daily activity energy expenditure and mortality among older adults. *Journal of the American Medical Association, 296*(2), 171–179.

Marr, L. (2004). Soft drinks, childhood overweight, and the role of nutrition educators: Let's base our solutions on reality and sound science. *Journal of Nutrition Education and Behavior, 36*(5), 258–263.

Mathematica Policy Research. (2006). *Problems start early in the diets of infants and toddlers: New analyses from Mathematica's groundbreaking feeding infants and toddlers study may help in fight against childhood obesity.* Retrieved September 20, 2007, from http://www.mathematica-mpr.com/Press%20Releases/fits06JADA.asp

Mayo Clinic. (2008). *Childhood obesity: Treatments and drugs.* Retrieved May 15, 2010, from http://www.mayoclinic.com/health/childhood-obesity/DS00698/DSECTION=treatments-and-drugs

MayoClinic.com. (2010). *Water: How much should you drink every day?* Retrieved September 19, 2010, from http://www.mayoclinic.com/health/water/NU00283

McDevitt, T. M., & Ormrod, J.E. (2010). *Child development and education* (4th ed.). Upper Saddle River, NJ: Pearson Education.

McNeil, J. (2003, March 24). When does brand loyalty start? *Adweek.*

Media Awareness Network. (2008). *Beauty and body image in the media.* Retrieve June 15, 2008, from http://www.media-awareness.ca/english/issues/stereotying/women_and_girls/women

Mellin, L. M., & Johnson, S. R. (2005). *Just for kids!* San Diego, CA: Balboa.

Michigan Department of Education. (2001). *The role of Michigan schools in promoting healthy weight.* Retrieved September 30, 2007, from http://www.michigan.gov/documents/healthyweight_13649_7.pdf

Moore, B. (2002). *Parent's guide for the assessment and treatment of the overweight child.* Washington, DC: Shape Up America!

Mundell, E. (2002). *Sitcoms, videos make even fifth-graders feel fat.* Retrieved June 16, 2008, from http://naturalsolutionsradio.com/articles/article.html?id=2817&filter=

Mundell, E. (2005). *Soap, music videos linked to teens' body image.* Retrieved August 6, 2008, from http://www.commonsensemedia.org/resources/body_image.php?id=1

Nader, P. R., O'Brien, M., Houts, R., Bradley, R., Bradley, R., Belsky, J., Crosnoe, R., Friedman, S., Mei, Z., & Susman, E. J. (2006). Identifying risk for obesity in early childhood. *Pediatrics, 118*(3), e594–e601.

NASPE. (2004). *Moving into the future: National standards for physical education.* Reston, VA: National Association for Sports and Physical Education.

National Alliance for Nutrition and Activity. (2002). *From wallet to waistline: The hidden costs of super sizing.* Washington, DC: Author.

National Institutes of Health. (2004). *Celebrate the beauty of youth* (NIDDKD Publication No. 04-4903). Washington, DC: National Institute of Diabetes and Digestive and Kidney Diseases.

National Institutes of Health. (2005). *Aim for a healthy weight* (NIH Publication No.05-5213). Washington, DC: U.S. Department of Health and Human Services.

National Institutes of Health. (2007a). *Tips for a healthy new year.* Retrieved December 28, 2009 from http://win.niddk.nih.gov/notes/winter07/winnotes_winter07.htm#res-not1

National Institutes of Health. (2007b). *Young and old alike benefit from exercise and physical activity.* Retrieved December 28, 2009 from http://win.niddk.nih.gov/notes/winter07/winnotes_winter07.htm#res-not1

National Institute on Media and the Family. (2008). *Media's effect on girls: Body image and gender identity.* Retrieved June 12, 2008, from https://www.mediafamily.org/facts/facts_mediaeffect.shtml

National Restaurant Association. (2002). *Industry at a glance.* Retrieved September 28, 2007, from http://www.restaurant.org/research/ind_glance.cfm

Nestle, M. (2002). *Food politics.* Berkeley: University of California Press.

The New Games Foundation. (1976). *The new games book*: Garden City, NY: Headlands Press.

New Hampshire Department of Health and Human Services. (2007). *How much sugar do you eat? You may be surprised!* Retrieved January 3, 2011, from http://www.dhhs.nh.gov/DPHS/nhp/adults/documents/sugar.pdf

Pangrazi, R. P., & Beighle, A. (2010). *Dynamic physical education for elementary school children* (16th ed.). San Francisco: Benjamin Cummings.

Peterson, K., Silverstein, J., Kaufman, F., & Warren-Boulton, E. (2007). Management of type 2 diabetes in youth: An update. *American Family Physician, 76*(5), 658–664.

Pitman, T., & Kaufman, M. (2000). *The overweight child: Promoting fitness and self-esteem*. Buffalo, NY: Firefly.

President's Council on Physical Fitness and Sports. (n.d.). *Get fit and be active! A handbook for youth ages 6–17* (Publication No. 41-462-20). Bloomington, IN: The President's Challenge.

Public Schools of North Carolina. (n.d.). *Limited English proficient (LEP) students in physical education*. Retrieved March 11, 2009, from http://www.ncpe4me.com/ pdf_files/limited-English-in-pe.pdf

Puhl, R., & Brownell, K. (2001). Bias, discrimination and obesity. *Obesity Research, 9*(12), 788–805.

Putnam, J., Allshouse, J., & Kantor, L. (2002). U.S. capita food supply trends: More calories, refined carbohydrates, and fats. *Food Review, 25*(3), 2–15.

Reisser, P. C. (2006). *Family health, nutrition, and fitness: Building your body, mind, and soul—one day at a time*. Carol Stream, IL: Tyndale House.

Rimm, S. (2004). *Rescuing the emotional lives of overweight children: What our kids go though—and how we can help*. New York: Rodale.

Rink, J. E. (2002). *Teaching physical education for learning* (4th ed.). Boston: McGraw-Hill.

Ritchie, L., Ivey, S., Masch, M., Woodward-Lopez, G. W., Ikeda, J., & Crawford, P. (2001). *Pediatric overweight: A review of the literature*. Retrieved October 1, 2007, from http://cnr.berkeley.edu/cwh/news/announcements.shtml#lit_review

Rizza, R. A., Go, V. L. W., McMahon, M. M., & Harrison, G. G. (Eds.) (2002). *Encyclopedia of foods: A guide to healthy nutrition*. San Diego, CA: Academic Press.

Robert Wood Johnson Foundation. (2010). *The state of play: Gallup survey of principals and school recess*. Retrieved February 21, 2010, from http://www.rwjf.org/files/ research/stateofplayrecessreportgallup.pdf

Roizen, M. F., & Oz, M. C. (2005). *YOU: The owner's manual*. New York, NY: HarperResource.

Roizen, M. F., & Oz, M. C. (2007). *YOU: Staying young: The owner's manual for extending your warranty*. New York: Free Press.

Schooler, D., & Ward, L. M. (2006). Average Joes: Men's relationship with media, real bodies, and sexuality. *Psychology of Men and Masculinity, 7*(1), 27–41.

Schwimmer, J. B., Burwinkle, T. M., & Varni, J. W. (2003). Health-related quality of life of severely obese children and adolescents. *Journal of the American Medical Association, 289*(14) 1813–1819.

Sears, W., Sears, P., & Foy, S. (2003). *Dr. Sears' lean kids: Lifestyle exercise attitude nutrition*. New York: New American Library.

Sesame Workshop. (2007). *Healthy habits for life*. New York: Author.

Shaibi, G. Q., Cruz, M. L., Ball, G. D. F., Weigensberg, M. J., Salem, G. J., Crespo, N. C., & Goran, M. I. (2006). Effects of resistance training on insulin sensitivity in overweight Latino adolescent males. *Medicine and Science in Sports and Exercise, 38*(7), 1208–1215.

Sharkey, B. J., & Gaskill, S. E. (2007). *Fitness and health: Your complete guide to aerobic fitness, muscular fitness, nutrition, and weight control*. Champaign, IL: Human Kinetics.

Shephard, R. J. (1997). Curricular physical activity and academic performance. *Pediatric Exercise Science, 9*(2), 113–126.

Shephard, R. J., Volle, M., Lavallee, H., LaBarre, R., Jequier, J. C., & Rajic, M. (1984). Required physical activity and academic grades: A controlled longitudinal study. In J. Ilmarinen and L. Valimak (Eds.), *Children and sports* (pp. 219–223). Berlin: Springer-Verlag.

Smith, J. C. (1999). *Understanding childhood obesity*. Jackson: University Press of Mississippi.

Stanford University School of Medicine. (2007). *Building "generation play": Addressing the crisis of inactivity among American children.* Retrieved February 21, 2010, from http://hip.stanford.edu/documents/4a.%20Stanford_Report_Generation_Play.pdf

St. Anthony Catholic School. (n.d.). *Mi vida activity challenge*. San Antonio, TX: St. Anthony Catholic School.

Statement from the American Cancer Society, the American Diabetes Association, and the American Heart Association on Physical Education. (n.d.). *Physical education in schools—both quality and quantity are important.* Retrieved March 11, 2009, from http://www.everydaychoices.org/082008/PE%20in%20Schools%20Statement%20 ACS%20ADA%20AHA%205.27.08%20_final_.pdf

Strasburger, V. C. (2007). First do no harm: Why have parents and pediatricians missed the boat on children and media? *Journal of Pediatrics, 151*(4), 334–336.

Strasburger, V. C., Wilson, B. J., & Jordan, A. B. (2009). *Children, adolescents, and the media* (2nd ed.). Thousand Oaks, CA: Sage.

Strock, G. A., Cottrell, E. R., Abang, A. E., Buschbacher, R. M., & Hannon, T. S. (2005). Childhood obesity: A simple equation with complex variables. *Journal of Long-Term Effects of Medical Implants, 15*(1), 15–32.

Sturm, R. (2005). Childhood obesity—What we can learn from existing data on society trends, part 2. *Preventing Chronic Disease: Public Health Research, Practice and Policy, 2*(2), 1–9.

Symons, C. W., Cinelli, B., James, T. C., & Groff, P. (1997). Bridging student health risks and academic achievement through comprehensive school health programs. *Journal of School Health, 67*(6), 220-227.

Tartamella, L., Herscher, E., & Woolston, C. (2004). *Generation extra large: Rescuing our children from the epidemic of obesity*. New York: Basic Books.

Terris, M. (1975). Approaches to an epidemiology of health. *American Journal of Public Health, 65*(10), 1037–1045.

Tershakovic, A. M., Weller, S. C., & Gallagher, P. R. (1994). Obesity, school performance, and the behavior of Black, urban elementary school children. *International Journal of Obesity, 18*(5), 323–327.

Texas Education Agency. (2009, March 9). *Physically fit students more likely to do well in school, less likely to be disciplinary problems*. Austin, TX: Texas Education Agency News.

Thompson, C. A., & Shanley, E. L. (2004). *Overcoming childhood obesity*. Boulder, CO: Bull.

Tiggemann, M., & Pickering, A. S. (1996). Role of television in adolescent women's body dissatisfaction and drive for thinness. *International Journal of Eating Disorders, 20*(2), 199–203.

Trust for America's Health. (2007). *F as in fat: How obesity policies are failing in America 2007*. Retrieved January 4, 2008, from http://healthyamericans.org/reports/ obesity2007/

Trust for America's Health. (2009). *F as in fat: How obesity policies are failing in America 2009*. Retrieved January 16, 2009, from http://healthyamericans.org/reports/ obesity2009/

UCLA Student Nutrition and Body Image Action Committee. (2008). *Body image*. Retrieved June 15, 2008, from http://www.snac.ucla.edu/pages/Body_Image/Body_ Image.htm

University of Missouri. (n.d.). *Recommended food pattern*. Columbia, MO: Family Nutrition Education Programs: Nutrition and Lifeskills for Missouri Families.

U.S. Department of Agriculture. (2000a). *Changing the scene: Improving the school nutrition environment*. Retrieved December 28, 2009, from http://www.fns.usda.gov/TN/Resources/guide.pdf

U.S. Department of Agriculture. (2000b). *Move it! Choose your fun!* Retrieved December 28, 2009, from http://www.fns.usda.gov/tn/resources/moveit.pdf

U.S. Department of Agriculture. (2000c). *Nutrition and your health: Dietary guidelines for Americans* (H&G Bulletin No. 232). Washington, DC: Author.

U.S. Department of Agriculture. (2001). *Foods sold in competition with USDA school meal programs: A report to Congress*. Retrieved December 28, 2009, from http://www.cspinet.biz/nutritionpolicy/Foods_Sold_in_Competition_with_USDA_School_Meal_Programs.pdf

U.S. Department of Agriculture. (2005a). *Anatomy of MyPyramid* (CNPP-16). Washington, DC: Center for Nutrition Policy and Promotion.

U.S. Department of Agriculture. (2005b). *Making it happen: School nutrition success stories* (FNS-374). Alexandria, VA: Food and Nutrition Service.

U.S. Department of Agriculture. (2005c). *MyPyramid: Steps to a healthier you*. Retrieved December 28, 2009, from http://www.mypyramid.gov/downloads/resource/MyPyramidBrochurebyIFIC.pdf

U.S. Department of Agriculture. (2007). *Promoting healthy eating behaviors: The challenge*. Retrieved September 20, 2007, from http://fns.usda.gov/tn/Healthyeatingchallenge.html

U.S. Department of Agriculture. (n.d.). *Why was the Body Walk Project developed?* Retrieved September 18, 2010, from http://healthymeals.nal.usda.gov/hsmrs/Illinois_Body_Walk/Manual/Timeline.pdf

U.S. Department of Health and Human Services. (n.d.). *Get fit and be active! A handbook for youths ages 6–17*. Retrieved October 13, 2009, from http://www.presidentschallenge.org/pdf/getfit.pdf

U.S. Department of Health and Human Services. (2000a). *Healthy people 2010* (SN 017-001-001-00-550-9. Washington, DC: U.S. Government Printing Office.

U.S. Department of Health and Human Services. (2000b). *Promoting better health for young people through physical activity and sports: A report to the president from the secretary of health and human services and the secretary of education*. Washington, DC: Author.

U.S. Department of Health and Human Services. (2001). *The surgeon general's call to action to prevent and decrease overweight and obesity*. Retrieved October 1, 2007, from http://www.surgeongeneral.gov/topics/obesity/calltoaction/CalltoAction.pdf

U.S. Department of Health and Human Services. (2003). *Statistics related to overweight and obesity* (Publication No. 03-4158). Washington, DC: National Institutes of Health.

U.S. Department of Health and Human Services. (2005a). *Aim for a healthy weight* (NIH Publication No. 05-5213). Washington, DC: Nation Institute of Health; National Heart, Lung, and Blood Institute.

U.S. Department of Health and Human Services. (2005b). *Dietary guidelines for Americans*. Retrieved July 30, 2008, from http://www.health.gov/dietaryguidelines/dga2005/document/pdf/DGA2005.pdf

U.S. Department of Health and Human Services. (2005c). *Finding your way to a healthier you: Based on the* Dietary Guidelines for Americans (HHS-ODPHP—2005-01-DGA-B). Washington, DC: U.S. Government Printing Office.

U.S. Department of Health and Human Services. (2005d). *Healthy people 2010: The cornerstone for prevention*. Retrieved December 28, 2009, from http://www.healthypeople.gov/publications/Cornerstone.pdf

U.S. Department of Health and Human Services. (2006). *Active at any size* (NIH Publication No. 04-4352). Washington, DC: National Institute of Diabetes and Digestive and Kidney Diseases.

U.S. Department of Health and Human Services. (2007). *Healthy eating and physical activity across your lifespan: Helping your child* (NIH Publication No. 04-4955). Washington, DC: National Institutes of Health.

U.S. Department of Health & Human Services. (2008a). *2008 Physical activity guidelines for Americans: Be active, healthy, and happy!* (DHHS Publication No. U0036). Washington, DC: U.S. Government Printing Office.

U.S. Department of Health and Human Services. (2008b). *Making a difference at your school! CDC resources can help you implement strategies to prevent obesity among children and adolescent.* Retrieved March 12, 2009, from http://www.cdc.gov/HealthyYouth/KeyStrategies/pdf/make-a-difference.pdf

U.S. Department of Health and Human Services. (2008c). *The effects of advertising on teenage girls: World of advertising and our girls.* Retrieved June 15, 2008, from http://hablemos.samhsa.gov/new/medialit.aspx

U.S. Department of Health and Human Services. (2010). FDA issues statement on IOM report. Retrieved September 23, 2010, from http://www.fda.gov/NewsEvents/Newsroom/PressAnnouncements/ucm209155.htm

U.S. Department of Transportation. (1969). *1969 National personal transportation survey: Travel to school.* Retrieved September 30, 2007, from http://www.fhwa.dot.gov/ohim/1969/q.pdf

U.S. Environmental Protection Agency. (2003). *Travel and environmental implications of school siting.* Retrieved September 30, 2007, from http://epa.gov/smartgrowth/pdf/schoo_travel/pdf

Vail, K. (2004). Obesity epidemic. *American School Board Journal, 191*(1), 22–25.

Voice of Play. (n.d.). *Physical benefits of play.* Retrieved May 15, 2010, from http://www.voiceofplay.org/imp_of_play/physical.asp

Wang, Y., Beydoun, M. A., Liang, L., Caballero, B., & Kumanyika, S. K. (2008). Will all Americans become overweight or obese? Estimating the progression and cost of the US obesity epidemic. *Obesity, 16*(10), 2323–2330.

Ward, E. (2005). *The new food pyramid: Commonsense advice that demystifies the new nutrition guidelines.* New York: Alpha.

Wenner, M. (2009, February). The serious need for play. *Scientific American Mind,* 22–26.

The White House Office of the Press Secretary. (2010). *Presidential memorandum—establishing a task force on childhood obesity.* Retrieved May 16, 2010, from http://www.whitehouse.gov/the-press-office/presidential-memorandum-establishing-a-task-force-childhood-obesity

Willett, W. C., & Skerrett, P. J. (2005). *Eat, drink, and be healthy: The Harvard Medical School guide to healthy eating.* New York: Free Press.

Williams, M. H. (2007). *Nutrition for health, fitness, and sport.* Boston: McGraw-Hill.

Witmer, D. (2008). *What is body image?* Retrieved June 12, 2008, from http://parentingteens.about.com/cs/bodyimage/a/bodyimage.htm

World Health Organization. (2001). *Men ageing and health: Achieving health across the lifetime.* Geneva: World Health Organization.

Young, S. (2010). *U.S. limits urged for salt in processed foods.* Retrieved September 23, 2010, from http://articles.cnn.com/2010-04-20/health/salt.guidelines_1_sodium-consumption-salt-consumption-iom-report?_s=PM:HEALTH

Zembar, M. J., & Blume, L. B. (2009). *Middle childhood development: A contextual approach.* Upper Saddle, NJ: Pearson Education.

Index

About the Author

David Campos (PhD, University of Texas at Austin) began his education career nearly 20 years ago when he started teaching second grade. He later entered graduate school, taught English as a Second Language, and worked in corporate training and development. He is an associate professor of education at the University of the Incarnate Word (San Antonio, TX) where he supervises student teachers and teaches undergraduate and graduate courses in special education, multicultural education, and curriculum methods. In 2004, he traveled to China on a Fulbright.

David has authored four books and coauthored two others. He was guest editor of a special issue of the *Journal of Hispanic Higher Education* (Sage), which focused on language acquisition as it relates to Hispanic students. His peer-reviewed articles focus on constructivist teaching and authentic assessment by way of African American visionaries.